IT ALL
FALLS DOWN

IT ALL FALLS DOWN

TRUST SERIES
BOOK THREE

DAINES L. REED

Printed in the United States of America

ISBN 978-1-7340526-4-0 (paperback)

978-1-7340526-5-7 (Ebook)

DLR Publications

*"Once you've ruined your reputation,
you can live quite freely."*

-Unknown

Acknowledgements

It is a testament to the faith, grace and encouragement of the people who love me, that I was able to complete this story. I could not have done it alone. Family and friends who checked in with me from time to time reminded me that they believed in my passion for storytelling. For that, I am deeply grateful.

Those closest to me, my husband, my parents, my best friends and my children, have endured so many conversations about the ins and outs of the publishing industry! I'm sorry! Sometimes I just need to talk it out! I'm grateful to each of you for the suggestions, advice, and listening ears.

I am eternally thankful for Mrs. Debra Rhodes who has called me Superstar since the day we met. You took a chance on me, putting me under the spotlight on the big stage at the Annual Author's Brunch in the beautiful city of Chicago. Thank you for allowing me a safe space to share my triumphs and my lessons learned. I cannot wait for the opportunity to work with you again.

However… the real salute, the real big ups go to my readers! Hey, listen, I was trying to keep this message professional, but we're friends, right? May I be honest with you? Every message from a reader, every request for a book club engagement, every review on social media was my motivation to keep writing. Your purchases and feedback forced me to write when I was tired or feeling a little insecure, and I thank you so much more than you could ever fathom.

Thank you to my book club besties: Read My Lips, My Sister's Secret Book Club, U.S. G.I.R.L.S. Book Club, Reading Between the Wines, Books and Beyond, Table 4 Queens, Lit Java, We Be Book'n, Joy Book Club, Sista2Sista, The Renaissance Girls Book Club, Alpha Kappa Alpha Sorority- Zeta Mu Omega Chapter, Alpha Kappa Alpha Sorority- Omega Kappa Omega Chapter, B.P.S. (Bonnets, Pajamas, and Slippers) Book Club, ECC Book Club, The TipTopThursday Book Club, and the Glory Girls Book Club. My heart has been filled to capacity after every single meeting. I cannot thank you enough!

I will continue writing stories (no more senseless deaths, of course) as long as you'll keep rocking with me.

Aside from book clubs, I have received personal messages from readers through email and social media. Thank you for taking the time to share your kind words.

If we have not connected yet, I'd like to say I'm honored to share my work with you. Thank you for your purchase! I pray you enjoy it!

PROLOGUE

She pulled into the valet lane at a restaurant situated 65 miles beyond the city's limits and brought her car to a hard stop just inches from the bumper of the Bentley Mulsanne ahead of her. The valet, a spindly kid dressed in a crisp white sports coat, black bowtie, and black tuxedo pants, waved to her, motioning instructions to wait while he attended to the cars ahead of her.

He ran from one car to the next, greeting guests, exchanging valet tickets for key fobs, and ushering the guests toward the revolving door at the front of the restaurant. When he returned, she was not inside her own, but a different car, rifling through the glove box.

Eyebrow raised, he leaned into the car and whispered, "Hey! What are you doing there? That's not your car."

She paused to glance at him and shrugged one shoulder. "Oh, nothing. It's subliminal. I'm here to avenge Michael Jackson's death."

She lowered her voice a bit and whispered, "At least, that's what they *told* me."

The young man, unable to make sense of the disjointed explanation, and too busy to question her further, ushered the woman out of the car and into the restaurant.

Inside, she approached the hostess and requested a table for one. She ordered a sixty-five dollar steak, medium rare, and a perfect Makers Mark Manhattan. Not long after, she noticed a lively group of seven friends, both men and women, laughing and drinking good-naturedly in the booth next to hers. She invited herself into the group. She

1

was smiling, friendly, exuding happiness. "Can I join you guys?"

They transferred an expression of mild surprise from one to another and decided they were just tipsy enough to add this interesting woman to their party. She chatted with them about the weather, astrological signs and the Illuminati. While her conversation didn't compute, her eccentric behavior amused the strangers.

They asked her questions: *So, where are you from?* And she entertained them with her answers: *I don't know. Mars?* She told them her mother was Earth, that the ocean was calling her. The strangers peppered her with more questions, encouraging her wild responses. *I know I look like I'm from Venus, but I'm actually from Mars.*

When they'd had their fill of fine foods and drinks, the party of seven strangers settled their checks and left. Alone at the table, she finished her own drink and made her way to the door, but a manager stopped her.

"Ma'am. How do you plan on paying for your bill?" he asked.

Her response was casual and light. "They paid for me."

"I don't think so," he replied. "We can't allow you to leave without settling your bill."

She didn't try to run. She wasn't hostile. She was carefree and indifferent, even as the manager detained her in the nearly empty restaurant. In an attempt to settle the $96 check, and having observed her curious behavior all evening, the manager asked her if there was anyone he could call.

CHAPTER ONE

2001

Her mother had pegged her as a daddy's girl from the moment she burst into the world as a hollering, defiant chocolate-covered ball of thunder. She'd been a tiny baby, all balled fists and big mouth, well-equipped to pound and argue for her place in the world, although the opportunity was never hers to seize.

The Daddy's Girl moniker was one Julene's parents had forced her to carry, and she did, eventually learning to own it publicly, even as she rejected it privately. As she grew from a fussy toddler to a headstrong little girl, it was true that she shared many similarities with her dad. She was quick-witted and intellectual, arguing her way through any dispute with cleverness and self-assurance.

When she challenged him and won on anything—from who decided which words were *bad* and which ones were *good*, to what makes bacon and eggs more acceptable than spaghetti for breakfast—he'd grin as though she'd just beaten him in a chess match. He was never angry with her, only amused, and he'd often bait her into a robust battle of the brains just to watch her flex her mental muscles. He was proud of her, after all, because he credited himself with everything exceptional about his daughter. She would grow to become just like him, but better. What more could a parent hope for?

"You're going to be a lawyer just like your daddy. The writing's already on the wall," Brad Davis often told his daughter.

Her mother, Layla, said these things, too, pride shining in her eyes while she hovered nearby, watching the nearly daily competitions between father and daughter.

At the dinner table, in the family room, or during a car ride, Brad relished the opportunity to test his daughter with brain teasers: *What's full of holes but can still hold water?*

It's as light as a feather, but the strongest person can't hold it for more than five minutes. What is it?

You're driving a city bus. At the first stop, three women get on. At the second stop, one man gets on. At the third stop, two children get on. The bus is green, and it's raining outside in December. What color is the bus driver's hair?

She'd shout answers, right or wrong, wanting to solve the problem quickly enough to shock him. His mischievous eyes would sparkle while he watched her mind work. Her nearly correct answers brought out a smile that forced his lips apart, showing off his brilliant white teeth. Her wrong-wrong answers drew his lips into a tight, challenging smirk. Her mother's answers, if she were in the vicinity, simply went unacknowledged. The husband's smile would disappear, taking with it the wife's.

While her parents recognized the remarkable dynamic between a little girl and her father, Julene observed a different dynamic, years before she'd be able to verbalize it. Her mother adored her father, but it was obvious he didn't adore her back. When he came home from work in the evenings, he'd bypass his waiting wife with little more than a nod, before dropping his briefcase and searching the house for his daughter. A quick game of hide-and-seek was their ritual daily greeting. He'd pretend not to find her and feign heart-stopping fear when she popped out from under a table or bed or out of a closet, and then they'd collapse, laughing until they were breathless.

Sometimes he'd chase her once she came out of hiding. She'd run with a child's wild abandon, no fear of slipping or falling, around corners and through one room after another, until she found her mother. The game always ended there, with Julene hiding behind a smiling Layla, with Brad hot on her heels until he found himself within arm's reach of his wife. That's when he'd concede defeat, unwilling to tag his daughter if it meant his wife was going to play along, too. Julene watched smiles fade, first Brad's and then Layla's, once their eyes met.

Julene, the only child and common denominator between a nearly estranged husband and wife, was magical enough to make smiles appear on two faces at once, but she had to work at it. Like a magician uses sleight of hand to distract the audience from the real trick, she had to keep them both focused on her, and not one another, to make it work.

In the middle of an odd love triangle, she learned to leverage her position. She'd play the role of the merciless little attorney, or the wiz kid, or the adult-in-a-child's-body, not because she was a Daddy's Girl, as was the assumption, but because her theatrics filled the void in her mother's eyes while, at the same time, circumventing her father's attempts to turn his attention elsewhere.

She mastered the craft of giving her daddy hell— under the guise of entertaining him—to punish him for not loving her mother enough. Somehow, during those early years, a daughter harnessed the power of embodying her father just to make her mother feel loved. Because, contrary to her assumed identity, she was, in essence, a *Mommy's* Girl. She was *named* a Daddy's Girl, but she was *born* to protect her mother.

Her mother was a liar— of this Julene been certain for as long as she could remember. She'd realized her mother was a liar the way most people realize Santa Claus isn't real— with slow suspicion at first, followed by confirmation, a pang of disappointment, but no loss of love. And, much in the same way people propagate the love of Santa, even after they learn he isn't real, Julene continued to adore her mother.

Her earliest recollections—before she knew enough to label her mother's methods as actual lies—were of subtle untruths. As a small child, her mother had trained her to memorize addresses in zip codes more affluent than their own to secure seats in the city's best primary schools. She learned to smile politely and not interrupt as she listened to her mother tell friends and acquaintances about European vacations she hadn't taken, parties she hadn't thrown, and shopping sprees her husband hadn't financed.

The falsehoods and untruths eventually moved to within a shadow of the actual truth as her mother worked determinedly to establish their family's position in the community. She convinced her husband to rent a stunning home in a luxury community. She pushed her daughter to make the right friends—only those whose parents were worth befriending. She aligned herself with the city's elite—serving on committees, hosting benefits, or borrowing money from her husband's credit cards and her own to make donations to high-profile political campaigns.

As Julene grew older and learned to discern fact from fiction, she also assumed a more active role in hiding the lies—even augmenting them whenever the need arose—to protect her mother's and her family's hard-fought reputation, unaware that, by default, she'd been groomed to become a liar as well.

She learned well how to manipulate her father, to avoid public humiliation at all costs, to speak and move and look like she belonged with the cream of the bourgeois. She learned how to keep her parents satisfied, even as it left her exhausted and increasingly disillusioned.

The days of hide-and-seek could have well belonged to a different girl, a different family, for theirs was no longer a home built around the love of an only daughter. It hadn't been fun for quite some time. Instead, it had morphed into a home of pretention, of sterility. It was as though they lived in a glass house, on perpetual display for the scrutinous eyes of Chicago's African American elite. Theirs was a home governed by a woman whose eyes no longer sparkled with adoration for her husband or pride in her daughter. The awe, envy, and approval of anyone in their swelling social circle became the elixir that gave her eyes their glow.

As a teen, Julene struggled to find the rewards in her efforts. It was 1996, at the age of 15, she'd already grown tired of her life as a show horse. Her mouthy antics were no longer cute, nor were they enough to hold her father's interest and her mother's affection—and the paradigm shifted considerably with her growing awareness. Her father was no longer a man who enjoyed riddles, or hide-and-seek, or playful bantering with his daughter. Where she'd once seen him as a giant man in living color, he'd become spiritless and monochromatic.

The girl who'd been born to love her mother grew to resent the woman who expected her to wear her public facade at home. She followed her mother's lead in public—saying the right things, appearing in the right places, associating with the right people—but at home she craved normalcy. For her mother, the public persona *was* normalcy. For Julene, it was not. For both, this was the bone of contention.

The concept of normalcy, of regularity, had been just an idea. It was just an imagined thing for Julene until the weekend of the baby shower. Her mother hadn't wanted to attend the family gathering at all. She'd done well to distance herself from her own reprehensible family, but Brad still held onto the fringes of his family ties, doing his best to show up at the most important occasions, like weddings and funerals, whenever he could.

He'd distanced himself from most of his family for a variety of reasons. Perhaps it was just the element of life in which one finds fewer and fewer opportunities for casual visits with aunties, uncles, and cousins as time passes. Maybe it was his wife, exceptionally comfortable in settings she deemed prestigious, and equally uncomfortable in settings that reminded her of her own humble beginnings. The issue could have been a paralytic combination of survivor's remorse and imposter syndrome. Why had he been fortunate enough to have built this privileged lifestyle with his wife and daughter while many of his family members remained tethered to a line just above poverty? If his affluent veneer were peeled away, who would be revealed? Would the person beneath be deserving of this station, these benefits of an opulent life?

Brad's extended family wasn't nearly as well off as his immediate family, and time spent with them required him, his wife, and his daughter to confront the cultural gap separating them from their relatives. It was uncomfortable for him, but for his pregnant young niece, the family member with whom he still maintained the truest connection no matter the distance between them, he'd stood up to his wife's resistance and won.

It happened on a Tuesday evening while Julene sat at the dinner table between her parents. Her father chattered about his frustrations at work, while her mother was preoccupied with the arrangement of the spoons, forks, and knives in her place setting.

"I wasted my entire day straightening out a half-assed petition for conservatorship for a case that was postponed until September," Brad said. "Why? Because no one thought to send me the updated court calendar!"

He yanked his napkin from beneath his silverware and snapped it open before trying to shove it into his collar. Feeling his necktie still knotted at his throat, he dropped the napkin into his lap and loosened his collar. "By the time I found out the hearing had been postponed, I was late for my afternoon meeting—a completely inconsequential discovery meeting that could have been addressed in a simple email! My billable hours are barely—"

"The secret to perfect steak frites is in the bearnaise sauce."

Layla's voice rose above Brad's rant and drew Julene's eyes away from the swirling pattern she'd been drawing in her ketchup with the tip of a French fry.

"Taste it! Tell me what you think," Layla encouraged. She leaned back in her seat and glanced from her husband to her daughter and back again, waiting for either of them to take a bite.

"I worked on this recipe for hours today."

Brad abandoned his unfinished story and cut into his steak. Julene lifted the French fry she'd been drawing with and popped it into her mouth, watching for her father's reaction to the steak bite he'd popped into his own mouth.

They chewed carefully, the room filled only with the sounds of their chewing, before Brad nodded with slow approval.

"It's good," Julene said, her voice echoing through the dining room louder than she'd have liked, although she appreciated the way it drowned out the sound of her father chewing meat. "But maybe it's kind of...chewy? I can't eat very much."

"Remember, we don't speak with food in our mouths, right?" Layla said. Her tepid voice betrayed her overachieving smile. Leaving no space for a response, she continued, "I'm not sure what you mean by 'kind of chewy', but this is fine dining. Your palate just isn't refined enough to know the difference, so you need to learn how to fake it until you make it. Never let your face show surprise or disappointment. One day you may find yourself dining with dignitaries and politicians—heads of state—and you'll need to maintain your poise, no matter what's on your plate."

"If I don't want it, why do I have to eat it?" Julene pushed her plate away and tossed her napkin atop the swirled ketchup.

Brad spoke then, after laboring to swallow and chasing it with a gulp from his wine glass. "Julene, don't disrespect your mother. She prepared this meal for us and if it isn't to your liking, you can respectfully excuse yourself while we finish our dinner."

The word *excuse* hadn't quite cleared his lips before Julene was up, happy to remove herself from the nightly torture of this dinner for three.

Their meal, which Layla had presented as pan-seared steak frites with bearnaise, was in fact a pre-made Encore microwavable meal. Earlier, Julene had seen the empty box in the garbage bin, although she'd never breathe a word to expose her mother's secret. Layla had plated the Salisbury steak and potato wedges on the same delicate dinner plates she'd owned when she met Brad back in college, dicing the beef patties and arranging them in the center of each plate. She'd even gone so far as to drizzle gravy on the plates with the flair of a Michelin chef, reserving the rest for the gravy boat that matched her dinner plates. The dinnerware was service for four, and she always set the table as such, even though they were only a family of three.

Layla, over-riding Brad's instructions, refused to let her daughter leave the room. "You are not excused. Please have a seat."

Her words pulled Julene back into her chair and sent Brad's left leg into a bouncing fit, something he did when he was nervous. Layla studied her family in silence while they fidgeted, and glanced at one another, arranging and rearranging their utensils until they finally surrendered and directed their attention toward her. After a moment, she cleared her throat, smoothed the napkin into her lap, and picked up her own knife and fork. "You know, when I was away at boarding school, we were taught to—"

"You never went to boarding school," Brad interrupted as he placed his napkin into his lap and shook his head softly as though he were correcting a small child.

His wife faltered for a moment, smiled at her husband and nodded, before continuing her story. "When I was away at boarding school, we were—"

This time, Brad interrupted by introducing a new subject, rather than debating with his wife. "Lucille is hosting a shower for Baby Mama and we've been invited. It's—"

"Who?" Layla's question was a live grenade, a quiet threat tumbling across the dinner table. She busied herself with a potato wedge, not bothered to lift her eyes in her husband's direction.

"Lucille. My *sister* Lucille. Her daughter Vanessa is expecting a baby and the whole family will be there to celebrate." Brad's words were measured, filtered, balanced on the edge of a virtual cliff.

Layla's voice was lighter, amused as she tossed a resolution across the table while balancing a small piece of a potato wedge on the tip of her fork. "Another baby, huh? I can see why they call her Baby Mama. I never understood why an adult woman with a name as beautiful as Vanessa would allow herself to be called *Baby Mama* in public, but it's starting to make sense. I'll find her a gift at Neiman tomorrow and drop it in the mail. What's the address?"

Brad stilled his bouncing leg and leaned back in his chair. "We're not mailing a gift. We'll deliver it in person. I told them we'd be there. The party is Saturday, the 26th."

"I'm sorry. I'm sure I've got another engagement that day. It just won't work. You'll have to give her our regards and let her know we must decline." Layla spoke slowly and distinctly, offering Brad the opportunity to memorize her scripted words and properly relay them to his family.

Brad's leg bounced again, but his voice held more resolve. "I'm going to be with my family on that day…"

"We're your family." Layla leaned across the dinner table for emphasis.

"…and I'd like for you and Julene to accompany me. But, if you don't—if you won't—I'll have to go alone." He paused and glanced at Julene. "Unless you want to go with me. The family would love to see you."

His leg no longer bounced. He stood firmly on the strength of his ultimatum, but a smothering silence hovered over the table. He tapped his knife on the edge of his plate while Julene watched for her mother's reaction, intrigued.

Her parents rarely argued. More accurately, her father rarely challenged her mother. Julene had seen his frustration simmer to the surface more than once, but he had never boiled over.

Layla leaned back and shook her head in disbelief. "You're not taking my daughter into that *environment* without me. She doesn't know those people! I mean, my God! *You* barely know them! Why is this so urgent? Why can't we go the next time? Surely this isn't the last baby for your precious niece." She looked toward Julene, eyes searching for an ally. Finding none, she softened her gaze and returned her attention to her husband. "Brad. Please. Is this really necessary?"

He met her gaze, placed his knife alongside his plate, and stood. "You've brainwashed yourself into forgetting about your own family. I won't let you erase mine, too."

Layla laughed out loud. She stood and began gathering the plates filled with uneaten food while Brad stood watching, unsure if the conversation was over.

When Layla reached Brad's end of the table, she paused to look up at him. "The people who raised me were never my family. I never belonged with them. I was different—I always knew I was. I always knew I was better, just like I knew you were better than yours. We've always had that in common. We left those people behind, and we created the family we always deserved. We created *us*—this is who we are now."

She waved her arms about. For a moment, she reminded Julene of the inflatable tube man she always saw flopping around outside the used car dealership near the highway. She suppressed a laugh.

Layla moved toward the kitchen, arms laden with dishes, and returned with a tray of coffee, still talking. "…deserve this, we earned this. We have nothing to feel guilty about. This is where we belong, and there's no need for us to go slumming around the *ghetto* with people we don't know just because we happen to belong to the same family tree." She placed the tray on the table and began pouring coffee into mugs.

"Here, sit and have your after-dinner coffee," she invited as she placed the mug near Brad's seat at the table. "We won't be attending your niece's *baby shower*. I've decided it. Please just give them our regrets and let's move on. I understand it's difficult for you to make the hard decisions sometimes, and I've been patient with you, but I'm becoming annoyed. Be a man just this once, and don't force me to push your hand. You'll only wind up embarrassed."

Brad's voice was a low growl, barely loud enough to reach the spot where Julene remained glued to her seat at the table. She'd been munching on a cookie but stopped chewing long enough to hear him make her mother a promise. "Push my hand? I invite you to do that. Embarrass me? I've been embarrassed before and I've survived. You'd better worry about *me* pushing *your* hand.

If you awaken the sleeping bear inside me, you'll pray you don't live long enough to regret it."

Layla's breath caught in her throat, forcing her eyes to widen before she gathered herself and found the smile she'd worn earlier in the evening. Laughter filled her voice as she picked up her coffee. "I won't worry about awakening this *sleeping bear* you speak of. If it hasn't been awakened yet, I doubt you'll ever be able to get it up."

Brad and Layla fell quiet, each having drawn a line in the sand, silently challenging the other to cross. Julene attempted to break the tension by changing the subject. "Mother, I was invited to a birthday sleepover for my friend Arlen. I think you met her family at the school fundraiser last month. Do you think it would be okay if I attend?"

Arlen had been adopted at the start of the school year, pulled from the foster care system by a wealthy family in their community and thrust into the private school Julene attended along with 1,364 elitist juveniles. She'd struggled to adapt to the culture, having come from West Philadelphia where she'd lived with her birth mother and a host of siblings, only to be taken into the custody of the Child Welfare system after her mother's arrest during a traffic stop.

Adopted and slow to make friends, Arlen ate lunch alone in the school cafeteria until Julene joined her. The two girls shared an art class together, eventually progressing to form a natural friendship. Theirs was an easy and refreshing friendship because although Arlen had been adopted, the air of privilege hadn't adopted her. Julene was drawn to the new girl's earthy nature.

Layla rolled her eyes. "Julene, you've got to be more selective about how you choose your friends. What can she offer you? What can her family offer? They're wealthy but they have no leverage. I mean, her father made a bid for Illinois Secretary of State and couldn't even get elected! When that family manages to achieve something worthwhile, maybe we can consider associating with them, but for now, the answer is no. Understand?"

Julene glanced at her father, found no support, then nodded at her mother, crestfallen.

Layla smiled again. "I'll make plans for you to have an outing with Madison, Brooke, Daryl, and Candace soon. I think they're better suited to be in your company." She exhaled as though she'd managed enough of her family's challenges for one day. "I'm tired now. I'll take my coffee in the study."

She disappeared into her 'study'—the spare bedroom she'd furnished with a chaise lounge and a few strategically arranged books selected more for their visual appeal than their literary content—and Brad withdrew into his own darkly-appointed office filled with shelves of identical leather-bound books, each one a volume of blank pages, selected for their aesthetic value once upon a time when he cared about making appearances just as much as his wife did. He softly closed the door behind himself, shuttering his rage and shutting out his wife's acrimonious taunts, his quiet aggression evidenced only by the click of the door lock.

Julene sat at the table alone with the remnants of her parents' conversation. The jangle of ice cubes tumbling into a glass could be heard on the other side of her father's door. The thick, muted sound of liquid sloshing into a glass came next, followed by a palpable silence. She imagined her father on the other side of the door having a long sip and rubbing his head, as he often did when he was stressed. She imagined her mother lying delicately along her chaise in her study, a tortured queen, self-appointed to reign supreme over a cardboard castle and her dissenting subjects.

Julene wished, as she had so often before today, for a sibling to share a knowing glance with right now. Someone who could recall the days when adoration and wanting for Brad lit up Layla's face, despite his disinterest. Someone who would remember the day the parents became housemates. Someone intimately involved enough to feel the change in temperature when the parents spoke to one another now—the cooling of the air when Layla flexed some hidden wild card, the heating of the air when Brad hinted at his own unplayed card.

A brother or sister, a shared partner in this experience, would wait until the parents had retreated, and then run with her, breathless, upstairs into a bedroom to whisper about what had just happened. A sibling, a built-in best friend, would be there to witness and dissect the issues that weren't meant to be discussed outside the home. They'd see the madness with their own eyes, not needing Julene to provide any explanation or backstory, and they'd help her make sense of it all. The task of shining light into the dark corners of their home, the burden of providing warmth to their frigid existence, required backup. It required support. She'd managed, as most only children do, to trudge this road alone, to shoulder the weight of loneliness and deeply seated dysfunction on her own, but in times like this, when she was left sitting alone at a massive dining table, the deficit in her life grew to become a gaping hole, magnifying the silence inside the house.

After another moment, having abandoned the daydream of having someone to scurry upstairs with for a *what-just-happened* conference, Julene drifted into her own room. She lay on her bed, mulling over her mother's words. *People who raised me. Family. Different.* These words opened the door for a stream of questions Julene had never considered. *Aren't the people who raise you your family? Do you just get to leave if you don't like them? Can you just make your own, new family if you accidentally wind up with the wrong one? And, if you ran away from your family, wouldn't they come looking for you? Wouldn't they miss you and want you back? Can you even go back?*

Her mother had certainly distanced herself from her own family—the people who raised her—and had ventured out to exist in a world of her own creation. She'd insisted on buying a home in a gated community, having an unpublished phone number, and private schools for Julene—decisions that enabled her to craft a new story, to paint a new picture, and reframe her upbringing and credentials, as well as her husband's. She'd birthed Julene into a world of make-believe, and she hadn't done it on her own. Brad, for all his sullenness and unveiled misery, remained by her side, a silent participant. He'd played his role without ceasing, tolerating the lies and disrespect well past the years when most of Julene's friends had watched their own parents navigate the realities of separation and divorce.

His rare expression of defiance, coupled with the thought of her daughter's exposure to such an unsavory environment, became the catalyst that put them all on the road to the baby shower. Despite her distaste for the extended family and her insistence on declining the invitation, Layla tapped on Julene's door and pushed it open without waiting for a response.

"I've decided we'll be able to attend the baby shower," she announced. "It's against my better judgment, but I'm not an irrational woman. I'm perfectly capable of mingling with ordinary people, and I'll teach *you* how to do it, too. But don't worry, darling, just follow my lead. We will make our appearance early and we'll be back here at home before the sun sets."

She said it all in one breath, as though she had rehearsed her declaration just before she stepped into the room, then she slipped away into the shadowed hallway, leaving Julene alone with new worries, new questions.

Though her mother was eccentric, Julene trusted her to keep her safe. Safe from what? From whom? Her father's family? Would there be drugs? Fighting? Liquor bottles and stray dogs? She'd heard her mother use the term 'lowlife' more than once. She imagined the homeless men she'd seen standing on the corners when they were forced to drive through the bad sections of the city. She remembered women in hair bonnets and house slippers sitting on bus stop benches, jostling fat babies or begging strangers for spare change—the people her mother had warned her she'd become if she didn't do as she was told. She obsessed about the growing anxiety over meeting these uncivilized relatives for the rest of that night, and the next, and the next, until the day of the trip was finally upon her.

On the afternoon of the baby shower, they drove the forty-three miles to the country in a Mercedes just like their own, but better. The day before they were to leave, Julene stood quietly while her mother insisted the service manager at the Mercedes dealership perform thorough diagnostic tests on their car.

"It makes a noise when I'm driving— not every time, but quite often. My daughter can tell you. She heard it for herself on the drive here just this morning."

Julene, upon hearing reference to herself, looked first at her mother and then at the service manager, before nodding in agreement. She hadn't really heard a noise to her knowledge, but she was well-trained in the art of following her mother's lead, even if she didn't know where she was going.

"Mrs. Davis, my guys are pretty backed up in the garage," the service manager said, removing his hat. He smoothed the thin veil of hair that lay across his forehead and replaced the cap. "I can't guarantee I can get it pulled into the bay for a once-over until Monday, at the earliest. Can you bring it back on Monday?"

Layla stepped backward and placed a hand on her hip. "You don't honestly expect *me* to drive my family around in this *death trap* until you have time to fix it. My husband has spent a substantial amount of money in your establishment, and now you're telling me you aren't willing to stand behind your own vehicle? You sold me a lemon and you won't be able to deal with it until *whenever*?"

She spoke in incrementally louder octaves, willing to make a scene, willing to insult the integrity of every vehicle on his lot, until he responded appropriately.

"Tell you what I can do," the poor service manager said. He exhaled, never having a fighting chance against this expert manipulator. "I can put you in a loaner for the weekend. I want you and your family to feel safe. That's our number one priority. I'll have my guys take a good look at your car and I'll personally call you when we know what the issue is. How's that sound?"

Julene's mother crossed her arms, glanced at her daughter, and then leaned in to read the man's name tag. "What's your name? Greg? You're not putting me in some filthy rental, are you, Greg? I expect you to provide me with a vehicle comparable to the one I currently own."

He turned to the pegboard behind him and flipped through the key fobs, checking the make and model of each vehicle. "Just a second. Let me see…"

"I also expect your *loaner* to come with a full tank of gas. I shouldn't have to be inconvenienced to put fuel in *your* car just because you don't have time to repair *mine*."

The service manager peeked at Layla over his shoulder. "You're a tough negotiator, huh?" He smiled at her and walked around the desk. "Here's what I'm going to do because I want to make sure you're satisfied. Pick the one you want."

He guided her toward the window and gestured at the line of Mercedes Benzes parked outside.

Layla tapped her daughter on the arm, pointing at the collection of cars. "Darling, why don't you pick a car for us?"

When Julene and her mother pulled the new Mercedes off the dealer's lot, she nudged her daughter and patted the steering wheel. "*That's* how you get a brand-new car for free when you need to impress the other side of the family."

And so, they drove the forty-three miles to the country in an upgraded, larger, late model version of their own certified pre-owned Mercedes. Julene had selected the same color—black—because it suited her mood. She didn't want to take the trip at all, having exhausted herself with her own worries about going to the ghetto. She'd begged her parents to let her stay home while they drove down and visited family members she barely knew. She was unsuccessful in her efforts, her mother holding firm to the idea that they looked "better together."

For as long as Julene could remember, Layla had preached her longstanding ideology that the three of them looked more aesthetically pleasing when they appeared at public events together. To argue that a distant family member's baby shower wasn't necessarily a public event would have been a wasted effort, although Julene had considered trying it anyway. In the end, she conceded, as her mother had weeks before, but for a different reason. She simply knew she wouldn't win.

She was quiet in the back seat, watching the city shrink away in the distance, until her mother began reciting her list of warnings and acceptable behaviors:

We're just going here to show our faces, support your father, and then we're leaving, so watch for my cue.

Don't eat anything before checking with me. I'm not sure what they're serving, and who knows how they're preparing the food. That's why we ate lunch before we left home.

Leave your purse in the trunk of the car. We'll lock it up when we get there. Just for safety.

I don't care what everyone else is doing. I want you to remember we are not like them. We have class, and I expect you to govern yourself accordingly at all times.

"So, why, if they're so bad, are we going?" Julene challenged.

Layla didn't answer, forcing Brad to explain the reason for a trip she wasn't interested in taking. He exhaled, long and slow, until he could correctly balance reason and authority in his tone. "First of all, they are not *bad*, they are *family*. Second, my niece needs to know her family supports her, and that includes us."

Layla, staring out of the passenger window, not bothering to face him, had a question. "How many fathers do her children have? I'd say she probably has all the support she needs."

There was silence in the car after that. No music. No road trip trivia or jokes. Only space for Julene to prepare herself for this afternoon she'd have to endure with *the family*. She smoothed her dress, an Ann Taylor shirt dress she'd chosen because her mother had advised her to dress down. Her hair, a smooth Doobie with a hump and a bump, still smelled of finishing spray. She wore brand new sandals, exclusive leather thongs by an emerging designer from New York named Tory Burch. Her shades, simple Ray Bans, were resting just above her forehead, ready to be pulled over her eyes should she find herself needing to avoid eye contact or potentially awkward conversations with these people whom she barely knew.

CHAPTER TWO

The music from the party had already traveled to the entrance of the neighborhood where Brad's sister, Lucille, had lived for thirty-three years. When their loaned Mercedes turned in, they could hear it before they could see it— a celebration that had spilled out of the backyard, right into the street. Cars, parked haphazardly along the curb and some homes' front lawns, made the street difficult to navigate, and after driving to the end of the street and turning around again, Julene's father ultimately pulled onto someone's lawn and parked next to some other cars.

The homes here were all the same—narrow, cookie-cutter dwellings without fences, or landscaping, or identities. All were white single-story boxes with wooden siding and black shutters. Each yard flowed right into the next, each teaming with parked cars and meandering people, making it impossible to tell which home was actually hosting the party.

Brad, Layla, and Julene followed the music, walking across lawn after lawn, as Layla whispered *God help us* under her breath every so often. Brad led the way between the houses, walking faster toward the sound of almost-forgotten voices, until they arrived in the backyard, greeted by a sea of smiling, laughing faces. There were tables and chairs of all varieties, some made for indoor use, some for the outdoors, all dragged into the yard for whomever needed a seat. A group of men surrounded the grill, one of them holding a pair of tongs, the rest holding beer cans, all holding a conversation at the top of their voices.

Children played off to the side, some on a trampoline, some on a rusted swing set, the front leg lifting from the ground and settling again whenever a child pushed toward the sky. A group of women sat at a table near the back door, swatting at mosquitoes, laughing about a story one of them was telling, pausing occasionally to call out to the children and remind them to play nice.

The small family stood for a second, taking in the revelry. Julene held the oversized gift box, wrapped by the associates at Neiman Marcus with silver paper, silver ribbon, and an ornamental gift tag. Her mother's distaste could not be contained.

"This isn't a baby shower!" she exclaimed. "They didn't even decorate. Not even a tent?"

An older woman appeared before them, all laughter and hugs.

"I'm so glad you all could make it! So good to see you after—how long's it been—doesn't matter!" the woman greeted. "You're here now! Make yourselves comfortable."

She ushered Layla toward the loose grouping of women, and Brad toward the men. Next, she looked at Julene and said, "I'm your Aunt Lucille! Just take that beautiful gift inside. Put it on the table in there and then come on out here and fix yourself a plate if you want."

"Thank you so much, but she isn't hungry. We had a late lunch," Layla explained as Julene disappeared inside the house.

"Juju! Is that you? You made it!"

A girl just about Julene's age grabbed her, tossed the gift onto the couch, and pulled her into a hug. She released her and grabbed her arm, pulling her into the kitchen. Aluminum pans of every conceivable size and shape covered the table and lined the countertops. Well-worn, industrial-grade pots occupied every eye on the stove.

"You don't remember me, do you?" the girl said. "I can tell by your expression, but that's okay."

Julene stared at the girl who resembled her so closely, who felt so familiar, though she couldn't say for sure. She *sounded* familiar, but her box braids, gold beads, nose ring, and belly piercing were not.

"It's me. Your cousin, Lori." she announced. "Remember when I came to your house that time with my mom? We were like, six, I guess? And we played in that big doll house you had?"

Julene smiled then, recalling the fun little girl who'd come to play with her nine years ago. Her mother had been livid. She'd heard her parents arguing about it later that her father had allowed someone from *that* side of the family to come over and bring her children without providing twenty-four hours' notice or even calling first. They were just in the area, he'd explained, so they stopped by. It's rude and presumptuous, her mother had shouted. Anyone with class would know that.

"I almost forgot about that!" Julene said. "It was forever ago. What have you been up to?"

"Just hanging out, you know?" Lori paused, taking in Julene's expression, her appearance. "Why're you dressed like a schoolteacher? You look uncomfortable."

Julene looked down at her dress and sandals, comparing her outfit to Lori's baby tee nearly overtaken by Tommy Hilfiger's logo, clingy jeans, bright, white Air Force Ones, and oversized gold hooped earrings. Her braids swept her backside when she moved. "I… my mother didn't know what—"

"I get it. I know your mom's real fancy. You didn't have to dress up, though," Lori said as she released Julene's arm and handed her a Styrofoam takeout container. "Let's make our plates now before all the good stuff is gone. I always hide my plate in the back of the fridge for later."

She lowered her voice to a whisper and glanced around to confirm no one else was in earshot. "Don't eat anything in the glass dishes, like that macaroni right there. It has no taste! You can tell by the color alone—no seasoning."

Lori nodded toward a Pyrex dish filled with milky-white noodles. "Aunt Elaine made that. She swears she can cook, but her food always tastes like water. It's easy for me to tell what she brought because she uses those glass pans."

She nodded toward a cluster of aluminum pans on the table. "Anything in those pans was made by Aunt Lucille. You can trust her cooking. She used to work in the school cafeteria when I was little. Everybody loved her cooking! When she retired, she brought her pots home. She said they were her trophies."

Lori giggled and pointed at the massive pots covering the stovetop. "Cousin, those pots are magic! Anything she cooks is dope. And look—" She ran to the oven and opened it. "Aunt Lucille's macaroni is in here. She puts real cheese in hers. None of that plastic government stuff. Let everyone else eat Aunt Elaine's. This one is for us. Come on."

Lori busied herself scooping the steaming, golden noodles with the browned edges into one half of her own takeout container before moving on to the table where she peeled the foil lids from the aluminum pans. She filled her box with barbequed chicken, Polish sausages, potato salad, and baked beans while Julene stood rooted in the doorway, clutching her empty container.

"What's wrong?" Lori asked as struggled to close the lid on her over-filled container, pausing when she realized her cousin hadn't joined in. "Aunt Lucille won't be mad. Trust me. She knows I get my food first every time we have a get-together."

"It's not that. I just—we just ate lunch so I'm not very hungry." Julene recited the script her mother had written, even as her stomach rumbled, screaming for a taste of everything Lori had heaped into her takeout box.

"Who eats *before* they come to a cookout? I only do that if I'm going to someone's house and I don't trust their cook—ohh…" Lori's face ran a gamut of expressions of confusion, enlightenment, and amusement in quick succession while Julene had to admit it sounded foolish. Maybe it was the growling deep inside her belly, a primal reaction to the promise of Aunt Lucille's cooking. Maybe it was the immediate connection she shared with Lori, a cousin she'd only briefly known long ago, who somehow felt like she could be trusted with a sister's confidence. Whatever the reason, it didn't feel like betrayal when she said, "It's just my mother. She's weird about certain things. She doesn't even eat at her friends' houses unless the food is catered."

Lori tilted her head and studied her cousin. "Are you hungry? Yes or no?" She burst into laughter and placed her takeout box in Julene's hands. "Try mine. If you like it, eat it. Your mom's outside. How's she gonna know if you eat food? I'll fix another plate for myself."

She handed Julene a plastic cutlery packet with a fork, knife, spoon and paper napkin. "Uncle Julius works at Jofra. He brings this stuff home by the case."

"Jofra…," Julene repeated slowly, allowing it to settle in her mind somewhere between familiar and foreign.

Lori, taking note of her cousin's dilemma, offered gentle clues to jog Julene's memory. "I know you know Jofra. You've heard of it. It's that big restaurant depo out there in Goose Island. You probably don't go to those types of neighborhoods that much, but I'm sure you've seen their commercials before—the ones with Jack and the Beanstalk?"

Julene immediately visualized the commercials and their slogan, Jack loves Jofra! "I know that place! I mean, I know the commercials. I used to love the one where Jack comes down the beanstalk to buy milk for his kids and ends up buying so much kitchen equipment that he can't carry it up the stalk. The look on his kids' faces when they come down the stalk and see him standing there wearing that chef's hat and apron and making sausage dogs and cotton candy is hilarious!"

"Right, right—that's the place!" Lori confirmed. "Uncle Julius is the warehouse boss there. He's not the big boss yet, but he basically runs the place. He used to get into a lot of trouble when he was younger—from what I hear—and people used to say he would never straighten up, but Aunt Lucille always said he was going to prove everyone wrong. She always believed in him."

Lori paused and tilted her head as though she were processing the words that had just come out of her own mouth. "Now that I think of it, Aunt Lucille says the same thing about me, too. She says that about all of us. She makes you feel like you can do no wrong and she will fight anybody who says otherwise." She laughed at the picture she'd drawn with her words. "Can you imagine Aunt Lucille fighting anybody? They said she used to be tough in the streets when she was younger and she was always protecting her family—especially your dad because a lot of people used to say he was—" She paused, searching her memory for the bits of conversation she'd heard over the years. "—soft? Or maybe he was small for his age?"

She shrugged, more interested in the gist of the story than the minor details. She continued rattling off her understanding of their family history. "I wish I could have seen Aunt Lucille throwing hands, but you know, this was way before we were born. Before she got all saved in the Lord. They said she would fight anybody who messed with your daddy. I mean, the big boys, too. Your daddy was something special to her. She definitely made a name for herself in the streets back then because now, as soon as people find out Lucille is your people, you get automatic respect."

Lori chattered on, repeating what she'd heard about how Uncle Julius could get the hookup on the items he stocked at work, explaining why certain family members were here at the baby shower and some weren't, and bragging about why she was secretly Aunt Lucille's favorite niece.

Her words fell on deaf ears. All outside distractions scattered into the peripheral when the first bite of Aunt Lucille's food crossed Julene's lips. Lori's voice was distant, muted, while Julene explored the flavors of the small buffet. She enjoyed each dish separately and then found even greater delight when they were combined: chicken with potato salad, polish sausage with macaroni, baked beans with meatballs—every combination was superb, every flavor a compliment to the next. The sound of Lori's giggle interrupted the intimacy she shared with the takeout container, and she looked up, dazed and hazy.

"You were doing a happy dance while you were eating." Lori rocked side to side, imitating Julene's movements. "I get it. Aunt Lucille's cooking will make anybody dance. Even your mom if she would try it."

That's when the shrieking began. A woman's shrill voice pierced through the music in the backyard. A low rumble of adult voices grew, overtaking the shrieking only for a moment before the shrill voice took the lead again. The energy of the commotion outside differed from that of a raucous spades game or a spirited open discussion. The girls sensed as much, and they ran to the window in time to see Julene's parents engaged in a very public argument.

They watched Layla pace the length of the yard, trailed by Brad, while the remainder of the party guests looked on, astounded. Layla's high-octave voice rang across the yard, *take me home take me home right now I want to go home right now,* while Brad's deeper voice pleaded, *calm down just wait just calm down,* cautiously, timidly, touching her arm, only to have her shrug him off, jerking her body away from him no matter which way he approached.

The argument escalated while everyone watched until two women approached the couple, offering Layla a glass of wine. Words were offered along with the wine, though the girls couldn't hear them, and the argument subsided for a moment, before Layla slammed the wine glass onto the ground and turned her back to her husband and the two women. The wine glass, no more than a plastic, Jofra goblet, bounced on the grass twice before rolling under a nearby table. Around them, hands lifted to cover mouths and eyes bulged at the shame of it all.

Brad reached out again, touching Layla's shoulder, only to have her jerk herself beyond his reach. His lips moved in a pleading fashion, his face pinched, and he extended his hand toward her again. This time, Aunt Lucille intervened, gently pushing Brad away, and positioning herself in front of Layla, waving a brown medicine bottle and offering a tissue. Layla accepted the tissue and declined the medicine bottle. From the kitchen window, the girls could see Aunt Lucille pleading, saying words that finally forced Layla's shoulders to drop, bouncing softly in rhythm with her sobs.

Lori turned to Julene. "Maybe we should go out there. I think those are Aunt Lucille's nerve pills in that bottle. She always feels better when she takes them. Maybe that's what your mom needs. Don't you want to check on her?"

"I can't go out there." Julene backed away from the window, not wanting her parents—or anyone—to catch her watching. "Daddy can usually calm her down, but I've never seen it this bad. When she gets upset like this, they always tell me to stay out of it." She looked over at the container of food she had abandoned. "There's still a lot left in there if you want it. I know she won't let me take it when we leave."

The girls exchanged quiet glances. The afternoon, once brightened by the glow of the cousins' unexpected bond, was instantly overshadowed by the rapidly inflated adult drama. Julene moved toward the door. "I guess we'll be leaving soon now that we've ruined the party. Maybe I can come back to visit sometime."

"Who's talking about going somewhere? Who's leaving?" Aunt Lucille slipped into the kitchen with quiet grace. Her presence commanded respect while demanding peace. She was a petite woman who exuded pure comfort and spoke with a soft voice. She hugged the girls, one on each side. "Your mother isn't feeling well. I think maybe the heat got to her out there. We haven't had a summer this hot since I was a little girl."

She used one hand to pull Julene closer and smoothed her hair. "Your dad is going to take her home and let her get some rest. You're going to stay with us tonight. That way he can focus on taking care of your mother. That okay with you?"

"I didn't bring an overnight bag," Julene said softly. She mentioned this detail, not in protest, but unsure if the logistics had been considered.

Aunt Lucille offered another quick hug and released the girls. "You can borrow some pajamas from Lori tonight, and she can give you something to wear tomorrow until your father comes back to get you. I always keep spare toothbrushes here—you never know who might drop in— and I should have an extra bonnet for your hair."

She smiled, turned her attention toward a plastic-wrapped tray of pound cake slices, and pinched off a piece.

Her smile faded while she struggled to swallow the bite, then she cleared her throat and whispered to the girls, "Tastes like Elaine made that cake. I wouldn't eat it if I were you. Not unless you got a whole jug of milk to drink behind it. If your Uncle Randy brings his Blueberry Delight later, save me a piece, will you?"

When the door closed behind Aunt Lucille and they were alone in the kitchen again, Lori hugged Julene and gave her a high five. "I'm glad you didn't have to leave! I mean, I hope your mom feels better, but I didn't want you to leave before we—"

The tapping on the kitchen window startled them both, interrupting their celebration. When they stepped to the window, Aunt Lucille was standing there. Lori lifted the glass. "I meant to tell you to start bringing the gifts out. Baby Mama should be here soon."

"Yes, Ma'am. Where do you want us to put them?" Lori asked.

Aunt Lucille had already begun walking across the backyard, out of earshot, but she pointed to a small table and chair decorated with blue streamers and balloons. Lori grabbed her takeout container and Julene's, stashing them in the furthest corner of the refrigerator.

"Late night snack," she whispered before skipping into the front room to grab an armful of gifts.

Julene followed, grabbing as many packages as she could carry, and then standing back to let Lori lead the way. The girls wound their way across the yard, finding a path through the loosely arranged tables and chairs until they reached the spot Aunt Lucille had designated. There, they piled the gifts on the table and turned to head back to the house.

"Don't leave! I need you to help me. I'm putting you girls to work."

Aunt Lucille appeared behind them, handing Julene a notepad and pencil, and tossing Lori a small roll of trash bags. "What I need you to do is write down each gift and who gave it," she explained, nodding in Julene's direction. "And you're in charge of grabbing all of the wrapping paper in these trash bags when she opens them."

She smiled at Lori. "Think you can handle that? I'm going to sit right here and rest my tired feet. I've been up since four-thirty this morning, cooking and getting everything ready. I hope this is the last baby shower I have to put on for a very long—"

She stopped mid-sentence and looked across the yard, a warm smile stretching across her face. Lori and Julene turned to look, too.

A small mahogany brown woman, all white teeth and well-rounded belly flitted across the yard in their direction, stopping to hug and kiss every guest she encountered along the way. Her outfit—an oversized t-shirt with the shimmering words Baby Mama airbrushed in hot pink across the front, black spandex shorts, and a pristine pair of Michael Jordan sneakers—left Julene stunned. Her father's favorite little niece, the day's Guest of Honor, looked like she'd stepped right out of a rap video. Her hair was molded into a flawless French roll, giving way to a cascade of soft curls that fell across one side of her forehead. A glittering crown etched with the words Baby Mama sat nestled among the curls in a way that reminded Julene of the Hollywood sign in California she'd fibbed about visiting last summer.

Given the venue, a sparsely decorated backyard, she hadn't expected this shower to be as sophisticated as the country club and ballroom showers she'd attended with her mother in the past. But, the sneakers, the tee shirt, the colorful, unapologetic flamboyance? She'd never seen anything quite like it. *Obnoxious* is what Layla would have said about her. Julene could practically hear her mother's words echo in her ears, although that title didn't reconcile with the woman walking toward her. This small woman with the enormous belly, the deep dark skin, the glowing white teeth, and the one-of-a kind outfit exuded confidence and love. Her energy, her very essence, rivaled Oz's Good Witch Glenda's, complete with the magic wand

and fairy dust, for the way she left a trail of goodness and joy in her wake.

Eventually, she made her way to Lori, whom she hugged for a long moment and kissed on both cheeks, and Aunt Lucille, whose hands she clasped in her own, swinging them side-to-side before releasing them and pulling her into a deep and playful hug.

"Mama!" she exclaimed. "Everything looks amazing! You know you really outdid yourself with this shower. You even got Uncle Donald here?"

She paused to glance around the yard, taking in the crowd of familiar faces once more, before leaning a little closer to Aunt Lucille to whisper, "I stopped in the kitchen to make my plates before I came out here." She rubbed her belly softly. "I'm eating for two, right? I hid mine in the bottom drawer in the fridge. I got a little bit of Aunt Elaine's food, too. I'm not eating it, but it'll make her feel good if she thinks someone tried it."

Their foreheads touched softly while they shared a laugh filled with history and understanding. Julene hovered behind Aunt Lucille, captivated by the tender moment between mother and daughter. She was caught by surprise when she locked eyes with Baby Mama.

"Julene? You guys came! I'm so glad. Your daddy said he would be here, but you know how that goes. I know he gets so busy. I understand it, but I'm glad you guys were able to make it this time. Look at how mature you are!" She turned to Aunt Lucille, and said, "Look at this beautiful girl!"

She spoke to Julene. "It seems like you were just a little girl, and the next thing I know, you've grown into a woman! I can't get over it!" Her words were threaded together in one glittering, breathless strand, forming a web that ensnared Julene even before the last word left her lips. In the same moment, she swept Julene into her arms, pulling her into an overly familiar embrace, ignoring the boundaries of personal space, and kissing her on both cheeks as she'd done with Lori. The delicate fragrances of Ivory soap, cocoa butter and baby powder wafted in the air between them like a magic potion. Julene understood then why her father adored his niece with such devotion. She was ethereal, magnetic, endearing.

A stream of thoughts flooded Julene's mind. *You smell nice. You're beautiful. I love you.* The words she ultimately spoke aloud were embarrassingly inadequate.

"I like your—shoes," Julene stuttered, cringing at the sound of her own voice.

Baby Mama didn't find the compliment awkward at all. "You like these? I know a guy who can get Jordans as soon as they hit the street—for cheap. What size are you? I'll find you a pair. And where is your father? I haven't seen him yet."

Her words flowed, smooth and fast, one into the next, as though she was speaking in cursive, as she surveyed the yard to see if she had overlooked Brad.

"He had to leave." Julene cast her eyes downward, wanting to pretend her parents' public altercation hadn't happened.

Stillness hung in the air between Julene, Baby Mama, Aunt Lucille and Lori.

Aunt Lucille spoke after a moment. "Brad will be back tomorrow. Layla wasn't feeling good, so he had to take her home. Julene is staying here with us tonight and he'll come back to pick her up tomorrow." She pointed toward the men still crowded around the grill, still laughing and slapping each other on the backs, and brightened her voice. "Let's get this party started. Go over there and tell Bootie to do the blessing so we can eat and then you can open your gifts."

Julene watched as Bootie, a tall, thin man, moved away from the rest of the men and stood in the open space near the center of the yard. He was older. She could tell by the way his thin skin clung to his bald head, high cheekbones, sharp nose and broad chin. He had the lean, brittle stature of an elderly man, and his large ears reminded Julene of an odd fact she'd learned in her biology class last year—the bones in the body stop growing after puberty, but the cartilage in the ears continues growing throughout our lives. Judging by the size of his ears, she guessed he must have been in his late eighties, but his face held no wrinkles.

It was as smooth and as deep and as dark as Lake Michigan on a calm night. Though he was an old man, he wore his rich, black skin like a tuxedo, proudly and confidently. His eyes were kind, and when she studied them, even from across the yard, a vague familiarity gripped her. She had known his eyes before this day, though she struggled to recall how.

Around her, and without words, the rest of the guests drifted toward the center of the yard, hands outstretched, reaching for another hand, until a lopsided circle began to take shape. Babies were hoisted onto hips, and small children wedged themselves into the spaces between the adults, breaking the chain to insert their own tiny hands. Julene watched Lori stand and grab Aunt Lucille's hand, and, unsure of what she should do, she mimicked her cousin, moving her hand outward in the direction of Aunt Lucille's free hand. Without hesitation, Aunt Lucille reached out to grab Julene's hand, giving it a soft squeeze.

The tail-ends of conversations, jokes, and laughter floated around the misshapen circle, fading to quiet as Bootie's voice rose:

Lord, we are so thankful for this day. We thank You for the way You woke us up this morning. We thank You for this opportunity to come together in celebration. We thank You that we were able to travel safely, that the food was prepared with love, that You have withheld nothing from us.

Lord, Your Word says a baby is a blessing and we are so pleased that You thought us worthy to welcome and protect this child. You picked us, God, to raise this child in the way of Your Word. You picked us, God, to be the community, to be the village for this child and for the mother-to-be, and we say yes! We say yes to Your Will and to Your way. We welcome this child as we welcome You, God. We thank You for Your mercy and for Your grace. And, as one family under one God, we say, amen.

Amen! The voices, young and old, rang across the yard and melded into one song. Julene, both fascinated and distracted by Bootie's eloquence, missed the queue. She mouthed the word 'amen' to herself while the circle morphed into a jagged line, snaking through the kitchen and out the side door back into the yard. She watched as paper plates, laden with food, paraded past her. Some were eaten at tables. Some were perched on knees where table space was unavailable. Some were eaten while standing, a greater testament to the goodness of the food, rather than a lack of seating.

Julene's pre-filled takeout container, hidden in the kitchen, beckoned to her, but Aunt Lucille's voice stopped her from going to find it.

"Julene, can you do Auntie a favor?" she asked, pointing at a basket near the gift table. "Grab that basket and hand those clothespins out to everyone. Give each person three pins. There should be enough for everyone."

Without waiting for Julene to accept or decline this task, Aunt Lucille called toward Lori. "Hey baby, come do Auntie a favor…"

The two girls, moving in different directions to do Aunt Lucille's bidding, shared a smile as they passed one another. Lori rolled her eyes before whispering, "I should have told you Auntie is going to work us to death! I'm her favorite, and she still doesn't give me a break."

The love for Aunt Lucille had been instant and profound, transforming any favor she requested into a privilege rather than a chore. The girls giggled each time she called their names, making faces at one another but never daring to object, pout or lollygag. While Lori disappeared into the house to complete another task, Julene began handing out the clothespins. She stirred the pins inside the basket with her hand, pulling up a handful, then letting the pins fall between her fingers back into the pile. She approached a table crowded with unfamiliar smiling faces and anxiety rose in her chest, but curiosity rushed in just as quickly. The sharp noses, the broad chins, the same rich dark skin, the same kind eyes—the similarities among the family members came into focus with the slow and certain clarity of a Polaroid picture, fuzzy at first, then emerging detail by detail until the abstract becomes tangible.

These were her daddy's people. She could see a different version of her father in each face. Male or female. Young or old. The difference—the factor that may have prevented her from appreciating the undeniable resemblance earlier—was their complexion. While they all shared the same lustrous mahogany skin, her father did not. His skin was as fair as lightly toasted almonds. In summer, if he was able to play enough golf, he could earn the coppery shimmer of warm peanut butter, though it never lasted. By Thanksgiving, even if his face still hinted at his heritage, his feet and legs would have paled to the brink of Caucasian.

She stood there, basket outstretched, imagining the way her father would look in different skin, when a lady about her parents' age spoke.

"You're Brad's girl, aren't you? You look exactly like him!" she said, and then nudged the woman next to her, who was cutting a burger patty into small bites for the toddler who sat on her lap. "Tootie, look. You know who this is? This is Brad's girl! Isn't she pretty?"

The lady stopped cutting the burger to look up at Julene and smiled. "Well, my goodness. Aren't you a sight for sore eyes! All grown up now, I see. You sure are your daddy's child. There's no denying that. What a beautiful girl."

The toddler in her lap grabbed for the burger and gripped the meat, tipping the plate over in the process. Food scattered across the table and Tootie shook her head. "This little guy is so impatient! Couldn't even give me time to say hello to my little cousin. He had to try and feed himself!"

She covered the little boy's face with kisses before she began scooping the spilled food back onto the plate. When she finished, she looked up at Julene again. "So, I'm your dad's cousin Tootie. This is my sister, Rosalind. Our dad is Bootie over there. He's the one who led the prayer earlier. He can preach a sermon if you get him going."

Rosalind spoke up then, and Julene realized they were twins. "You haven't been around us much, and there are a lot of us, but basically, everyone here is your cousin. Our dad Bootie and your dad's father—your grandfather— were brothers. That makes Bootie your dad's uncle and that makes him your great uncle, I guess. Back in the day, everyone said your dad looked like he should have been Bootie's son, except for that light bright, almost white skin."

Rosalind laughed and Tootie paused from feeding the baby again to laugh with her. "I remember that! Daddy used to say 'my genes are too strong to produce a boy that light!' But your daddy sure loved himself some Uncle Bootie when he was growing up. That was his favorite uncle. We used to say daddy loved Brad more than he loved us. He was the son daddy never had."

The sisters shared another laugh, and then motioned toward the basket Julene still held. In unison, they asked the same question. "Are we playing a game?"

Julene glanced into the basket and back at the sisters. "I guess so. Aunt Lucille asked me to pass these out. She said everyone gets three."

The sisters laughed again and Rosalind said, "She told you to do what? You don't have to walk around doing that! Let's just take some and pass the basket around."

Rosalind lifted the basket from Julene's hands, took three pins for herself and passed three to her sister. Then she handed three more pins to Julene and passed the basket to the table behind them. She smiled at Julene. "See? Easy as that! Auntie will definitely put you to work if you let her."

"I don't mind. I like helping," Julene replied as she watched the basket make its way across the yard, and then glanced behind her to see Lori sitting on Aunt Lucille's lap and Baby Mama taking her seat near the gift table. She walked over and pulled a chair close to Lori and her aunt.

As soon as Julene sat down, Aunt Lucille stood up and threw her voice across the yard. "Alright, everyone! Time to have some fun! While Baby Mama opens her gifts, we'll play a little game. Everybody's got three clothespins, right?" She surveyed the yard, smiling, winking, and acknowledging everyone's participation before continuing. "Okay, so you know how it goes. If someone hears you say the word *baby*, they can take your clothespin. When the shower's over, the person with the most clothespins wins."

"What do we win?" one of the twins—Tootie or Rosalind, Julene had already forgotten who was who— shouted across the yard.

The other twin piped up. "Why're you asking? You know I win every time. Lu, you may as well go ahead and run me my prize right now."

Everyone laughed, including the men sitting on folding chairs and overturned milk crates under the buckthorn trees near the back fence. Julene absorbed the scene with her eyes. The family was playful, boisterous, noisy. Young and old, they teased one another, shouting out, interrupting Aunt Lucille's instructions with more questions and comments until she was doubled over with laughter as well.

Lori leaned over, laughing, and whispered to Julene. "Aunt Tootie never wins anything. That's why they're laughing. Whenever we get together and play games, she's always the first one out. She loses at everything and then she whines about it and tries to change the rules or says she was cheated. One time Aunt Lucille said Aunt Tootie deserved a prize for being the biggest loser."

The girls giggled, and Aunt Lucille moved closer to them, motioning for them to hand her a small paper bag sitting nearby.

"Watch this," Aunt Lucille said with mischief making her eyes dance, laughter begging to tumble from her lips. She held the bag high in the air. "Tootie, you're right. You deserve to get yours right now."

The surprise gift clipped the tail-end from Tootie's laughter, and she hoisted the toddler she'd been feeding onto her hip as she made her way to meet Aunt Lucille halfway across the lawn. She opened the bag, peeked inside and a new laugh bubbled up from within her. She laughed until her belly jumped up and down in a way that reminded Julene of Jolly Old Saint Nick. The toddler on her hip reached for the bag, managing to grab a corner of the paper, but Tootie pulled it just out of his reach, leaving him with a handful of paper, which he immediately pushed into his mouth with his fist and spit it out when he discovered the flavor of brown paper bag.

Tootie placed the toddler on the ground, careful to make sure he was steady on his feet, and then wiped a tear from the corner of her eye before pulling the surprise from the bag. She pulled an oversized, golden pacifier from the bag and held it in the air. The yard erupted into fresh laughter. Julene watched, studying the dynamics of this high-spirited clan. Their laughter was infectious and when the giggles began deep within her own belly, she couldn't help but let them out. One giggle at a time, and then strings of them flowed from her lips, until the muscles in her stomach clenched, working to push more laughter to the surface. Her eyes fell on Lori, who was grasping at her own belly, suffering from the pain and surprise of a gut-wrenching laugh, and when the girls made eye contact, they laughed harder.

Aunt Lucille leaned in and hugged Tootie, and then pulled away to give her a high-five. Their hands slapped together, and they interlaced their fingers for a moment while they giggled together, enjoying this long-running joke. "The biggest crybaby wins the biggest pacifier!"

Still pressing the backs of her wrists against the corners of her eyes to blot the laughter tears, Aunt Lucille returned to her spot between the girls and the gifts. "As I was saying, I do have a prize for the winner." She turned toward her daughter. "Baby Mama, go ahead open your gifts, then we'll have cupcakes."

Julene reached out and tapped Aunt Lucille's elbow, and then pulled her hand back as though she'd touched a hot iron.

"What is it, baby?" Aunt Lucille asked, her voice softening when she paused from her instructions to acknowledge her niece.

The yard was dead silent, and Julene, furious at her own hand for tapping Aunt Lucille, shook her head and said, "Nothing."

Aunt Lucille tipped her head just a little, perhaps sensing Julene's need to say something. "You tapped me just now, didn't you? Do you need something?"

"You, um…" Julene pointed at the clothespins clipped to her aunt's dress. "You said the word. You have to give me your…"

She dropped her hand to her lap, and then reached down to scratch a phantom itch near her ankle. She was awkward in the silence, regretting her impulsive decision to call Aunt Lucille out in front of everyone. She'd allowed herself to be swept up into the festive atmosphere, to become part of the family, to be like everyone else. A faux pas. Her mother had always ingrained in her the importance of remaining self-aware, to avoid any lapse in poise or decorum. The sin of committing a faux pas would be virtually impossible to recover from.

Unable to physically vanish into thin air or rewind the clock to the moment just before she'd opened her big mouth, she glanced toward Lori, desperate for a reprieve. Lori was already bouncing in her seat. "That's right, Auntie! You said it! Julene got you! Go ahead and give up that pin!"

The smile that spread across Aunt Lucille's face—it was as though a cloud had burst open to reveal a magnificent ray of sun, the bold and bright type of sunbeam that, as a little girl, Julene had believed could be climbed right up into heaven. Aunt Lucille's smile was so wide it revealed a gold tooth right at the corner of her upper lip. It told Julene there was no such thing as a faux pas, that she was entitled to play the game, that she could play to win, even if her opponent was her newly beloved auntie. Lucille unclipped a pin and placed it into Julene's hand.

"You actually said it three times. You said it when you gave Aunt Tootie the pacifier, you said her name," Julene said, pointing at Baby Mama, "and you called me it, too."

Julene held her hand outstretched, fingers wiggling gently, waiting to collect all of Aunt Lucille's remaining pins.

"Go on, Lucille! Give them up! She got you! Your own niece beating you at your own game," Tootie shouted, cackling from across the yard and slapping Rosalind's knee with one hand, while holding her jiggling belly with the other. Everyone chuckled around her, smiling and agreeing that Aunt Lucille should surrender her pins.

When Aunt Lucille placed her remaining pins into Julene's hand, she leaned down, drew her niece into an affectionate hug, and whispered into her ear, "I'm glad you won my pins. I'd rather lose to you than to Tootie."

She pulled away just a bit and petted the side of Julene's knee, her smile accented by that gold tooth again. "Plus, I can say the word baby as much as I want now. Who's going to check me, boo?"

She was sweet and sassy, warm and funny. She wore the fragrances of Dove soap and fresh laundry the way top models wore luxury Eau de Parfum, and Julene found herself captivated by every detail about Aunt Lucille. She also found a small but mighty kernel of empowerment, permission to let loose, and permission to win.

As Aunt Lucille kept the events of the day in motion, masterfully balancing the tasks of entertaining and hosting, Julene kept herself busy mingling with the guests, learning their names, connecting the dots that made them relatives, and collecting their clothespins.

CHAPTER THREE

W hen dusk descended and the sky took on the rusty, faded orange hue typical of late summer evenings, Lori and Julene found themselves relegated to the swing set. They'd trailed behind Aunt Lucille for most of the day and she'd finally shooed them away, advising them to find something else to do. The yard was still sprinkled with guests chatting, playing cards, and enjoying the fresh air. Some had drifted inside the house to watch the escalating Uno game happening in the dining room.

The girls loitered outside, twirling on the swings, using their feet to turn themselves in tight circles. The ropes twisted until only their toes touched the ground, the sides of their seats pulling upward into the shape of a U and squeezing their legs together. They then lifted their toes from the ground and held on while the ropes silently unraveled, slowly at first, then gaining momentum until they separated and crisscrossed in the opposite direction.

Julene, having won the most clothespins, fourteen in total, had linked them all onto a piece of ribbon she'd torn from the tail of a balloon and hung around her neck like a necklace. Each time she lifted her feet from the ground and allowed the centrifugal force of the spinning swing to whip her into a blur, her right hand rose to the base of her throat to protect her makeshift necklace. She hooked her left arm around the swing's rope to anchor herself as she twirled, challenging herself to hang on one-handed, or risk tumbling to the ground.

Twirling on the swings soon evolved into a rudimentary game of who could hang on longest. As Lori spun herself into a tight spiral, Julene watched, counting each rotation, shouting for Lori to hold on tighter, to lift her feet higher as the swing jerked her this way and that, until she came to a complete stop. Lori did the same for Julene, rooting her on, and shouting out suggestions for more rotations, more hangtime. "Let go of your necklace and hook your other arm around the rope. You'll be able to hold on better."

Breathless from the thrill of nearly being thrown to the ground on her last spin, Julene shook her head. "It feels like my clothespins are going to fly off if I don't hold them down."

Lori sprung from her swing and grabbed Julene's hand, pulling her toward the house. "The clothespin game is over anyway. Let's take your clothespins to Auntie and get your prize. It's a Sony Discman—I saw it when she was wrapping it. It's nice, too. It even plays bootleg CDs like the ones they sell at Swap-O-Rama. Now, that's important because my friend Sade got a knockoff discman for her birthday and it won't play any CDs unless they're from the actual record store. We even tried ordering some CDs from that mail-order company—if you have the coupon from the newspaper, you can get ten brand-new CDs for a penny! They won't play on a knockoff disc player though, but you won't have that problem with yours."

Inside the house, the girls found Aunt Lucille sitting in a well-worn recliner strategically positioned in the front room near the opening that led to the adjacent dining room. From her vantage point, she could watch the evening news on TV and also monitor the escalated Uno game at the dining table. The girls lingered for a moment to survey the game, covering their ears when the good-natured shouting reached a crescendo, before approaching Aunt Lucille.

"I was wondering where you girls got off to! I figured you were down the block, hanging out with your crew," Aunt Lucille said, gesturing toward a modern-looking flat-screen TV sitting atop an outdated floor model television. "Turn that down for me, baby."

Lori's protest was weak, half-hearted. "Auntie! You have the remote right there on the table next to you. You can just reach over and…"

As Lori spoke, Julene moved toward the TV sets and turned down the volume.

"You see? See that?" Aunt Lucille pointed at Julene and shook her finger at Lori. "You see how that baby just does as I ask? She doesn't give me backtalk like you! Here you are trying to run my pressure up, and I thought you were supposed to be my favorite! I'm not so sure anymore."

Julene watched Lori's face burst into a smile as she draped herself across Aunt Lucille's lap, burying her face in the warmth of her aunt's neck. Lori laughed, repeating herself over and over again, "I am your favorite. I am your favorite," making Aunt Lucille giggle like a teenaged girl.

"You're just a big baby! Get off me and tell me what you really want. I know you didn't come in here just to sit up under me," Aunt Lucille said, pushing Lori from her lap and peering at Julene. "What's that around your neck? Clothespins? You won them all, didn't you?"

Julene's hand went to the necklace again, clipping and unclipping the first pin on the right side. "Yes, Ma'am. I have fourteen altogether."

"Congratulations, baby. Throw your pins in that basket over there, and your prize is sitting right there on the table." Aunt Lucille pointed to the side table where the basket of clothespins sat next to a small package wrapped in a colorful page from the newspaper's comics section.

Julene did as she was told, carefully placing her makeshift necklace into the basket and scooping up her prize. She considered asking Aunt Lucille if she could keep her clothespin necklace but decided against it. "Thank you for the CD player. I really love it."

She held the colorful package gingerly, taking a moment to appreciate the concept of newspaper as giftwrap material. The simplicity and creativity of the idea was endearing.

"What do you mean, you love it? You haven't even opened it yet." Aunt Lucille's face was angled toward Julene, but her eyes rolled left, targeting Lori. "How did you know it was a CD player? Somebody with a really big mouth must have told you."

"No, Ma'am, she just—" Julene stammered, her mind scrambling for a way to tell the truth without betraying her cousin.

"Oh, now, don't lie for her. I know she told you," Aunt Lucille said, waving her small fist in Lori's direction. "Go on back there, get washed up, and get ready for bed. Church is in the morning."

Lori glanced toward the dining room—the Uno game had boiled down to just two players—and opened her mouth to protest, to beg for just five more minutes, but Aunt Lucille wouldn't allow it. "Don't even ask. Do what I said and don't use all the hot water."

Julene nudged Lori toward the bedrooms, implying she should lead the way, and the girls made their way to Lori's room. Lori skittered down the hall, Julene in tow, into a room no larger than a closet. A bed—just a frame and mattress draped with a too-small comforter—occupied most of the wall near the window. Seven pairs of sneakers, all neatly displayed on top of their respective shoe boxes, lined the opposite wall. Another row of sneakers, perched atop their boxes, lined the top shelf inside the closet. Pictures of people in groups—family and friends, perhaps—dotted the walls, unframed, held in place with scotch tape and thumbtacks.

While Julene worked to make sense of her cousin's bedroom, Lori scooped a pile of clothes off the bed and tossed them atop an already-full laundry basket before flopping onto her bed. "You wanna get your shower first? I have some shorts and a T-shirt you can wear to sleep."

Julene sat at the foot of the bed and shrugged. "That's okay. You can go first."

"Are you sure? I take like an hour in the shower." Lori was already standing, tucking her hair into a plastic shower cap. She gathered her pajamas, deodorant, lotion, and baby oil, cramming them under one arm while she grabbed a portable stereo with her free hand. She smiled at Julene. "I can't take a shower without music. Can you pass me that CD?"

She nodded toward a small bookshelf where a plain disk lay on top. Someone had used a blue marker to scrawl *Jodeci* on the surface.

"This one?" Julene leaned to grab the CD, using care not to mark it with her fingerprints, and knocked another disk from the pile. Each was labeled with the same blue handwriting, all with different titles, none recognizable to Julene.

Lori lifted her chin and motioned for Julene to tuck the CD underneath, arms too full to carry it any other way. "Yup. That's the one. It's their old album, but it's my favorite. Sometimes I listen to the whole album while I'm in there. I love this band, so my friend burned it for me for my birthday. Who do you listen to?"

"Um, I like Celine Dion, Eric Clapton…," Julene listed, noting the subtle change in Lori's expression—a barely perceptible disconnect in their musical preferences. She thought hard for a moment, pushing away the names of artists her parents preferred and making space for any name that would seem relevant to Lori. "Oh! I also really love Mariah Carey!"

Recognition returned to Lori's face. "Now, you're talking! Look through that stack of CDs. I'm pretty sure she's in there."

Julene tucked the CD under Lori's chin and watched her cousin trot off to the bathroom directly across the hall. When the door closed, she heard running water and then a guitar riff so loud it drowned out the noise from the shower. Lori strained her voice to match the band's harmony and Julene could hear her bellow the words clearly, maximizing the acoustics in the shower: *you're everything I doooo…. Oh, yeah….* In seconds, Aunt Lucille was at the door, tapping her knuckles, softly at first, and then harder, until Lori could hear her. "Turn that music down, girl! Where do you think you are? And hurry up in there! Other people need to use the shower tonight!"

The volume of the music decreased by half and Aunt Lucille, satisfied with herself, turned to walk away when she noticed Julene sitting at the foot of the bed in Lori's room. She leaned against the doorway, smiling. "That girl is something else. I tell you, she wears me out sometimes."

She tilted her head slightly, taking a closer look at Julene. "Are you okay? Don't worry about your mom. She's doing just fine. I spoke to your dad a little while ago and he said they'll be here to pick you up by the time we get home from church, okay?"

"Yes, Ma'am, thank you. I'm okay," Julene replied, picking at the loops in the crocheted blanket on Lori's bed. "I'm actually having fun with Lori. I wish I got to see you all more. I was thinking of asking my mom if Lori could come and sleep over at our house one day, or maybe for a whole weekend since it's kind of a long drive. Do you think that would be okay?"

Aunt Lucille looked down, smoothing the front of her blouse. She lifted her wrist to slide her watch band into a more comfortable position, and then slipped one hand into her pocket before rewarding Julene with her reassuring smile. "I bet Lori would love that. You girls seem to get on very well together. I'll have to speak to your mother about that and see if we can get you girls together again before school starts."

Turning to leave, she walked face first into the cloud of steam billowing from the bathroom. A fully refreshed Lori emerged. "Your turn!"

Aunt Lucille tussled playfully with Lori for a moment, and then doubled back to give Julene instructions. "Leave your dirty clothes in there when you finish, and I'll wash them before I go to bed tonight so you'll have something to wear home tomorrow. Lori will give you something to sleep in. And here," she said, tossing a silky hair bonnet onto the bed. "Put this over your hair."

When she disappeared down the hall, Lori rummaged through her laundry basket, pulled out an oversized T-shirt and a pair of gym shorts, and tossed them to Julene. "You can sleep in these tonight. I put a towel and washcloth next to the bathroom sink for you and I left the boombox in there so you can listen to music."

Julene thanked Lori and walked to the tiny bathroom. She turned on the shower and the boombox, just as Lori had done—but not as loud—and leaned against the closed door, breathing in the mixture of steam and candy-coated Victoria's Secret fragrances Lori had left behind. She closed her eyes for a moment, the adrenaline of the day fading, and imagined this life. She hadn't even known anyone who lived this way before today. This way of living had a certain *feel* to it. One she couldn't quite pin down. It was as though she were looking at the negatives from a leftover roll of film, where everything dark becomes light, and everything light becomes dark. Flip-flopped. Pared down. Simplified. Clear. She could see herself as Lori, a less rigid version of herself.

She considered Aunt Lucille's home—cluttered and comfortable, but well-loved. There was no pretense here. No pressure to remove shoes or speak in lowered tones. Aunt Lucille, herself, was the antithesis to the qualities Julene's mother had always taught were vital to a woman's presence. She wore no makeup, expensive jewelry, or private label clothing. She gave hugs and kisses, she played games, she welcomed her family into her home without hesitation.

"Hey, are you okay in there? I thought *I* took long showers, but you've got me beat."

Lori's voice on the other side of the door roused Julene from her wandering thoughts. She moved away from the door and jostled the shower curtain a little for effect before she answered, "I'm almost finished!"

In seconds, she was undressed, her clothes folded into a neat pile at the edge of the sink. She stepped into the shower and washed quickly, then jumped out to dry off. Lori's lotion, Pomegranate Pouf, was lying on the shelf above the toilet, and Julene slathered herself with the sweet, thick cream before pulling on her T-shirt and shorts.

Lori's bedroom was dark when Julene opened the door. A narrow beam of light from the hallway spilled across the room through a space just wide enough for

Julene to squeeze through. The light, landing squarely on Lori's face, who was already in bed, forced her to throw her hands in front of her face as though she were under an interrogation lamp.

"I thought you were gonna stay in there all night!" Lori said with a sleepy laugh as she pulled the covers back to make a space for Julene. "Get in. We have to get up early in the morning. Auntie likes to go to Sunday School *and* the regular service."

"Where do I put this?" Julene asked, holding up the boombox. "I didn't want to leave it in the bathroom."

Lori's arm motioned in the darkness, crossed the swath of light in front of her body, and disappeared into darkness again. "You can just put it on the floor over there. Wherever you want." Her voice was waning, drifting at the end of the sentence, and then she was breathing in the steady rhythm of deep sleep.

Julene pushed the bedroom door closed and crawled into the bed, slightly breathless with the anxiety of sharing a bed with Lori—with anyone—for the first time. In her lifetime, on the rare occasion she was invited to a sleepover, her mother had warned her to stay in her own sleeping bag, to never get under the covers with anyone. Now, in the alternate reality of Aunt Lucille's home, she lay next to her cousin in the dark, flat on her back, holding her body stiffly, crossing her arms over her chest so as not to accidently invade Lori's personal space in the twin-sized bed. She focused on smoothing out the rhythm of her own breathing, slowly matching it to Lori's unlabored breaths.

At some point, having drifted to the very edge of sleep, Lori nudged her shoulder, timidly at first, and then with more urgency. "Hey. You gotta turn on your side or something. I can see your outline in the dark and it's like you're laying in a—" She dropped her voice to a whisper. "Like you're in a *coffin* or something. It looks scary."

"What?" Julene turned, propped herself on one elbow to face Lori and giggled. "I can't lay on my back because I look *dead*? I mean, I usually sleep on my stomach or my side, but it's kind of awkward getting comfortable in bed when I—"

Lori patted Julene's pillow. "Get comfortable. Don't worry about it. I sleep wild so it doesn't bother me if you accidentally bump me."

Under the covers, she moved her feet and legs as though she pedaled an imaginary bicycle. Julene pedaled her own imaginary bike, and the girls engaged in a brief foot fight until Lori's voice was thick with the promise of sleep again. "I'm just kidding about the coffin thing. Sleep however you want. But I am afraid of stuff that looks dead."

Sleep came easily for Lori, and Julene lay, flirting with slumber for what must have surely been hours. Long bluish-black hours, punctuated by shape-shifting shadows along the walls and ceilings, distant sirens, cat calls and barking dogs. A point came when she abandoned the possibility of sleep and lay awake thinking of home. She didn't miss it. She didn't miss her bedroom, or parents, or the echoing of their three voices in the minimally furnished house. Her thoughts of home lulled her to sleep—and maybe even a brief dream. She knew this, not because she remembered falling asleep or dreaming, but because she woke up. She needed a moment to orient herself with her surroundings, with the smell of Aunt Lucille's home, with her backside pressed against Lori's backside. She turned slowly, taking care not to pull the covers from her cousin's shoulders, and positioned herself on her back. She finally rolled to her side again, ditching the coffin-esque style, giving herself permission to relax.

She drifted again into thoughts, out of thoughts, lingering at the edge of sleep as one might dally at the edge of the seashore, until Lori tapped her shoulder again. "Hey."

"*I'mnotinacoffin.*" Julene's words were slurred, proof she'd finally fallen asleep.

Lori's laughter caused the bed to shake gently. "It's time to get up. Aunt Lucille made breakfast and she likes us to eat first so we can get dressed first."

In the kitchen, Aunt Lucille sat in a wooden dining chair, pulled close to the open oven door, legs outstretched as though she were sunbathing. With her legs exposed this way, housedress pulled up mid-thigh, Aunt Lucille appeared both immodest and extraordinarily natural. No pretense, comfortable at home in her own skin. Her smile assured Julene this bit of exposed skin was okay.

The kitchen, warmed by the open oven, smelled of… charred meat? Toast? Coffee? The aromas melded together in a way that made Julene's stomach rumble softly, anticipating more of Aunt Lucille's exquisite cuisine. Julene stood, rooted at the edge of the kitchen doorway, inhaling, trying to decipher each scent, while Lori skipped across the small kitchen to plant a kiss on her aunt's cheek. Julene opted for a good morning hug rather than a kiss, and then took a seat at the table across from Lori.

Between them lay an aluminum pan half filled with chunks of strategically burnt sausage links. The casings of the fried pork burst in various places, hinting at the savory juices inside. The other half of the pan was filled with a version of scrambled eggs unfamiliar to Julene. They were darker in color than the pale yellow eggs she'd always been accustomed to eating.

The girls took their places at the table, and Lori, surveying the prepared food, bounced in her seat. "You made dirty eggs? My favorite!" She motioned to Julene. "Try some. You're gonna love it! Auntie fries the sausage in the cast iron skillet first—she knows I like mine sorta burnt—then she takes the sausage out and fries the eggs in the same pan. It's like it gives the eggs a special flavor."

Aunt Lucille stood up and slid a dish towel from her shoulder, using it to remove a pan of toasted dinner rolls from the oven. When she placed the pan on the table between the girls, she picked up a stick of butter, peeled its waxy paper wrapper halfway back, and rubbed the stick across the tops of the rolls until it began to liquify. Saliva pooled inside Julene's mouth while she watched, fully entranced.

"Everything smells so good and looks delicious," Julene said. "I've never heard of dirty eggs before, but I can't wait to have some."

She sat straighter in her chair and pointed at the rolls. "What kind of bread is that?"

Aunt Lucille pushed a plate toward Julene. "Those are just some old Brown 'n Serve rolls left over from the party last night. I just didn't have it in me to make biscuits this morning. Go ahead and get what you want, but make it quick. I need you two to eat and get dressed so we can get out of here on time. I'll drop you off at Sunday School and then meet you in the sanctuary for the main service."

Mild panic stirred in Julene's belly, pushing away her craving for buttered rolls and dirty eggs. She glanced at Lori and then looked to Aunt Lucille. "What if my dad comes for me while we're at church? Maybe I should just wait here for him."

Valid concerns regarding this unplanned sleepover and her uncertain departure time concealed her shameful truth: she'd never been to Sunday School, let alone an actual church service. Yes, she could recall the handful of times she'd dressed in outfits that complemented her parents and sat quietly in the pews of the most prominent African Methodist Episcopal church in the city. However, these visits were typically motivated by fundraisers, guest speakers, and charity events hosted within the historic sanctuary. She'd been *inside* the church, but she'd never been *to* church.

Aunt Lucille chuckled and busied herself scooping food onto Julene's plate. "There's plenty of time. Brad knows I don't ever miss my church service. He'll be here to get you afterwards. Go ahead and eat, now. We'll be leaving shortly. Your dress is hanging in the washroom."

Lori, oblivious to Julene's worries, motioned across the table. "Look," she said, holding up the masterpiece she'd just created, "I like to split the roll open and put a piece of sausage inside. When you bite into it—"

Lori abandoned her words and sank her teeth into the small sandwich, rolling her eyes upward in sensual deliberation before extending the remaining half toward Julene. Her mouth stuffed, she pointed at her food, nodded and muttered, *"Yougottatrythisit'ssogood."*

The girls laughed. Lori used her free hand to keep food from escaping her pursed lips, while Julene tore open a roll and stuffed a piece of sausage inside. Aunt Lucille swatted Lori with her dish towel, playfully fussing about talking with a full mouth, threatening serious repercussions if they were late for church.

True to her word, Aunt Lucille had cleaned, pressed, and hung Julene's dress in the bathroom, and laid out a brand-new toothbrush. After breakfast, the girls stood at the sink side by side, brushing their teeth and washing their faces, and then dressing quickly. Julene wore her dress and sandals again, not sure when she'd last worn the same outfit within 24 hours, and Lori wore a denim skirt with a blouse and gym shoes. They met Aunt Lucille, who was dressed in white from her pillbox hat down to her white pantyhose and white loafers, at the front door.

"Auntie, I didn't know you were ushering today," Lori said, assessing her aunt's outfit and nodded approvingly. "You look nice."

Aunt Lucille returned the compliment by pressing her cheek against Lori's and blowing a kiss. She did the same to Julene, and when she came close, she smelled of white soap and baby powder. Julene inhaled the heady freshness left in her aunt's wake and marveled at the way these basic toiletry staples could add such a delicate and ladylike air to a mature woman's presence. She'd never considered it until now, but the smell was so natural, so honest, that it seemed to accentuate her all-white attire.

When the three stepped out onto Aunt Lucille's front porch—each dressed fiercely independent of each other—they were greeted by a late model Volvo coupe idling in the driveway. Lori skipped down the driveway and opened the passenger door, and then pushed the seat forward to make room for herself in the back.

"Hey, Rosalind!" Lori's voice filtered through the open car door.

Julene squinted her eyes to see the driver. She recognized her as the twin cousin from the night before. When Rosalind waved at her, she realized she must have been staring and offered up a tentative wave with a smile for good measure.

"Go on, girls. Climb in while I lock up," Aunt Lucille said. Her keys jangled while she worked to secure the front door, the storm door, and a wrought-iron security door Julene hadn't even noticed until now. She watched as Aunt Lucille knelt down on one knee to snap a padlock closed. When she stood up again and headed toward the car, she waved her hands in Julene's direction, motioning for her to get into the car, huffing for breath as she approached. "I'm getting too old to be down on the ground tussling with that lock, but I don't want to come home to any surprise visitors, you know?"

Aunt Lucille muttered to herself about the crime rate and the changing neighborhood while she waited for Julene to climb into the back next to Lori. "Hey, Rosalind. Thanks for picking us up. I had asked Meechie to take us to church, but his car is in the shop."

Rosalind eased the car out of the driveway and replied, "I don't know why you had to move all the way out here anyway. We used to be able to walk to church from your old house, remember?"

The ladies chatted in the front seat and Lori tapped Julene's knee in the back seat, motioning for her to lean closer. "Auntie doesn't drive anymore so someone always has to pick us up for church and shopping. Also, she's ushering today, so we can sit wherever we want. There're no cute boys in children's church so I usually stay in the sanctuary with the adults. It's the best place to see who's going to catch the Holy Ghost, and the deacons always slide me some candy if I ask."

The church, just a ten-minute drive from Aunt Lucille's house, was nothing more than a windowless office suite squished between a Schwinn bicycle repair shop and a bustling Polish bakery. With its pressed fiberboard wood paneling, threadbare blue Berber carpet, stackable auditorium chairs, and laminated oak podium, the understated room brought to mind the makeshift campaign headquarters where Julene and her parents had once shown up, anticipating a photo op.

She'd listened to her mother persuade her father to attend for weeks prior to that event. The candidate, Russell Ward, a used car dealer-turned-politician, had been arrested and had once served time for money laundering.

Four years after his twenty-two-month jail sentence, he had returned to the community and begged for a chance at redemption, desperate to make new and powerful connections.

The plan, as Layla had convinced Brad, was to be captured in photos with the candidate and his wife and build a connection with their friends. Networking, Layla explained, was really the only way to get ahead in Chicago.

When they arrived at the event—complete with well-coordinated outfits and well-rehearsed conversational topics—they were stunned into silence. The room that served as the campaign headquarters was sparsely furnished without even the hint of opulence from heavily funded donors. There were no cameras, no media outlets, no recognizable society faces—just a frumpy middle-aged woman sitting in the far corner of the room sorting and cutting stacks of paper.

She looked up when they entered the room, offering a smile and waving them inside. "You must be the volunteers! Come in. Come in. There's a lot to do. My name's Fatima."

Layla moved into the room hesitantly. "Are we early? Where is everyone? Where is the press?"

Fatima, dressed in poorly fitting blue jeans and a faded 40th Ward Democrats sweatshirt, laughed and continued cutting slips of paper. "That's what I said. Where's everyone? Russell was called away on some campaign business and no volunteers have shown up. I've been stuck here cutting out handbills all day! I'm happy to have your help."

She stood from her chair and retrieved a new stack of papers, handing them to Julene. "The real unsung heroes are usually the ones behind the scenes. No glory for us, right? But it's all for the greater good. Whatever it takes."

She pointed toward a pair of scissors lying on the table. "Grab those and start cutting along the lines. Russell is my nephew, you know? I know him better than anyone. None of the rumors about him are true. They said he has ties to Russia and all sorts of crazy things, but it isn't true. He's a genuinely good guy."

She paused and glanced from Layla to Brad, who hadn't moved from the doorway. "You aren't here to help, are you? I should have known! Look at you all—dressed in your fancy outfits, hoping to use our campaign as a networking event, I'm sure. You aren't the first to try that."

Brad stepped forward, extending his hand. "Hold on just a moment. We didn't mean to—"

Layla moved in front of him, pushing his hand down. She slipped her hand into his pocket and produced his checkbook. "Darling, of course we aren't here to work. We're merely here to make a donation to a worthy cause. You do accept donations, don't you?"

Fatima's expression softened and she pushed a can of campaign ink pens closer to Layla. "My apologies. We do accept donations. You'll just need to make your check out to The Committee to Elect Russell Ward."

Layla selected a pen and signed a check. "Five thousand should be enough to give this campaign a boost. If Russell needs more, please have him call us." She slid the check toward Fatima and motioned for Julene to leave the stack of papers on the table, and then smiled at Brad. "We can go now, honey."

Grabbing the scissors and holding the papers in the air, Julene pleaded with her parents while her eyes surveyed the boxes of papers and campaign materials cluttering the room. "We can still cut these. I don't mind helping."

Layla, finding it unnecessary to address Julene's comment, ushered Brad out of the room.

Julene placed the papers on the table and offered Fatima an apologetic smile before racing to catch up to her parents, who were holding a terse conversation in the hallway.

"We don't have five thousand dollars to donate to this campaign! That was never the plan! What were you thinking?" Brad said, pacing the hall, hands snapped to his hips in a way that caused the back of his sportscoat to lift slightly. It exaggerated the contour of his already prominent rear end in a way that reminded Julene of the bustles worn by women in the late 1800s. Under different circumstances, she would have laughed about it aloud.

Tonight, however, with her parents on the precipice of a fight, laughter seemed inappropriate.

"Obviously, the plan changed. If you're going to make it in this world, you've got to know how to change course from time to time." Layla, replied. Already several steps ahead of her husband, she doubled back in his direction and grabbed his arm, which he yanked from her grasp as if she'd electrocuted him.

He walked ahead of her. "I never should have let you drag me into this! I don't give a shit about this guy! He's a con artist and he's most definitely connected to the Russians. Everyone knows that. His aunt is delusional, and he's a scumbag. And now you've given him five thousand dollars that we cannot afford to give without so much as a single photo? If no one sees us give the money, then we might as well have not given it at all."

Layla quickened her steps until she was able to walk in step with her husband, peeking back to make sure Julene was following. "Honey, listen, this was an admittedly failed attempt to make some important connections for both of us, but I'm working night and day to move us into the right circles. Obviously, I was operating on inaccurate information and didn't know there would be no candidate and no media here tonight. But I'm not an ignorant woman. Do you really think I'd give one thin dime to his campaign? That check will never clear the bank, but I'm sure Aunt Fatima is on the phone with Russell right now, telling him how much we contributed and making sure he knows our names. No one can keep it hush in this town, especially when money is involved."

Brad cast an incredulous glance in his wife's direction before flinging the door open and stepping into the empty parking lot. "So, your plan was to make sure they know our names right before our bad check bounces? Brilliant, Layla. We'll definitely be the talk of the town."

Layla paused at the door, waiting for Julene to catch up. "Darling, would you listen to your father? Such a drama queen. Such a worry wart. Where would he be without me?"

She linked her arm through her daughter's and walked to the car, waiting for her husband to open the door. He had opened the doors and stood back, aloof, waiting for them to get in. Then he slammed the front door with force, barely allowing Layla time to pull the hem of her dress inside. He closed the back door with less irritability once Julene was inside, and then let himself in on the driver's side.

Once Brad had buckled his seat belt and pushed the gearshift into drive, Layla placed a hand on his shoulder. "Honey, the check won't bounce. I'm way too classy to commit such a faux pas. It simply won't clear the bank. I wrote the number five thousand dollars in the box, but I wrote the words *five thousand cents* on the line. The two amounts won't match, and the bank will hold the check until the error is resolved. They won't flag it for insufficient funds, though. They'll just contact you to sort it out."

She patted his leg and laughed. "Of course, you'll be too busy to return calls from the bank and eventually you'll just have them stop payment on it. By then, Russell will have added us to all of his guest lists because he'll think of us as generous donors who may have more to give."

She turned to look at her daughter. "Julene, darling, your mom is a mastermind, no matter what your father thinks."

Julene found it difficult to decipher the looks her parents exchanged in that moment, but she saw her father's shoulders relax and her mother returned her attention to her daughter. "Follow my lead, dear daughter. I'm like a chameleon. I can turn myself into whomever I need to be in order to get whatever I need to get. You're learning from the best."

Julene shifted in the back seat, some portion of her consciousness struggling to reconcile her mother's words with the Golden Rule her favorite teacher, Ms. Malinda, had taught her when she'd been in second grade: *treat others the way you'd like to be treated. Every lie you tell, every selfish gesture you embrace, rips a thread from your moral fabric.* The teacher had explained that we all possess a tiny piece of fabric in our guts, which helps us to do the right thing. She had warned the children to make good choices and to protect each thread of their moral fabric at all costs because the repair process was known to be difficult and painful. She had impressed upon them the importance of standing up for what is right, even when it seems scary or unpopular.

"Mom, I—"

"Mother." Layla never missed an opportunity to prune Julene's words.

"Sorry, Muh-therr. I was just going to say it seems a little dishonest to say you're going to give them money but not really give it. When I was in elementary school, the teacher told us to always think before we do something to someone, to ask ourselves how it would feel to have someone treat us the same way."

Layla allowed her head to rest against the headrest and sighed. "Darling, that is a perfect lesson for children. Children should be kind and obedient. But this is a grownup lesson: everyone is dishonest—especially people with money. Everyone is looking out for their own best interests. Everyone wants to be on top, so we all fake it. It's okay to play little tricks from time to time if you need to get ahead. That's all I'm doing—showing you how to get ahead in this world."

"We could have stayed and helped Miss Fatima, though," Julene protested. "She was all alone. We could have cut the papers for her."

Layla offered a patient response to balance her daughter's naiveté. "You want the finer things in life, don't you? You want to enjoy life's luxuries and privileges, right? You won't get there by cutting paper alone in some low-budget storage room without even one media outlet present, like some average person. It's my job as the woman of our household to save us from becoming average."

She spat the word *average* with unconcealed contempt. As though the word wasn't even worthy of floating around inside the car.

Julene sat back in her seat, working to reconcile her parent's words and actions. She noticed her father's eyes in the rearview mirror, focused intently on the road, then glancing up to meet his daughter's stare.

He looked over at his wife before addressing his daughter. "It might sound strange, but it's true. It's all about who you know, who owes you a favor, how you can gain a competitive edge, and how to get people to buy whatever you're selling, even if what you're selling is just a better version of yourself."

Julene shifted her gaze to the outside, her eyes taking in the buildings, people and traffic racing past her window. "What's wrong with the regular version of yourself? Why wouldn't anyone want that?"

Now it was Layla's turn to answer. "Regular is the same as average, and I have just explained why it just isn't good enough." After a moment, Layla spoke again. "Also, Julene, darling, you must learn to keep your mouth shut. The next time I say let's go, drop whatever you're doing and follow my lead. Don't ever challenge me publicly again. Do you understand? You're too mouthy, and that isn't an attractive quality for a young woman who needs to be accepted by the right people."

Julene shook her head now, clearing that memory from her head as though it were an Etch-A-Sketch drawing. The campaign incident had happened years ago and, although the room looked the same, the scene unfolding before her eyes today was far different.

CHAPTER FOUR

J ulene stood just inside the doorway to the sanctuary, watching the congregation file in, and listening to the musicians warm up. Aunt Lucille's voice echoed from the foyer, where she handed out programs for the morning's service. Lori flitted around the sanctuary, hugging many of the older church members, and accepting pieces of hard candy and sticks of gum along the way.

The sanctuary filled and the air stirred with powdery fragrances, hugs, kisses, and morning greetings. Julene peered around the room, observing as an outsider at first, then slowly realizing she'd seen some of these faces at yesterday's baby shower. Family was here. Cousins. Aunties and uncles. She released a soft breath and drifted toward Lori, smiling politely and offering her hand to the older women and men who grasped it in their own, patting it warmly and smiling as they bid her a good morning.

She was stopped by a woman whom she recalled from the day before, although she couldn't remember her name. "Good morning, young lady. Don't you look pretty! Go on up there and get a seat. Service will begin soon."

She pointed toward an empty space on the second row of chairs and paused expectantly. Julene's eyes darted from the second-row seat to the corner where she had just seen Lori, but she wasn't there. She looked behind her, to no avail. Hesitant, but obedient, she slid into the designated seat next to a husky boy in a crisply pressed, short-sleeved plaid shirt and well-worn khaki pants. He was on his knees, facing his chair with his face buried in the screen of a handheld gaming device. He appeared to be only a year or so younger than Julene and Lori, far too old to be permitted to crawl about the floor of the sanctuary playing video games. At least in the real world, she knew he'd be chastised, but here, no one seemed concerned. A woman, his mother, she guessed, sat on the other side of him, bouncing a baby girl on her knee while she carried on an animated conversation with a woman to her left.

Distracted by the boy's failed attempts to master the video game, Julene didn't notice when a woman had taken the seat to her right until it was too late. She'd planned to save that seat for Lori, who had reappeared in the far corner of the sanctuary but hadn't thought to put her purse on the seat to show that it was reserved. Without the courage and authority to inform the woman the seat was taken, Julene twisted her body discretely, hoping to catch Lori's eye. She was gone again.

A boy who appeared to be a teenager took a seat at the organ and began to play softly. Julene watched, intrigued that everyone seemed to know what the music meant. They began to shuffle toward their seats, filling in the spaces around Julene, isolating her from Lori and from Aunt Lucille. Already being seated, she hadn't needed to understand the meaning of the musician's cue, but what was next? Acutely aware of the fact she didn't know how to conduct herself during a church service—when to stand, when to sit, the words to the hymns— she focused her attention on the man seated directly in front of her. A horizontal line was etched into the back of his head, from ear to ear, and she imagined it was from the pressure of a too tight ball cap. She decided to follow his lead to blend in as much as possible without drawing attention to her churchly inexperience. Even still, with her plan to follow along, anxiety crept through her body, tickling the spaces behind her knees, itching in the pits of her underarms, swelling in her throat.

Her thoughts raced home, to her mother, to her dad, wondering what instructions they'd have if they were here. They'd taught her poise. They'd trained her to see and be seen, to speak properly and exist with confidence in elite social settings. They had not taught her how to survive a traditional church service.

A woman about her mother's age stood at the podium and looked around the room, smiling and nodding at various members of the congregation before addressing them all. "Good morning!"

The congregation's response was inharmonious and sluggish.

The woman paused, looked back at the organ player and drummer, then returned her attention to the congregation. "Maybe you didn't hear me." She tapped the microphone with her fingernail. "I said, I'm so glad God woke me up this morning! Just to wake up, knowing He is on my side is enough! God is good!"

The congregation, finally settled into their seats and able to provide her with their undivided attention, responded in unison, "All the time!"

The woman nodded her head and smiled broadly. "And all the time?"

Voices rang out around Julene. "God is good!"

The man in front of Julene bobbed his head and nudged the woman seated next to him, who also nodded hers in agreement.

The woman at the podium, satisfied with this more enthusiastic response, leaned into the microphone. "Well, let's give God a hand, then!"

The drummer and organist offered an energetic melody while applause thundered through the church. Julene, just a beat behind everyone else, followed their lead, clapping until the applause died down, and then watching for a cue from the man in front of her.

After a moment, the woman spoke again. "Your pastor has prepared a tremendous sermon for you this morning. Before we get to that, we will have the children come to the front to recite their scriptures, we'll share some announcements, then have a song, and then we will worship through giving. Sound good?"

She paused for another brief round of applause. "Alright. Let's have the children come up front."

The boy to Julene's left handed his video game to his mother and walked up front, falling into line and jostling playfully with another boy. Julene sat back in her seat, wondering, as children from various locations in the sanctuary made their way toward the front, what they had prepared.

A gentle nudge from the lady on her right, who pointed toward the front and mouthed the words *you, too,* startled her.

"I'm not... I don't..." Julene stammered, shaking her head slowly, unsure of what was expected.

The woman at the podium spoke into the microphone, looking directly into Julene's eyes. "That's right. Let's have every child come to the front. Even the visitors. Let's make some space for each one of our little blessings."

Julene rose from her chair slowly, her hands tingling with anxiety as she searched the room for Lori or Aunt Lucille, the only people who could save her now. She excused herself as she stepped sideways along the row of chairs, doing her best not to step on the toes of the adults who were fortunate enough to have remained seated.

At the end of the row, she fell into step with Lori, who linked arms with her and whispered. "Don't look so scared. We do this every Sunday. The kids have to come up front and recite a Bible scripture. You can say any verse you want."

This bit of information, meant to reassure, flooded Julene's body with a new wave of anxiety. She whispered back to Lori, "I don't know any scriptures."

"You don't know any?" Lori asked, studying her cousin's face. They reached the end of the line of roughly twelve children. "Okay. Say 'Jesus wept', John 11:35. That's easy to remember, right?"

"Jesus wept. Is that all I have to say?" Julene asked. She turned the scripture over and over in her mind, testing it for quality before deciding there was no time for any other option. She had never learned a single Bible verse. She'd have to trust her cousin to guide her.

"Yes, that's all. Jesus wept, John 11 and 35. Don't forget to say that part," Lori whispered, her arm still linked with Julene's. A little boy who couldn't have been more than five years old took the microphone. "The little kids always like to show off. Watch him."

After heaving into the microphone, the boy's breath echoed for a moment throughout the sanctuary before he said, "For God so loved the world that He gave His only begotten Son, that whosoever believeth in Him should not perish, but have everlasting life. For God sent not His Son into the world to condemn the world; but that the world through him might be saved. John 3:16 and 17."

He spoke rapidly, his words running together as though tumbling downhill, and the congregation exploded with applause and shouts of approval. He smiled broadly, pleased with himself, before passing the microphone to a little girl on his left.

She grasped it with both hands and brought it close to her mouth. Her eyes surveyed the congregation until they landed on a woman, perhaps her mother, whose reassuring smile encouraged the little girl to speak.

"Children, obey your parents in the Lord: for this. Is. Right! Eat peas in six and one," she recited, smiling sweetly when she finished and looking toward her mother who whisper-shouted from her seat, "E-fee-she-ans... Ephesians 6 and 1."

Some adults chuckled, amused by the small girl's effort, and the little girl, self-satisfied, passed the microphone to her left.

The children continued on in this way, the little ones delighting and entertaining the elders while the older children mumbled their verses as quickly as possible, giggling playfully at each other once their turns had passed.

When the microphone reached Lori, she cleared her throat dramatically and smiled at Aunt Lucille, who had appeared in the doorway at the rear of the sanctuary, one white-gloved hand tucked behind her back. "Trust in the Lord with all thine heart, and lean not unto thine own understanding. Proverbs 3:5."

She passed the microphone to Julene and gave her a nurturing smile.

The microphone was heavier than Julene had expected. She cradled it in her hands, just as the smaller children had done. Her trembling voice was magnified through the speakers. She was annoyed by the sound of herself, but she forced the words out as clearly as she could manage. "John 11 and 35. Jesus wept."

Unsure of what to do next, she shoved the microphone back into Lori's hands just as Aunt Lucille began to clap. The rest of the congregation joined in, shouting words of encouragement to all of the children. The organist and the drummer played a short tune while the children were dismissed to their seats.

Lori linked her arm through Julene's again, leading her past her empty seat on the second row and pulling into the last row, where there were still four empty seats.

"You didn't tell me we would have to do that!" Julene whispered to Lori, lowering her voice a bit when she noticed Aunt Lucille was watching from the door. "Then you left me sitting up there alone. Where were you?"

"I was getting snacks for us. I know who to hit up for good candy, and look," she said, opening her purse and holding it toward Julene to display the contents. "Strawberry hard candies, communion bread, and wine."

Inside the purse, just as Lori had claimed, were five pre-filled communion cups, no larger than the size of the single-serve coffee creamers that Julene sometimes played with at her father's office. She blinked at Lori, confused. "It looks like coffee creamer."

"It's better than coffee creamer. You peel back the top and there's a cracker inside. It has grape juice in the bottom part, but I like to pretend it's wine." Lori unzipped a side pocket on her purse and revealed an assortment of candies and gum. "Plus, I have all this. Next time, stick with me. Why did you sit all the way up front? I never sit up there because you can't talk without getting caught."

The girls giggled and hunkered down in the back row, eating strawberry hard candies and Tootsie Rolls and chewing gum as the church service continued. They paused and lowered their voices momentarily when Aunt Lucille appeared at the end of their row, passing the offering plate their way. Julene pulled her wallet from her purse without hesitation and flipped through the crisp bills tucked inside. She used her fingertips to rifle through the money, uncertain about how many to withdraw, then finally plucked out two bills and placed them on the plate. She passed the plate toward Lori, who watched, dumbfounded, and then discretely grabbed the two twenty-dollar bills Julene had laid atop the plate and stuffed them back into Julene's purse in a crumpled wad. "Forty dollars? That's too much! Don't you just have a dollar? Or even some change?"

Julene's ears burned hot while she flipped through her wallet again, searching for any smaller denomination before finally settling for a five. She placed it in the plate and passed it to Lori for a second time. This time, Lori slipped two one-dollar bills onto the plate and handed it off to the first person on the next row. She patted Julene's knee with motherly warmth. "Who are you trying to impress? We're kids. We don't have to give that much. And when we get home, don't let anyone see your money like that. We're family and everything, but…"

She paused, considering the gentlest way to teach this lesson, and continued, "Just don't ever let anyone know how much money you're handling. It's just not—that's not what we do at home or in the streets."

While the pastor captivated the congregation with biblical lessons, the girls slouched in their seats, sharing stories of school and boys and food and music. Combined, their stories were in sharp contrast to one another—prep school versus neighborhood school, predominately white versus predominately Black, fine dining versus potlucks, cotillions versus house parties, Brittany Spears versus Mary J. Blige—but like one person with two personalities, the girls found balance and common ground in their experiences.

Their stories blended like seasonings in a decadent, layered recipe, savory and sweet, acidic and spicy, to complement and enhance each girl's view of the world through the other's eyes.

"So you actually went to Michael Jordan's house?" Lori asked, her eyes bugging and toes tapping the pew in front of them. A lady turned around and threatened her with a stare, and Lori stilled her toes and bucked her eyes at Julene. "You mean, you went inside his house? How was it?"

"It was okay." Julene shrugged. "Just a house. They served us some hor d'voures and let us hang out in his game room while the adults were talking."

"Hor d'voures? They give that to kids? What was it?" Intrigue pushed Lori's voice into a strained whisper.

Julene paused and racked her brain for the memory. "Um, I think it was crab cakes, king crab claws and oysters Rockefeller."

Lori slid to the floor and pulled herself up again, gasping for air. "What? Snow crab claws? I only had those once, when Uncle Jeremiah came home from Germany. He had money, and he brought us some. I know they were expensive. Why were you at his house?"

"I think they were doing some kind of fundraiser for cancer or something."

Lori grasped Julene's hand. "Was it the Stomp Out Cancer thing? Uncle Julius was working at that event. He said the whole service staff had a party inside one of Jordan's garages. He has like eight of them, you know? So, he had a Grill Master making burgers and Italian sausages for the service staff. He said there was a bartender doing tricks and making drinks, and there was a dance floor and a DJ, and it was all free! I guess he really is rich, huh?"

Julene nodded, envisioning the scene, considering the contrast between the event she'd been forced to attend and the one Uncle Julius had reported. "That's cool, a party with burgers and dancing. Sounds like fun."

"What? That's a normal party around here—except for the part where Michael Jordan pays for it—but burgers and sausage are like the bare minimum for a party around here. I would have been more excited about being inside his house and eating oysters Rockefeller. What is that, anyway? It kinda sounds nasty now that I think of it."

Lori's face contorted in perfect comedic timing while her thoughts raced to reconcile with the words spilling out of her mouth as the girls giggled. Julene nodded her head. "It *is* nasty! It has no flavor at all, but everyone just eats it and pretends to love it."

Lori dismissed this foreign idea immediately. "That's weird. That must be something rich people do. Around here, if we don't like it, we ain't eating it."

Julene nodded and explained, "So Mom and Dad say pleasure and enjoyment are low class. It doesn't matter if you like it or not. Actually, you're not supposed to look like you're enjoying yourself too much, even if you do like something. There are certain things you can express an appropriate amount of pleasure in, but don't get too carried away. And there are also things you're not supposed to enjoy at all. For example, they say its low-class to enjoy junk food unless its chocolate. Chocolate is okay."

"So, except for the oysters, the food was good, but you couldn't *say* that?" Lori struggled to make sense of this thought process.

Julene thought for a moment before answering. "No. Well, yes. I said, *this is very nice*. I just couldn't say *oh my God! This is delicious!* Mom says that's too much. She said it's embarrassing.

Lori shook her head. "You rich people. I don't get it. You have all the good food, all the money, you're at Michael Jordan's house, and you can't get excited? Doesn't make sense to me. The service workers probably had more fun than you, and all they had was burgers in a garage."

Julene tossed this around in her mind for a moment. "You know, Dad says we aren't rich. He says we are wealthy, and wealthy people must behave appropriately, even if it isn't fun. Honestly, before yesterday, the last time I had real fun was…"

She couldn't think of a time. There were memories of enjoyable times. Times she would have categorized as fun prior to her time at the baby shower. The baby shower had been really fun, and if that was the definition of actual fun, then anything that had come before lacked in comparison. She sat there examining her circumstance, imagining life in Lori's shoes, wondering if it was wrong to hope her parents wouldn't come back for her.

Lori's voice interrupted her thoughts. "Rich and wealthy sound like the same thing to me. I don't know about all this 'act appropriate' and 'this is very nice' stuff, but the rest sounds awesome. I'm going to be rich—I mean wealthy—one day, but I'm still going to be—"

She stopped mid-sentence and stood abruptly. Julene stood as well, mimicking her cousin, and bowed her head as the pastor moved down the center aisle of the sanctuary, shouting, "Will you come? Will you come? The doors of the church are open! Come now. Come forward. Let us meet you where you are. Will you come?"

A few individuals slipped from the pews and made their way toward the front.

The command to come forward was so compelling. Julene glanced over at Lori, prepared to walk to the front if Lori did. Lori, sensing Julene's stare, peered at her sideways. "We don't go up there unless you want to get saved. Unless—do you want to get saved?"

Julene watched as Aunt Lucille took a spot at the front of the sanctuary, receiving anyone who approached her with a warm hug before directing them through a door at the left of the pulpit. She glanced over at Lori and shook her head. "I'm not going up there."

When the pastor reached the rear of the sanctuary, he turned and faced the congregation. "Let's join hands now, family. Let's lay our burdens at the altar together. You may stay where you are, but reach out and join hands with the person on your left and on your right. Let's make a circle here."

Soft music played as the congregation shuffled about and joined hands across the pews and around the sanctuary. The music faded, and the pastor's voice took on a soothing, gentle tone. "God, we thank you this morning. Where would we be, if not for you? What would we have if not for your precious son? Which words are appropriate for giving you thanks? Lord, sometimes there are no words strong enough to express our appreciation, so we use our hands, we use our feet, we use our music, we—"

"Amen! Yes, God. Thank you, God!"

Whispered words of affirmation wafted across the sanctuary until the pastor's prayer evolved into a rhythmic call-and-response among the parishioners. The growing rhythm of the piano and the drums punctuated the pastor's words. The woman to Julene's right side began trembling, gently at first, growing stronger with the rising energy in the sanctuary. Julene, unsure if she was to keep her head bowed and eyes closed, gripped Lori's hand on the left while holding the lady's hand on the right. She peeked at the woman and noticed her entire body was shaking. Having heard of the Holy Ghost before and witnessing someone become so freely consumed by the spirit of God were two entirely different things. The woman shook and trembled so erratically that Julene was barely able to hang onto her hand, but no one else had broken the shapeless circle, and Julene wouldn't be the first.

She peeked at Lori, whose head was also bowed, but her eyes were open, surveying the increasing chaos of a sanctuary gone off into a state of unchoreographed praise and worship. The girls grinned at one another, Lori's twinkling eyes assuring Julene they'd talk about this later.

Julene returned Lori's mischievous smile and noticed her cousin's expression shift into one of concern.

Julene watched Lori's eyes settle on something behind her, and Julene, sensing something was wrong, turned slowly to peer over her shoulder. Aunt Lucille was coming, white-gloved hands motioning for another usher and a deacon who was stationed at the rear of the room. When they pushed their way to the end of the pew to attend to the lady, who was now convulsing uncontrollably, Julene peeled her hand from the woman's damp grasp. The girls watched as the woman's eyes rolled toward the ceiling, saliva pooling at the corners of her mouth. There was quiet panic as Lori gently pulled Julene away from the commotion and the girls watched the adults tend to the woman in silence. Words like *seizure*, *tongue*, and *ambulance* swirled around the room, blending with the pastor's stern instructions to *give her some space, let's all take a step back, I need someone outside to flag down the ambulance*. A group of church members assembled themselves in a far corner of the room and began praying aloud, grasping hands and bouncing lightly on their toes every few moments as though they could add a sense of urgency to their request of God.

Ambulance sirens began softly in the distance and grew louder in what seemed like seconds. Tears streamed down Julene's face and only when she reached up to wipe her cheeks did she realize she was still clutching Lori's hand. As soon as her hand was free, Lori pressed a wad of toilet tissue into Julene's palm. "Here. It's okay. Aunt Lucille always makes me keep tissue in my purse, but all I had was toilet paper this morning. You can use it."

Julene pressed the tissue against her face. It smelled of Aunt Lucille's house. She held it to her nose and inhaled, closing her eyes for a moment to drown out the bustle of activity around her. When she opened her eyes, Aunt Lucille was walking toward the girls, her hands no longer gloved, her hat askew. She smoothed her dress, took a deep breath, and ushered the girls outside.

"Can you believe that? Sister Andrea knows she needed to eat something before she came to church this morning. She'll be okay once they get some sugar into her. She should have never—"

Aunt Lucille paused to peer into Julene's face. "Have you been crying? That must have been scary for you. She's going to be fine, though. No need to cry."

A fresh stream of warm tears flowed from Julene's eyes, exceeding the absorbent capabilities of the shredded tissue. She wiped her face with the back of her hand. "Am I in trouble?"

"For what?" Lori responded before Aunt Lucille could process the question.

"Why would you be in trouble? What did you do, baby?" Aunt Lucille asked as she wrapped her arm around Julene's shoulder and guided her to the edge of the sidewalk, further away from the crowd that had formed in front of the church. Lori followed.

"I was holding her hand. I felt her shaking and I didn't say anything. I thought she was—I thought she had the Holy Ghost." She blubbered the last few words, her tears flowing down her cheeks before merging with her lips. The saltiness made her mouth water.

Aunt Lucille cupped Julene's chin with one hand and pulled her face upward. "Listen. This was not your fault. Sister Andrea has a health condition that can get out of control sometimes. How could you have known? You are not to blame here, understand?"

She waited until Julene nodded her head in confirmation, and then continued. "What you can learn from this is to use your voice. If something feels wrong, sounds wrong, seems wrong, you say something, okay? Don't hold your tongue, even if you're afraid. You can still speak up for yourself or for someone else."

Lori piped up then, wedging herself under Aunt Lucille's free arm, wrapping her arm around her aunt's waist. "Don't be afraid to say something. Just think. If you had spoken up when she first started shaking, we could have gotten out of church a whole lot sooner."

"Good grief, child! What am I going to do with you?" Aunt Lucille swatted at Lori's backside, laughing when Lori skipped just beyond her reach. Julene found a smile, too, and the girls drifted toward the window of the Polish bakery next door while Aunt Lucille watched the paramedics gather their belongings and pile into their truck.

The girls peered into the bakery window and Lori began pointing out her favorites—cheese pockets, Bavarian creme doughnuts, paczki, cheesecake loaf, kolaches—but a simple birthday cake decorated with a picture of Tweety Bird caught Julene's eye.

"That's what I would get," she said, tapping the glass softly. Lori paused to consider the cake.

"Are you a Tweety fan? Me, too. I had a cake kinda like that when I turned seven. The old guy who used to run this bakery made it. I think decorating was kind of like his specialty. I think his sons run this place now. It's still good, though."

"I always wanted a fun cake like this with Tweety or Barbie or Hello Kitty, but I never got one." Julene sighed heavily, thinking of the gold-dusted, multi-layered statement cakes that had been chosen for her over the years when all she'd wanted was a kid's cake like this one.

Lori shrugged. "I always thought you were the luckiest girl in the world. I was sure you could get whatever you wanted. I'm surprised you didn't have a seven-layer Tweety cake with a real, live Tweety bird performing at your party. What was the problem? Is Tweety too low-class?"

Julene laughed and bumped her shoulder against her cousin's. "Yes! Now you get it. I never had childish things like cartoon characters on my birthday cakes. My birthday parties were big, but my parents and their business partners had more fun than me. I always wanted the sneakers with Velcro straps and cartoon characters on the side, but it's the same as the cake situation."

"Low-class." The girls giggled the words together.

Aunt Lucille appeared behind them. "Let's get a move on, you two. I need to get home before the riffraff tears up my kitchen. I know they're hungry." She guided them toward Rosalind's car, idling at the corner.

The girls climbed into the backseat and Aunt Lucille buckled herself in the front. They sat quietly, listening as Aunt Lucille recounted the morning's melodrama to Rosalind who had been busy in the back room, volunteering at Children's Church.

When they were just a few blocks away from Aunt Lucille's street, Lori leaned forward and shook her aunt's shoulder with urgency. "Can we walk home? Please?"

Aunt Lucille peered over her left shoulder at Lori and exhaled. "Why would you want to walk home? We're almost there."

"Because it's fun! Uncle lets me do it sometimes. We'll come straight home. Promise." Lori clasped her hands under her chin, pleading.

Aunt Lucille glanced over at Rosalind, whose smile was sympathetic, before turning to face the girls again with a stern order. "Straight. Home."

In another moment, Rosalind had pulled close to the curb and the girls were out of the car, standing on the sidewalk, waving and smiling. They giggled over having won that battle with so little effort. Aunt Lucille and Rosalind pulled away from the curb, the gravel crunching beneath the car's rear tires.

CHAPTER FIVE

A unt Lucille gives you anything you want just like that?" Julene gestured toward the car as it approached the stop sign at the end of the block. "Is it because you live with her?"

Lori's face said she'd never considered this until now. She tilted her head to one side and pondered Julene's questions. "I don't live here. I really just come here on Fridays, but I usually stay through the weekend. Sometimes she lets me stay until Monday and sometimes, if I get lucky, she lets me come over on Thursday after track practice. I'm only here on Thursday, Friday, Saturday, Sunday, and sometimes Monday—unless I come after school on Monday. Then, she lets me stay the night and I go home on Tuesday after school. Unless I promise to go to Bible study with her on Wednesday, then she lets me stay Wednesday night."

"Sooo, you live here. Your stuff is here."

Lori tilted her head to the other side. "I guess I do kinda live here."

She chuckled a little. "I never looked at it that way. I just like being here all the time. But she doesn't give me whatever I want. She doesn't really have a lot to give. But, if I beg enough, she lets me do stuff."

"She gives you freedom," Julene stated. She looked over at her cousin, really studied her face for a moment, searching for some change of expression to show Lori truly understood.

Lori, oblivious to Julene's observation, linked her arm through the crook of her cousin's arm and tugged her toward the corner store.

"Let's get some wine."

Julene stopped mid stride, resisting Lori's gentle tugging. "We can't buy—I mean, I don't drink. Won't we get in trouble?"

Lori laughed, circling behind Julene to push her into the convenience store. "It's not real wine. It's sparkling water, and they come in different flavors. We always pretend like it's wine, but it isn't."

She nudged Julene a little harder, "We have to hurry. If we take too long to get home, Aunt Lucille will come looking for us. And she doesn't mind embarrassing us!"

Inside the store, Lori skipped to the beverage cooler, grabbed two glass bottles—one with raspberries on the label, the other with mangoes—and placed them on the counter near the register.

The store clerk, a young Latino guy wearing a Run DMC T-shirt, smiled while he scanned the drinks. "Lori, my love, would you like paper or plastic?"

Lori stepped back from the counter, snapping her hand to her hip. "Don't play with me, Angel! How much you charging me for these? I only have a dollar. Plus, my cousin Skeet said you still owe him money, so really, I shouldn't have to pay at all."

While Lori haggled with Angel, Julene unzipped her purse, reaching for her wallet, only to be stopped by Lori. The girls made eye contact and Lori's smirk prompted Julene to zip her purse closed again.

Angel pushed the drinks across the counter and when he smiled, dimples appeared at the corners of his eyes. He placed his hand over his heart. "Lori, mi amor, you're breaking my heart. Give me your number and anything in my dad's store is yours."

"Aw, Angel, you know I'm not allowed to give my number out." She grabbed the drinks, shoving one into Julene's hands before linking arms with her and skipping toward the door. She blew a kiss in Angel's direction on her way out. "Thanks for the drinks. I'll see you tomorrow."

Outside, Julene took a long swig from her drink and squeezed her eyes when the carbonation burned her throat and nose. "What just happened?"

Lori, after a long swig from her own bottle, shrugged and led Julene toward Aunt Lucille's house. "He likes me. He never makes me pay for anything. I see him at school sometimes—he's a senior—but I'm not trying to date him. It's just this little game we like to play."

She paused long enough to trade drinks with Julene, her face crumpling from the intensity of the carbonation. She smacked her lips. "Ahh, this is good stuff."

She poked Julene in the belly. "What about you? Who are you crushing on? Better yet, who's crushing on you?"

Julene sipped the drink Lori had shoved into her hands, decided she didn't love it, and swapped drinks with her cousin again. "I'm not really crushing on anyone. I spend a lot of time with my best friend Tristan because our parents know each other. I guess we kind of like each other. Other than him, my parents don't want me talking to any boys until I get my Jack and Jill membership. They said there will be plenty of boys to choose from after I get in."

"I don't know what you're talking about," Lori said. "You don't need a membership to Jackson Gill or whatever you just said! You just flirt with boys at school and have fun."

Lori shook her head as they approached Aunt Lucille's house. Many of the cars from the day before had returned. The girls took a shortcut across her lawn. "Cousin, I see you really need my help. I've gotta show you how to be a regular kid."

She opened the front door and ushered Julene inside. Friends and family members filled the space from the living room, through the dining room, and into the kitchen. The smell of cooked food made Julene's stomach rumble in recollection of yesterday's cookout. The girls wove their way through the rooms until they found Aunt Lucille sitting in her favorite kitchen chair, bouncing a baby on her knee. "What took you two so long to get here? I was just about to send someone to find you. I told you to come straight home!"

"AuntieAuntieAuntie," Lori sang, smothering Lucille with kisses. "We came straight here just like you told us. I swear!"

Julene stood back watching and grinning. Her heart fluttered a bit when Aunt Lucille winked at her. "You came straight home, did you? So where did you get those drinks?"

Both girls swung their hands behind their backs, knowing full well they'd been caught.

Lucille shook her head and lifted the baby, turning him toward her face. "Who do these girls think I am, huh? Do they think Auntie was born yesterday? Yes, they do, don't they? They were probably pretending they were drinking wine, weren't they? Should I whoop them? Should I put them over my lap and teach them a lesson?"

The baby gurgled gibberish in response, amused by Aunt Lucille's conversation. Lucille blew raspberries into the baby's belly until he giggled, and then spoke to him again, smiling as though he could understand. "Tell your cousins to get out of my face before I put them to work. I'm sure there are dishes to be washed."

Before she could enforce her threat, Lori and Julene turned and ran, laughing all the way to the bedroom and collapsing onto the bed.

"Everyone comes over after church to eat on Sundays," Lori explained. "Auntie always has a full house, but the kids usually stay outside."

She jumped to her feet and pulled Julene up, too. Then she shed her church clothes and changed into a baby tee and shorts. "Everybody is hanging out down the street. We don't have to hang around here with these old folks, but you can't be wearing that. You wanna wear something of mine? I can find something for you."

Lori pulled a stack of plastic storage containers from the closet, tossing the lids aside. She tore into the first one and then the next, digging inside, searching through a mess of clothing, jeans, and shirts. She held them up, considering their potential, before discarding them on the floor.

"How about this?" she asked, displaying a bright pink baby tee similar to her own and a pair of cutoff denim shorts. "It's Donna Karan. My friend works at Macy's. She lets me use her employee discount sometimes."

She looked at Julene's feet. "Your sandals are dope. I like different stuff like that, but I think my Jordans would look better. I'm a six, so I usually buy a size four in kids. It's the same shoe, but like thirty dollars cheaper! What size are you?"

Julene was already shedding her clothes, slipping the baby tee on, wiggling into the cutoff shorts. She kicked the sandals off. "I'm a seven."

Lori reached into the closet and tossed two sneakers in Julene's direction. "That'll work. They'll be a little tight, but it'll be fine."

Julene changed clothes quickly and the girls slipped back outside without being spotted by Aunt Lucille.

With feet crammed into borrowed sneakers, Julene followed her cousin down the block, becoming, with each step, a girl crammed into a borrowed life. At the corner, near a green electrical box, they reached a crowd of teens. There were maybe seven in total, a potpourri of guys and girls, laughing and talking, and teasing one another. Some sat atop the electrical box, some stood on it, some stood around it. One girl chased a boy, both of them breathless with laughter, around and between the others. The group paused when Lori burst into the center with an announcement. "Hey, everybody, this is my cousin, Julene. She's cool."

Julene lifted a hand, offering an uncertain wave to the crowd, while Lori introduced everyone. "That's Fats, Shayna, Aaliyah, Vaughn, Bone, Breeze, and Yara, but everyone calls her Ra-Ra." One of them, before Julene could try associating names with faces, pushed a boy from his seat on the electrical box. "Move! You see the girl needs somewhere to sit!"

Soon, the kids were laughing and joking again, teasing one another, comparing Beyonce to Ashanti, Jay-Z to

Eminem. They made room for Julene, including her in their debates, offering to braid her hair, while periodically breaking from their conversations to chase and tag and slap box one another.

In what seemed like the blink of an eye, the streetlights, glowing softly at first, grew to a flame, attracting large, swirling insects and providing a spotlight for the teens while pushing the street filled with white box houses into the shadows. The smell of barbecued burgers and fried fish filled the air, and when the lure of food was too strong to ignore, Vaughn and Ra-Ra raced back to the house, returning with plates of hot dogs, burgers, macaroni, and potato salad, bags of chips, and bottles of Green River pop. They passed the snacks around, unconcerned with clean hands or utensils or who was deserving and who wasn't.

Time was of little value. The teens would have occupied that corner until early morning, were it not for the cars, one at a time, and then two, and then many, backing off front lawns and pulling away from curbs, signaling the conclusion of the Sunday evening ritual. They watched the cars go by, waving at some, laughing at others, drinking in this summer night until a car stopped on the street in front of them. A woman's voice shrieked from inside the shiny, black Mercedes sedan with the front passenger window barely cracked open.

"Julene! My God, Julene! We've been searching all over for you! We were about to call the police—and you're *here*? Hanging on the corner like a—"

The slight gap in the car window closed abruptly, as the driver—Julene's father—did his best to minimize the offensive generalizations his wife hurled recklessly at the kids. He unbuckled his own seatbelt, stepped out of the car, and leaned over the hood to call to his daughter, but she'd already run off, dragged back to the house by Lori. They ran hand in hand, both hysterical with laughter, cutting across lawns. They took the front steps of the house in bounds and ran to Lori's room, where Julene shed the clothes, but not the exhilaration, and replaced them with her dress.

When the girls appeared on the front step, flushed from the thrill of their antics, the Mercedes was already idling in the now-empty driveway, headlights glaring. The passenger window rolled down again, the shrillness in Julene's mother's voice reduced to a husky bark, "Let's go. Right now."

Her father stepped from the vehicle again, stopping Julene to look into her eyes as she made her way to the car, saying nothing. He hugged Lori, draping his arm over her shoulder as they disappeared inside the house for what seemed like hours, though it couldn't have been more than a very long minute.

Inside the car, Julene sat with her mother, neither one exchanging words, until her father returned to his place behind the wheel. When they'd backed out of the driveway and pointed the car toward home, her mother was the first to speak, peppering the side of her husband's face with her fury. "What took you so long in there?"

"It was only a minute, Layla. I was saying goodbye to everyone. You could have come in to say goodbye as well." His voice was one notch above a whisper, a telling mixture of embarrassment, stress, and exhaustion. His wife, uninterested and indifferent to his explanation, redirected her wrath toward the backseat.

"Julene, what were you thinking, dressed like a prostitute, hanging on the corner with those thugs?" She spoke the words as though pickle juice coated each one of them.

"They aren't thugs, Mommy. They're regular teenagers like me. And I wasn't dressed like a prostitute. I had on shorts and a T-shirt, like a normal teenager. Lori let me borrow an outfit so I could feel more comfortable. Why is that a crime?"

Layla turned around in her seat, unbuckling her seatbelt to face her daughter squarely. "Because you are not regular. You're not regular, you're not normal or average, and you're not one of them." She straightened in her seat, satisfied in knowing her declaration required no response, only understanding and compliance.

Julene resisted the urge to leap from the car at the stoplight and run back to the electrical box at the end of Lori's street, where she'd left a piece of herself. The piece that felt the most real, felt the most accepted, felt the most normal. Back there with the kids who spoke in incomplete sentences without reprehension, ate with their hands outside, laughed with the full volume of their voices. She kept that thought tucked deep inside, though, to avoid her parents' condemnation, were they ever to discover that their well-bred daughter aspired to be regular.

They returned home that night, one of them too humiliated to attend another family function for quite a while, one of them resolved to never attend another such a family function ever, and one who'd both lost herself and also found herself at this particular family function.

Julene walked the line her mother had drawn—no longer conforming out of love, as she had when she'd been a little girl—until the day it led her out of her parents' home. When she graduated high school and left for college, her plan was never to return. In the meantime, to relieve the pressure that comes from a lifetime of keeping up appearances, and to lay down the burden carried by daughters who overcompensate for their parents, she'd disappear with Tristan whenever the opportunity presented itself.

CHAPTER SIX

Tristan Scott, the crowning achievement of his parents' failed marriage, was the product of a magnificent—albeit broken—family, an asset that was not overlooked by Julene's parents. If their daughter sought the company of this admirable and well-connected young man, they encouraged her wholeheartedly.

Tristan and Julene were friends who bonded over aromatic marijuana smoke, naked truths about dysfunctional families, and marathon video game sessions. They were teenagers. Two black sheep from two reputationously quasi-prominent black families. They *got* each other. She, because of her smart mouth and increasing difficulty in conforming to the rules. He, because he'd let his weed habit take precedent over the literal certainty of a college and eventual professional basketball career. *Them*, because they'd grown tired of contorting themselves to the images their families presented to the community.

So, they smoked together until she exchanged her endless words for quiet introspection and he traded his introverted demeanor for the mouth of an extrovert. Until they could have hours-long discussions about the lyrics of an Usher song. Until they worked up voracious appetites for snacks, giggling and gobbling until they fell asleep.

And sometimes—not always—they'd explore one another. It wasn't the teenage sex their parents had warned them about. It wasn't about breaking the rules, or lust, or even love. It was just what felt right when the buzz of the spliff made their skin come alive.

Marijuana and sex were simple elements of their self-prescribed survival kit— a tool they used to prevent themselves from spiraling further outside the boundaries set by their families' positions in the community. To her credit, she didn't pop pills like most girls her age. She'd found weed to be a miracle drug. It provided the same relief as the Zoloft, Xanax, and Adderall she'd seen passed like extra chewing gum amongst the kids at her school.

He, on the other hand, enjoyed the simple joint whenever he smoked with her, but didn't shy away when his friends passed around chunky blunts laced with a sprinkle of their parents' cocaine.

They didn't realize, perhaps because they were only teenagers, that an outward spiral, no matter how carefully suppressed, can only be postponed. Never prevented.

They couldn't have known they'd created storms inside themselves, swirling tornadoes like the dance of marijuana smoke, which would eventually become impossible to hide.

The first hint of trouble became evident when he started sleeping in his car. He'd had a fight with his mother—an increasingly frequent occurrence—about his inability to pass a simple drug test in order to continue playing basketball.

Mom, marijuana isn't even a real drug. It's practically legal in some states!

Tristan, I don't care if it's legal or not. It's preventing you from going to class and playing sports at school. It's an embarrassment.

What if I don't want to play ball, Mom? Huh? What if I just want to relax and be a normal teenager?

You aren't here to 'relax.' You are here to make a name for yourself. You are here to impress your coaches and scouts. You are here to secure your seat at the table and—

What table, Mom? I don't want a seat! I don't want to impress anyone! I never even wanted to go to that stupid school in the first place. All the kids get high, just like me. Their parents just pay enough to make the faculty look the other way. Why are you making such a big deal out of it when I'm not any different from the rest of the kids?

Because you are *different. You're my son, and I expect you to be better than the rest. I expect you to abide by my rules. You will stop with the drugs, you will go to class, and you will get yourself reinstated on the basketball team. Sports are a very important part of your resumé.*

I'll move in with Dad.

Good luck with that. He's in Dubai every other month and you're a fool if you think he'd give up his lifestyle just to raise his son! He was never interested in being a parent. I mean, he left you, didn't he?

He didn't leave me! He left you, not me!

He pulled his cellphone from his pocket then, turning his back to his mother as he dialed his father's number over and over, ending the call each time the voicemail picked up. The text message came through only seconds later: *Can't talk now. Out of the country until next month. Will call you later.* He flipped the phone shut, pissed that his mother had been right, and had stormed halfway up to his room by the time her ultimatum reached his ears.

You'll do as I say, or you'll leave my house.

Empowered by self-medications, he considered the options his mother had presented, and chose the latter. With no job, no diploma, no father and frozen assets, he slept in his car until she brought him back home, frightened by the thought of her friends spotting her son around town, living like a vagabond.

But Tristan's temporary homelessness wasn't even the worst crack in the facade. The worst crack came in the form of a positive pregnancy test.

CHAPTER SEVEN

She chose morning to tell her parents about the pregnancy. It just made sense to get the issue out in the open and tell them her plans, rather than allowing the anticipation to simmer in her belly all day.

Rightly, she'd expected some pushback from her parents, maybe even some raised voices and tears, but she'd prepared herself.

"If you think I'm going to stand by and watch you become a teenage mother—throw your future away—" her father shouted and then stopped short. He snatched his briefcase from the table and turned toward the door. He dropped the briefcase and scrubbed his face with his hand, scratching a spot under his chin with unwarranted intensity.

He exhaled. "Listen to me. You have your whole life to have children. Have a bus load of babies if you want! But not now, you understand? You don't throw away your entire future because you were too irresponsible to prevent an unwanted pregnancy."

Julene, full of the same spicy spirit that had entertained her father when she was seven years old, wrapped her arms around her small belly and announced, "I will still have a future. I'm going to college whether or not I'm a teenaged mother. You can't stop me from doing both. And what makes you so sure this baby wasn't planned?"

His mouth dropped open and he took a step toward his small, but mighty daughter, when Julene's mother appeared between them, pushing a travel coffee mug into her husband's hands. "Shh, you haven't had your morning coffee yet."

She turned slowly, exhaling as though she could push away the tense energy in the room simply by breathing, and faced her daughter. "Julene, honey, we can manage this…unfortunate circumstance. Is it Tristan's? He's more than capable of taking care of you."

She reached for her daughter's hands, and Julene backed away, refusing the unsolicited empathy.

"Ugggh! Don't try to manage my life like it's a snafu in one of your charity functions! My baby is not an unfortunate circumstance. It's my choice!" She huffed for air, unsure if this was a side-effect of the pregnancy or a symptom of the exhaustion she experienced every time she tried to reason with her parents.

Julene grabbed a handful of college acceptance letters from the credenza near the front door, waving them toward her parents like a threat. "You see these? These colleges want *me*! These letters don't say—"

She held one up, pretending to read through the envelope, "—no baby's mothers allowed."

She took her time placing and arranging the envelopes neatly on the credenza again, her demeanor that of a prosecutor considering her next question in a cross-examination, before she looked up to address her parents again.

"You two need to understand something. Times have changed. My pregnancy might not be the best look in this phony, bougie little world you've created for yourselves, but out there," she said, motioning with a flourish toward the world on the other side of their front door, "no one blinks twice at an unwed mother pursuing a college education."

"Unwed?" Layla breathed the word that had not entered her mind until this very moment. "It *is* Tristan's baby, right? You two love each other, I know you do! Do you mean to tell me you don't want to marry him?"

Never had Julene seen her mother's face look so childlike, so innocent, as it did right now. The naivete pierced Julene's heart but failed to lessen her resolve.

Instead, she laughed, perhaps to ease the mania of this morning's heaviness.

"As I said, I am going to college. I'm not interested in being a *wife*—" she said and then stopped, letting her eyes measure her mother's example of a *wife's* depressing existence. "Tristan and I *do* love each other, but we are not *in love* with each other. He's my best friend. That's it. By my calculations, the baby will be due in July. College will start in August. Even if I have to hold off for a semester, I can take online courses and be on campus by the winter."

She pulled her backpack onto one shoulder and made a brave attempt to squeeze past her father, having laid down the law for both of them. But he hissed into her ear, with a nastiness she'd only heard reserved for her mother, "You're going to college, huh? I'd like to see how you plan to pay for it."

With that, with Julene's feet now glued to the imported tile on the foyer floor, her father brushed past her, leaving the house and slamming the door behind him.

In the silence, she turned her eyes toward her mother. When the water in her eyes drew her mother out of focus, she shifted her sights to the pile of college admissions letters on the credenza. Maybe it was the movement of her eyes, searching for a safe place to land, or maybe it was the hormones, working feverishly on behalf of her growing baby. Whatever the reason, the tough girl couldn't stop the tears from sliding down her cheeks.

Her backpack slipped from her shoulder and dropped down the length of her arm, where it hung slackly from her wrist, and it was her turn to have pure innocence bear itself on her face. "He's not paying for me to go to college? Just because I got pregnant? What does that have to do with…"

Layla took her daughter's hand and led her to the sitting area in the front room. When they were seated, Layla used her eyes to center Julene's attention.

"You're going to be a mommy," she said with an endearing, encouraging smile, "You can't get yourself all worked up about things during this time. You have a child to consider now. Your father, he doesn't know how to deal with his feelings, you know? He flies off the handle when he feels embarrassed, but don't worry about him right now."

Julene shook her head, knowing with certainty she'd heard her father correctly. "Parents are supposed to pay for college. Like, is he so angry about my baby that he doesn't want me to get an education? How is that fair?"

Layla straightened her back and used her knuckle to lift her daughter's chin just a bit. "He's angry. No, he's disappointed, I'm sure. We wanted the fairytale for you, you know? But things have changed. You're making a grown woman decision right now—having a baby—and now I have to tell you some grown woman truths. You're not a little girl anymore."

She exhaled heavily, never taking her eyes away from her daughter's. "He can't afford to pay for your college. He's had some financial troubles over the years, and he's never quite recovered. He's embarrassed about it. We were hoping you'd have gotten some scholarships and you wouldn't have ever found out, but the money just isn't there. That's the reality. So, listen, what you're going to do is—"

"But what about my college fund?" Julene interrupted. "Don't I have one? I did my part! I made good grades, I joined clubs, I pretended to be graceful for those stupid debutante balls, I never embarrassed you in front of your friends—and you can't even send me to college? What was it all for? What was the point?"

Fresh, hot tears coursed down Julene's face, and their endlessness only infuriated her further.

Layla remained calm. She'd long been an expert in projecting poise under pressure. When her daughter ran out of breath, she laid out the game plan. "What you're going to do is this: you're going to marry Tristan. He comes from a nice family. His mother fared very, *very* well when she divorced his father. As Tristan's wife, you'll have access to a financial life that your father just can't provide."

"I don't want—" Julene's protests went unheard.

"You don't want to be a *wife*," Layla mocked her daughter with air quotes. "You might not want to, but you need to learn how to play the hand you've been dealt."

She gripped her daughter's shoulders and shook them gently, tenderly. "You're pregnant by a rich boy who is also your best friend. You've hit the jackpot. Make it work. For the baby. For your future."

Julene wiped her face with her sleeve and breathed deeply. "I'm not like you, Mother. I would never scheme to trap a man with a baby just for the money. It didn't work out for *you* very well, did it? *Your* husband's *broke* and he doesn't even appreciate you! You don't even *like* each other! Why would I want that?"

Julene stood up, finished with this conversation, mumbling more to herself than speaking to her mother now, "I'll just get a student loan. People pay for college all the time with student loans. He's gonna feel like shit for sending me out into the world with student loan debt. I bet none of his friends—"

"You're in bankruptcy. You'll never get approved for student loans," Layla interjected. She waited patiently for Julene to return to her seat. " Why are we spending time talking about this when we could be celebrating the blessing of a pregnancy with a wealthy boy? You have always been headstrong and determined to be treated like an adult, and I can no longer shield you from the entire truth, but we can make this situation work to your advantage if we can leverage Tristan's family's position in the community."

Julene sat, stunned into numbness, while her mother explained the business venture her father and his partner had tried and failed. He'd tried using Julene's social security number to establish a line of credit for a business loan. The venture, while appearing promising on paper, hadn't been insulated from risk in real life, and had tanked before it could turn a profit. With a slew of investors backing it, and no way to salvage the plan, her father and his partner made the decision to claim bankruptcy as a bailout. They'd abandoned the business and tried several more, banking on the fact that the bankruptcy would be expunged from Julene's credit report before she was old enough to need it.

"You put the business in my name? That was your best alternative?" Julene's voice screamed inside her own head, though it was barely a whisper as it traveled the distance from her lips to her mother's ears. She was weak with disappointment.

"I can acknowledge your anger, but there's so much you don't understand," Layla said as she reached for Julene's hand again, only to have it snatched away. "We'd already lost the house. We'd mortgaged it several times. We don't hold the deed anymore, so technically, we're renting. Your father's credit was ruined. He'd borrowed against his retirement and his future earnings with the firm, we'd exhausted my credit, too—yours was our last lifeline."

Her mother's words reached her ears, but they were incomprehensible. Julene stood to leave, gathering her bookbag and purse, and announced a promise to her mother as much as to herself. "I will never, ever exploit my child the way you've exploited me."

She left the house unsure of her next steps, but certain she'd figure it all out.

Hours later, as she lay on the obstetrician's table under the slippery wand of an ultrasound technician, she struggled to find clarity in any point of the morning's conversation. Her parents were the worst kind of liars, she was bankrupt, and the possibility of college had all but completely fallen off her radar.

Her eyes began to water again with the gravity of it all, and she squeezed Tristan's hand, fighting against the tears at the very moment the ultrasound technician announced there were two heartbeats on the monitor.

CHAPTER EIGHT

The summer the babies were born, just as soon as the obstetrician would permit her to resume her normal activities, Julene and Tristan packed their belongings and moved into one half of the rental duplex awarded to his mother in her divorce decree.

Too stubborn to get married and clutching educational credentials no more prestigious than high school diplomas, neither could manage to secure jobs that would support the lavish lifestyles they'd been accustomed to living. Instead, they lived as a small family, sharing the responsibilities of raising their precious twin daughters while managing his mother's luxury rental properties in exchange for rent and living expenses.

"Tristan!" his mother exclaimed. "You smell like a pack of reefer cigarettes! Is this why you haven't finished the move-out inspection at the Norwood property?"

Ramona Scott stood, trying to read her son's hooded eyes, before finally walking right up to him, grabbing his collar and pulling it up to her nose. She released the shirt and pushed him away. "You said you were done with that stuff."

She shifted her gaze from Tristan to Julene, who stopped folding baby clothes to stand up, prepared to defend herself.

"Don't look at me! I don't smoke that stuff," Julene said. "I would never do that to my babies. Plus, I'm taking care of everything around here for you, scheduling maintenance for your tenants, collecting rent payments, answering complaints, writing and posting the rental advertisements—and you think I have time to sit around and get high?"

Ramona rolled her eyes in her son's direction and stepped a little closer to Julene, dropping her voice an octave. "Let's get this straight, you wayward little princess. You do *nothing* for *me*. The responsibilities I've given you two aren't even enough to cover the rent in this condo, not to mention the car I let you two drive, the insurance I pay, the groceries I buy. You don't even pay your own cell phone bill!"

She grabbed her keys and headed toward the front door, not even kissing the babies goodbye as she left. As she walked out, she looked back at them and said, "But I do these things because you two immature children will not embarrass *me* in this community, because these babies need a safe place to live, and because I'm still responsible for my son, no matter how much of a disappointment he's determined to be."

When they heard her car drive away, Julene sat down to fold the last of the baby clothes, and Tristan drifted out the back door to finish his joint. With a mother like his, one who wasted no opportunity to emasculate and ridicule her only son, Julene sometimes found it difficult to blame him for seeking the rapid decompression his weed provided.

At least he doesn't drink, Julene rationalized. *He's not a drunk or a hardcore drug addict. At least he's a good father. He's a good person.*

She wanted to walk out the door behind him, hug him tightly, tell him she was still his best friend, tell him his mother was a complete bitch. But she didn't. She knew Tristan better than he knew himself. She opted to give him his space.

When she had folded the last of the baby clothes, Julene moved to the kitchen and placed a pot of water on the stove. As she waited for the water to boil, she browned a package of ground beef, diced onions, peppers, and minced garlic, and sauteed it all together with a jar of marinara sauce. She tossed a handful of spaghetti noodles into the boiling water, and a package of cocktail shrimp into the simmering sauce.

Just as she began spreading four pieces of bread with her homemade butter and garlic spread, an incoming call set off her ringtone. Before she could grab a towel to clean her hands, Tristan was wrapping an arm around her waist and grabbing her phone with his free hand.

He glanced at the screen, silenced the call, and dropped his nose into the crook of her neck. His voice was a silky drawl, and it made her smile. "You got it smelling so good in here. I love it when you make ghetto spaghetti, and I'm starving right now."

"My spaghetti is *not ghetto*! I had to use what's left of the groceries to make something for us to eat! Your mother hardly gave me any money this week, so," she explained with a shrug, "I had to do what I had to do."

He rolled his eyes at the mention of his mother. "Speaking of the devil, that was her calling you just now."

"And you hung up on her?" Julene asked with a laugh as she slid the garlic bread under the broiler. "So now she thinks I'm the one who hung up on her. You need to call her back and tell her it was *you*."

When she turned around to say she was serious, he was disappearing down the hall, tossing a joke over his shoulder. "What're you saying? I can't hear you! I think Jada and Jacinta are calling me!"

"They're eleven months old. They aren't calling you. What I need you to do is come get this phone and call your mother back!"

When Tristan returned to the kitchen, carrying one baby girl under each arm like footballs, she couldn't help but laugh. They both stopped mid-laugh when Tristan's phone began to vibrate on the kitchen counter. Peeking at the screen together, they jumped backward at the same time and pointed at each other.

"I'm not answering it! You answer it!" they said in unison.

They burst into laughter again, shouting, "Jinx!"

Before they could decide who said it first, the phone stopped vibrating and they fell silent. In a split second,

Tristan's face broke into a smile, and he shrugged. "She'll be alright. She probably didn't want anything anyway."

He disappeared into the pantry and popped out again. "Where's the baby food? My girls are hungry!"

Julene moved the spaghetti from the stove to the strainer in the sink and dropped her head over the rising steam. "Ahh! It's in the trunk of your mom's car. She told me to get it out of her car when she got here, and I forgot. That's probably why she was calling."

"OkayOkayOkay," he resigned. "I'll call her and see if she can swing back through with the baby food. She could have carried the bag in herself."

He mumbled this as he dialed her number. He held the phone to his ear, pulled it away to make sure he'd dialed the correct number, and placed it to his ear again. A second later, he tossed the phone on the counter, disappeared into the pantry again, and returned, mouth filled to capacity with cheese puffs. Jada and Jacinta clutched cheez puffs in their chunky hands, too, struggling to press the orange-powdered treats into their mouths.

Without a word, he fastened his daughters into their matching highchairs, sprinkled dry cereal onto their trays, and filled their sippy cups with milk.

Julene watched quietly, reading the fury in her best friend's eyes, knowing well enough to say nothing. She watched him pull another blunt from the tin can he kept above the fridge and head toward the back door.

"I'ma go out here and cool off for a minute, and then I'ma take a ride over to mom's house," he said. His voice was deep—gruff, if she stretched her vocabulary. An uneasy quiver took root in her gut.

"Wait. What's wrong?" She pulled the garlic bread from the broiler and rushed to meet him at the door, positioning her small body in front of his.

"Mom turned off my cell phone—turned off *our* phones," he replied. "I know she did it out of spite and I'm sick of letting her get away with it. But I gotta calm down first."

He touched Julene's arm, letting his hand slide down to hers. He squeezed it slightly and tried to slip past her.

She squeezed his hand back, keeping him from walking out the door.

"Okay, listen," she said. "You don't need to drive *anywhere* right now. Just chill right here. *I'll* drive over to the house and find out what's wrong. Like it or not, we need her help, so let me just say whatever to make her happy and let's keep it moving."

She grabbed his other hand, glanced toward the babies and looked at him again. "As soon as I can figure out how to pay for college and you can figure out your next move, we can tell her to kiss our asses and never look back, okay?"

When he didn't answer, she gripped his hands a little harder, pulling his six-foot, four-inch frame down to eye-level. "Okay?"

"Yeah, alright." He exhaled and smiled the brilliant smile that had made the girls in her class go bananas when they were in school. He kissed her forehead, tucked the blunt behind his ear, and walked over to his babies' highchairs. "Gimme some of that milk! Give daddy some cereal!"

The babies giggled. Tristan dropped to his knees in front of them, begging for handouts. Julene snatched her keys and purse from the counter, pausing only for a second to allow the hot flash and the swell of nausea to pass before walking out the front door.

CHAPTER NINE

Twenty-five minutes later, having burned a precious eighth of a tank of gas, Julene parked her Range Rover alongside the mailbox in front of Tristan's mother's house. Though Tristan's mother had made it very clear the Range Rover was not a gift, but a loan, Julene had grown accustomed to pretending she alone held the title to the truck. It was the same year and model as several of Julene's friends', and they'd made a habit of calling themselves the Range Rover Girls whenever they all got together for brunch.

Tristan's mother wouldn't allow her to park the gorgeous truck in the driveway when they visited, though. There was a leak neither Tristan nor Julene could afford to have fixed, and his mother had been livid the day it dripped oil on her pristine driveway. *You won't have people thinking my car is a clunker! From now on, you park that thing on the street until you get it fixed.*

She sat in the car for a moment taking deep breaths and practicing her smiley-face before walking up the long driveway and ringing the doorbell. On the other side of the door, she could hear her children's grandmother laughing with someone on the phone. More than a few minutes passed before the door finally opened. Julene waited patiently, a sweet smile pasted on her face, until she was waved inside.

Tristan's mother placed a finger to her own lips, instructing Julene to keep quiet while she finished her conversation. "Okay, that's perfect…Yes. I prefer the black linen napkins because they don't leave lint on our clothes…The bouncy castle, not that tacky ball pit…Right…Oh! One more thing! Find out who did the cake for The Pattersons' wedding last summer… Yes. The one with the edible gold flakes. Wasn't it decadent? I have to have it."

When she ended the call, she sighed and smiled to herself, before finally acknowledging Julene. She batted her eyes pleasantly and sat down to give Julene her undivided attention. "And what can I do for you, Ma'am?"

"I just came by to get the baby food from your car. I forgot to take it out when you came over earlier."

Julene added a smile to her words, desperate to keep the peace.

"Oh! The *baby food*! Yes, I realized you'd forgotten it. I called you as soon as I left but you didn't answer. Your phone went right to your voicemail. I called Tristan, too, but he didn't answer, either."

The older woman met the younger woman's eyes squarely.

"You must've called when we were getting the babies up from their nap." Julene had rehearsed this answer, complete with soft, innocent eyes, on the drive over.

Tristan's mother's face was stone cold, and she filtered her voice carefully. "That makes sense! At first, I thought you were avoiding my call. Why didn't you just call me back?"

Julene worked to match the older woman's honeyed voice. "Tristan tried to call you right back, but he said the phones were turned off."

"Not *my phone!* I was just using my phone with no problems." She paused, as though she'd realized her own mistake. "You know what? I must've put a block on your lines by mistake. I was just trying to figure out why I couldn't get through when I called. Now I'll have to figure out how to reverse that."

She sat patiently, allowing Julene time to digest her bogus rationale. The younger woman rallied back with her father's quick tongue. "I figured it must have been something like that. I knew you wouldn't purposely turn our phones off knowing your grandchildren are with us. I mean, what if there was an emergency? We couldn't even call for help. It's okay. You're getting older and your mind isn't as sharp as it used to be. These accidents are bound to happen. It's part of the aging process, I guess."

The older woman smiled at the unveiled insult. Julene thought of how her father used to look much the same way whenever she caught him off guard.

"Darling, my mind is sharper than ever. It's certainly sharper than yours, what with you in this *condition,* shacked up with a worthless boy, and depending on me for support. I mean, honestly! What would you do without me?" the older woman replied. She shook her head slowly, then piped up again. "That reminds me! I have everything in place for the twins' first birthday party. Or are *you* going to handle that? Were your parents planning to pay for it? No?"

She didn't allow time for a response. "You don't have to thank me. Just make sure your *boyfriend* is there, looking respectable. Use my credit card to get him a nice linen suit if he needs one, and dress my beautiful babies in the outfits I'm having delivered on Wednesday. If you need a new dress, let me know. I've got a stylist coming by later with a few pieces, and I can have her bring something for you, too. I'm throwing the party of the year for *my* granddaughters, and I want everything to be perfect. There will be lots of important people there. Your parents can come, too."

A well-trained actress by virtue of her own mother's grooming, Julene rose from her seat and planted an air-kiss on each side of the older woman's face. "What would I do without you, Mrs. Scott? If you need me to do something for the party, just let me know. I'll grab the baby food on my way out and could you please turn our phones back on?"

"Of course, my love." The older woman wrapped her arm around Julene's shoulder and walked her toward the door. She took her keys from the hook and aimed them at the car. With the click of a button, the trunk popped open. "The baby food is in there. I'll have your phone turned on by the time you get home. I'm sure my aging brain can figure it out."

The women embraced in the doorway, and the older woman whispered a rhetorical question in the younger woman's ear. "Now, what are we going to do about the fact that you're pregnant again?"

The surprise of Mrs. Scott's words made Julene's stomach clench. A new wave of nausea threatened to ruin the front steps, but she was too willful to let it show. Instead, she smiled as she walked to the car and pulled the shopping bag from the trunk and shrugged. "It's no big deal. When you already have two babies, what's one more?"

She smiled and waved goodbye as she pulled away from the curb. When the large house had vanished in the rear-view mirror, she pulled over and threw up.

CHAPTER TEN

From the day Julene had walked out of her parents' home, a rap song by an emerging young Chicago rapper played like a quiet anthem in the back of her mind. The song about a rebellious young girl caught between her parents' expectations, the pressures of social scrutiny, and her own ideals about the life she deserved seemed to speak to her almost relentlessly. She couldn't get it out of her mind. The lyrics painted a picture of a lost girl in living color. She struggled against crippling self-consciousness, her responsibilities as a young mother, the uncertainties of college, her affinity for a certain standard of living, the elusive nature of the American Dream, and the dangers of becoming a statistic when it all falls down.

It was as though a program had been allowed to run endless loops in the background of her computer for years. The song's presence and message didn't bother her; she'd simply gotten used to it in much the same way she'd gotten used to the neighbor's cat taking a shortcut across the yard every day.

It occupied a fair amount of space in her brain's hard drive, but she didn't turn it off. In fact, sometimes she used it. It kept her pumped up on the inside. It kept motivating her to find a way out of the life she'd inherited, especially on the dark days when her actions didn't match her feelings, when she was acutely aware that her life didn't reflect her spirit. Things weren't right—of this she was certain—but on a good day, she succeeded in pushing the uncomfortable thoughts away.

Sometimes, on the days when she could barely support the weight of the mask she wore—that of a happy woman who was not a fraud and a liar—she was ashamed of herself for even singing the lyrics out loud alone in her car. Sometimes, on days like today, as she drove the car she didn't own to the home she didn't own to tell her baby daddy he was going to be daddy to another baby, instead of motivating, the song seemed to taunt her.

On those difficult days, she longed for Aunt Lucille, though she was too embarrassed to contact her. She'd craved one more night of feet-fighting in bed with Lori, with whom she'd not spoken to since the night her parents had whisked her away in disgust. She missed the feeling she'd enjoyed for little more than twenty-four hours when she'd spent time with her father's family a few years ago— the time when she'd been comfortable in her surroundings and comfortable in her own skin.

She shushed the song, if only for a short while, by deciding the only way to take control of her life for now was to fall in line. She'd play her part as the woman she'd been groomed to be until she could be the woman she *wanted* to be. She convinced herself that for the sake of the greater good, for her children and for her reputation, that she could learn to live a life of hidden contradictions.

Though she would never admit it, she'd recently come to admire Martha Stewart, who'd become so comfortable in her contradictions. She was a crafting and baking home economist, and a convicted felon who enjoyed a genuine friendship with Snoop Dogg. Martha, having grown very comfortable with herself, was doing what she liked to do, undefined by a husband or long-term boyfriend (at least in the public eye), was free to enjoy her unconventional friendship with Snoop, bringing him into her world rather than assimilating herself into his. She didn't flaunt fussy hair or makeup and didn't have labels and logos all over her body. Julene imagined she was a woman who spent money on the finest things in life, be it kitchen utensils or cannabis, but only if they were sensible and of the best quality—not because she regarded them as symbols of status.

If the conversation were worth discussing over brunch, Julene's friends would argue that Martha was just old as hell and old people can do whatever they wanted. But she would argue that maybe Martha had found the secret to happiness and had created a life that she loves, regardless of what the world would think.

She would tell her friends to imagine how life would be if we created lives that we love *now*, rather than waiting until we are too old to care? It was an argument that would never leave her lips, however, because, according to their social media profiles, they WERE living the lives they loved. One would need only to shine a light on the truth to see they were all living the lie, but like vampires, they'd learned to keep it shrouded in darkness, only revealing the parts they'd designed for the world to see.

And Julene—especially after having not one, but *three* babies in the two years after high school—pushed her own truths into the shadows as well, though the heroic effort to keep them there strained her moral fibers until they nearly gave way. So, she'd put the Beyoncé concert tickets on the one credit card extended to her by Tristan's mother after a friend had begged her to fly to Vegas for the show at the last minute.

She might have instead preferred to get tickets to Snoop and Martha's Cooking with Cannabis live-taping, but the Beyoncé concert was great for optics, especially under the bright lights of Las Vegas. After Vegas, as her friends booked excursions to the Essence Festival, Coachella, NBA All-Star Weekend, and New York Fashion Week, Julene could blame her growing belly rather than her growing inability to pay as her reason for avoiding the spotlight.

She appreciated the absence of the social scene as she and Tristan devoted themselves to their children. They'd managed to create a simple, organic family life filled with bubble baths, crayons, sandboxes, storybooks, and the addition of baby Jamison, where the only disruptions were directly related to the ebb and flow relationship between Tristan and Ramona.

Like the gravitational contest between the moon and the Earth influences the rise and fall of the ocean along with all the living things in the ecosystem, so too did daily life for Julene and the children respond to the pulling and pushing matches between Tristan and his mother.

Behind closed doors, a churning rip current existed, and Julene watched her friend fight to keep from being pulled into the undertow. In the days before their baby boy approached his first birthday, Tristan and Ramona's rift reached new, unsustainable levels of frequency and intensity.

CHAPTER ELEVEN

The day after baby Jamison's first birthday, Julene busied herself by sliding new key tags on her set of townhome keys. Replacing the key tags wasn't on her to-do list, but the task afforded her an excuse to linger in the living room while she eavesdropped on the hushed and harsh exchange taking place between Tristan and his mother at the front door.

She could tell from her friend's tone he was agitated. She could tell from his mother's tone she was antagonizing. *Why can't he just stop talking and why won't she just leave?* Julene asked herself for the zillionth time in twenty-four months, and still, she had no answer.

"Is it so difficult, Tristan?"

"That's not the point! It's like you don't listen to me!"

"You need to tell me something that makes sense."

"I just didn't have time! Do you really expect me to drop everything and come running when you call?"

"For what I'm paying you—for all I do for you—you should damn well stop everything when I call! I should be able to depend on you."

"I'm not your husband. I'm your son! I have my own life to live. I shouldn't have to live yours, too!"

"Boy! You couldn't be an adult for ten minutes, much less 'live your own life.' If I wasn't here to…"

A tremble vibrated through the house when Tristan walked out, slamming the door in his mother's face. The walking out and the slamming of doors after a shouting match had become a more frequent occurrence, too. While

Julene had learned to master her tongue and tamp down her anger in dealing with Mrs. Scott, Tristan had not.

Julene took her time, arranging and rearranging the keys, waiting, listening for the sound of Mrs. Scott leaving. Instead, the older woman's voice, just two feet away, made her jump.

"You think you know him so well. That boy has some demons you can never overcome. I know you two are close, but I'm his mother. I was once close to him, too—closer than you think you are. Colleges were lined up, begging him to join their teams despite the drugs. They were willing to look the other way. He could have been a star in the NBA by now! And look at what he's become! Worthless at anything except giving me more grandchildren."

Julene, caught between the responsibility of placating her financier and defending her best friend, ultimately chose her friend. "Why would you want to force him to do something he hates? We both know he never wanted to play basketball."

"He doesn't hate it! Now, maybe he didn't love it, but he wasn't thinking about his future. Even at the college level, his basketball career could have opened tremendous doors for him! And for you too, had you been able to motivate him properly. Did you ever think about that?" Mrs. Scott walked across the kitchen and back again, stopping to watch Julene's face, wanting her to take some responsibility for Tristan's failure to excel.

"How do you even know if he wanted to go to college to work for *free* as an athlete? It's slave labor! Why assume he couldn't have opened doors for himself doing something else? Something that God purposed for him to do? What if he tried to be happy instead of trying to be the next Michael Jordan? Doesn't he deserve to choose his own path?"

Up to this point, Tristan's mother had assumed a defensive stance, ready to fight this battle and determined to win. But this time, she sat down at the kitchen island, gently and deliberately, looking across at her son's girlfriend with genuine pity. "My goodness, you still believe that old hippie gypsy stuff about going where your spirit takes you and following your heart, don't you? You haven't grown up at all. It's sweet—you're sweet— but you're deluding yourself and my son, too. When will you wake up?"

To this, Julene had no response. She'd grown tired of the mother-son feud for today. She swallowed her pride yet again, and hugged the older woman goodbye, silently vowing to minimize contact with this toxic woman for a little while for her own sanity as much as Tristan's.

The vow of avoidance ended much more abruptly than Julene would have liked when, after going to sleep and waking in the morning, she'd yet to hear from Tristan. He had left on foot— the Range Rover remained parked in the driveway. She hadn't expected him to travel very far. He'd walked out in the past, staying away for hours sometimes to cool off after a confrontation with his mother, but he'd never stayed away overnight.

She spent the next day checking social media and making up bogus excuses to contact his friends, hoping to locate him. Then, late in the evening, after she'd coaxed her three children to sleep, her phone pinged with a text message: *Don't worry about me. I'm just in a dark place. Need time to figure things out.*

The message frightened her right away. Reading his sparse words, she could hear his pained voice trying to sound braver than it was.

She calmed herself before replying, *I'm here for you. Come home.*

When she could see he'd viewed her message but hadn't responded, she added, *The babies miss you.*

Tell them daddy loves them. I'll be back when I can be the father they deserve.

She tried to maintain the appearance of normalcy by going about her daily routines as though her best friend hadn't vanished, but she worried. By the end of the week, he no longer answered her texts or her requests to FaceTime with the children. Against her better judgement, but out of options, she called Mrs. Scott.

"I'm just worried about what has really happened to him," she told Mrs. Scott. "You may not know this, but he spirals into deep depression and withdraws from his friends, and even me sometimes, especially after confrontations with you. No offense intended, but I know I'm his *person*, the only one who understands him and can get through to him. But I can't find him without your help. Could you at least check the phone bill to see if he's been calling anyone?" Julene held the phone and her own breath, not wanting to believe a mother could be so unconcerned about her missing son, no matter how unpleasant their last visit may have been.

Mrs. Scott spoke sharply and with no pretext. "I don't have time to play private investigator, and I know much more than you think about his *spirals*. You may think I'm a witch for handling him the way I do, but you don't know him the way I do. He's gone too far, though. He can't come back here, and I won't waste a second looking for him. For God's sake, he left because he wanted to leave. I won't take responsibility for that!"

Tristan's mother paused and then continued, her voice more composed. "I have an investor who is interested in this property, so I'll need your unit vacated ASAP. I know you have the babies and everything, and I'm not completely insensitive, so you and the kids can stay here until the end of next month, but then you'll have to find somewhere else. And just forget about Tristan. He can't help you, and you can't help him. My advice to you, as a woman and as a mother, is to move on, find your own place, and get used to taking care of your own children. Don't be like him and expect your parents to take care of you for the rest of your life. From what I hear, they're busy with their own problems."

The older woman's words stung in the way of an open-handed slap to the face of an unconscious person. Tristan's instability couldn't be ignored, and though she could hope for his transformation, she hadn't enough time to wait for it.

That evening, sitting on the toilet long after she'd finished using it, Julene tried to push the problems to the furthest part of her mind, allowing space to reflect on her choices and plan her next move. She racked her brain to come up with a plan for escaping the life that had become her prison.

She imagined she was a rapper, coming up with the lyrics that would make sense of complicated circumstances. She could almost hear the beat of the song that always played in the recesses of her mind— the beat alone emboldened her— and she could see the Chicago rapper leaning over his notebook, thumping his pencil against the paper, bobbing his head hypnotically as he captured the essence and nuances of a life that doesn't turn out as planned.

In her mind, he'd taken the first step with his song. He'd taken the issues, the concerns that no one voiced aloud, and laid them on the table in plain view. He'd begun to pull the curtain back, casting an honest light on the insecurities and dysfunctions of all people, no matter how wealthy or self-assured they may appear, but his song didn't help address the next step. How do we fix it? How do we save ourselves?

These weren't new questions. The need to gain independence over her life had been a goal for as long as she could remember. She'd just never had a deadline like the one Tristan's mother had proposed until now. She would have to move out. The idea of finding a new home for herself and the babies seemed to make time shift into high gear. Time was racing forward now. Toward what? Toward the slow and certain death of a life defined by inauthenticity and social restrictions? The thought of it all made her heart race as fast as the words in the song.

Think!

Her feet tingled softly, and she shifted on the commode to wake her sleeping limbs. She closed her eyes, searching the darkness behind her lids for an answer.

Mommy, Maaameee….

She had left the bathroom door open, and her baby appeared. She needed only to take one glance at her beautiful baby boy's face to know what she had to do.

It took her nearly three weeks to actually do it.

CHAPTER TWELVE

When Julene finally picked up the phone and called her mother, she hadn't decided if her best approach was to fight or grovel. She'd barely spoken to her parents since she moved out, punishing them with occasional interactions with their grandchildren, and distancing them from the Scott family's social (and financial) currency. She considered fighting, using guilt as a razor blade: *What kind of parents would set their own daughter up for failure? What about my children? What must your friends think of you?*

Her alternative was to grovel: *I've learned my lesson. I was wrong to blame you when you've always tried to help me. I'm sorry if I embarrassed or upset you.*

In the end, she did neither. She lied. The story tumbled out of her mouth as though it had been rehearsed, but it hadn't.

"Hey, Mom," she greeted. "Tristan will be out of the country for a few months working on a real estate deal for Mrs. Scott. While he's gone, she's having our duplex renovated so I'll need to move out. I could use help with the kids, and I know you've been wanting to spend more time with them. I was thinking we should come and stay with you and Dad for a little while."

Silence crept in while Julene's mother digested the proposal, and then she laughed and breathed a sigh of relief. "Of course, darling! Of course, you and those beautiful babies can come here! You don't know how long

I've prayed that we could put all that old drama in the past. It'll be just like it used to be!"

"No, Mom, it won't be like it was," Julene stated. "I never said I'd forgiven you two for what you've done to me, but I'm trying to work through it. And I don't want my anger to keep the kids from having a relationship with their grandparents. They see Tristan's mother more than enough. I want to learn to be the bigger person."

Her mother, barely acknowledging Julene's declaration, began making plans. "I'll call the movers and have your things placed in our storage unit. Just bring what you need for the children. I'll have the two rooms upstairs set up when you get here."

Julene sat for a moment, relieved when the call ended. It had gone better than she'd expected, and the last-minute lie would make it much easier for her to push the rest of her plan into place.

Four days later, sitting across the dining table from her parents, she skipped the pleasantries and asked the hard questions. She addressed them both, but her eyes never left her father's. "How could you both have lied to me for all these years? How did you think I wouldn't find out? I mean, bankruptcy in my name? You screwed me! How is that even *legal?*"

Her father was the first to speak, placing his palm across his chest with sincerity. "Sweetheart, I'm an *attorney.* I can make anything legal on paper. *It's paperwork!* Now, I've been apologizing to you for three years. It was terrible judgment on my part, but, as I've learned in business, you can't dwell on the past. You have to dust yourself off and—"

"The past? This isn't my *past!* This is my *now!* And thanks to you, I can't *dust myself off!* I can't do anything because you ruined my credit before I ever had a chance to get started. You cost me my college education! I can't get a job to support my family!"

"First, let's calm down. You always were one for the theatrics," her father said, unmoved by his own responsibility in the matter. Instead, he explained the facts.

"As I said, it was a bad business decision. Had the business venture worked out, the outcome would have been tremendous for all of us. Unfortunately, I put my trust in an unscrupulous partner and it cost me dearly—much more than it cost you."

Julene laughed out loud, feeling herself come undone. "Are you serious?"

He held up a hand to quiet her and continued, "I invested my entire life's savings in that venture, and when my cash ran out, I leveraged a substantial amount of debt as well. When my partner bailed on me, I had to restructure the business, add you as a partner and shift the ownership to you *on paper only*. It relieved me of the financial burden. Otherwise, we would have been homeless or worse, they could have arrested me. You were fifteen at the time and I knew the Chapter 7 bankruptcy would fall off your credit by the time you turned twenty-two. I'd expected to recover financially well before then, and I'd have been able to pay for your college."

He stopped speaking and sighed deeply. "I'm sorry to say, I'm still trying to recover or else we wouldn't be having this conversation at all."

Before Julene could unleash her rebuttal, her mother touched her arm lightly, "And Darling, things aren't as bad as they seem. Maybe disappointing, yes, but you don't need credit and a job. You don't need to stress yourself. Tristan's done a fine job of providing for you and the children. Let him be a man. Why don't you concentrate on raising your children? The time goes so fast, you know, and they'll be all grown up before you realize it."

"Because," she snatched her arm away from her mother's touch, "I need to make sure I can depend on *myself*. If you two have taught me nothing else, you've taught me *that*."

She turned to her father and unrolled the final piece of her plan. "So, Dad, I want you to put me on at your firm. The least you can do is give me a job. Everyone has always said I'd follow in your footsteps, so my working with you will look like a compliment."

He scoffed. "That's not the way it works, sweetheart. The firm doesn't—"

"Make it work. If you can't, I'll go to the police to report identity theft and bankruptcy fraud." She stood from the table with a ferocity much larger than her tiny stature and walked upstairs to start the bath for her babies.

By the end of the week, Julene's father walked into her room and sat at the end of her bed, just as he'd when she was younger. He looked around for a bit, taking in the decor with tired eyes, before loosening his tie and unfastening the top button of his collared shirt. "You took your pictures down."

"And I got rid of the canopy on the bed, donated the stuffed animals, and moved the beanbag to the kids' room," she said, abbreviating the small talk. She had done her best to strip the room of the lie that was her childhood. She had no plans of staying for very long. She'd be twenty-two soon, free from her disfigured credit history, so she'd taken no interest in giving the room a proper makeover, though her mother had offered repeatedly.

Her father used one foot and then the other to kick off his shoes, wiggling his stocking feet into the carpet's high pile. "I pulled some strings and got you a job at the firm. It's not much. There was no room in the budget for much of a salary, but we were able to crunch some numbers to get you onto the payroll. It's essentially a paid intern position, but we've given it a...," he paused and searched for the right word, "a more refined title."

Julene sat in the corner window seat she'd fallen in love with from the moment she moved into the home with her parents so many years ago. The home had five bedrooms upstairs, a master bedroom downstairs, and an in-law suite situated off the Florida room behind the garage, but this was the only one with the window seat. As the only child, her parents had given her the liberty to choose any room she wanted, and though this one wasn't the largest, the window seat had made it the best.

Tonight, suddenly a grownup mother of three, she sat in her favorite spot, pulled her feet up onto the seat, and rested her chin on her knees. She used one finger to lift a slat in the window shade and peered outside. She studied her reflection in the glass. Darkness had long since fallen outside. Behind her, she could see her father's slumped shoulders, pushed down into shapeless mounds from fatigue, or depression, or both. She couldn't be sure.

"Thank you," she replied, pushing the words through her lips with barely enough enthusiasm to make them audible. She waited for her father to respond. When he didn't, she turned to face him directly and spoke louder. "Thanks for getting me the job. What will I be doing?"

He'd been using his feet to brush the carpet pile in one direction and then the other, but he stopped abruptly to offer his daughter a weak smile. "Well, we've got a flagship marketing program to attract new clients for our firm's estate management attorney, Ms. Saultina Dyer. As her administrative assistant, you'll be managing the marketing program. She'll tell you all you need to know. Think you can handle that?"

"I'm not going to be running into you in the office all day, will I? That would be weird." She turned back to study her reflection in the window again.

"Probably not. I'm typically on the fourteenth floor. You know where my office is. You'll be with Tina on eleven," he replied before returning his attention to the pattern he was sculpting in the carpet.

"Then yes, I can handle it." Her answer had come out sounding more unappreciative and sarcastic than she intended, but if it had hurt his feelings, she couldn't take it back and undo the damage any more than he could take back the pain he'd caused her.

CHAPTER THIRTEEN

Saultina Dyer, also known as Tina, a frizzy-haired blonde in a monochromatic navy pantsuit and navy flats, reminded Julene of a grown-up Shirley Temple—if Shirley had grown up to become an attorney, and if she had retained the chaotic afro and shed all other evidence of childhood.

Tina gave Julene a tour of the eleventh floor, pointing out the restroom, the coffee maker, and the supply room before showing her to her desk.

"You'll be responsible for creating reports to track the performance of our client acquisitions marketing program," she said. "We have a remote team who is responsible for running advertisements, landing pages, and subscription forms to capture leads online. I'll need you to organize their data, track which methods are performing effectively and which ones aren't. Make sense?"

Julene nodded and shook her head at the same time. "You want me to...what? I'm sorry, how do I know what they're doing?"

Tina smiled, tousling her hair into a frenzy before smoothing it into a more organized state of chaos. "Here, look."

She sat at Julene's desk and beckoned her to look over her shoulder. "You log in here."

Tap, tap, on the keyboard.

"You click here, and here, and then here to open the dashboard," she explained. She paused, looking up to confirm Julene was following along. "Then you open this little envelope."

Tap, tap, on the keyboard.

"And this analysis screen opens. You'll see it when you click on this drop-down menu." She looked at Julene again and smiled. "Simple, right?"

Julene returned the smile and thought of the computer technology class she'd taken in high school. The steps to get to this point in the software could have been shortened by at least half, but she wouldn't insult her boss on the first day by pointing it out. Instead, she asked, "Do you just want me to print this screen for you every day?"

Tina turned toward Julene and laughed softly, the coffee from her breath wafting past Julene's nostrils. "No, thank you. I don't have the time or patience to read any of this. That's what you're here for. Just boil it all down for me: if there is positive data, if something is working, increase the budget for it a little. If something is not converting, if it isn't working, let the team know. They'll either fix it or we'll axe it."

"Do you want me to meet with you when I have the data, or help you prepare documents for your clients, or…" Julene asked, needing to believe her job in a law firm would involve something fundamentally related to the practice of *law*.

Tina stood up and extended her hand toward the now-vacant seat, inviting Julene to sit. "That won't be necessary. You can just email me if you run into an issue."

She smiled at Julene and tousled her hair into an afroed confusion before smoothing it again. "This is a simple job—I know—but it's new for us, so we need someone to focus on making sure it works. If it succeeds, you'll have the opportunity to replicate the system in other departments. If it *really* takes off, you could lead the training programs in our sister offices in the region."

When Tina walked away, Julene sat for a moment, familiarizing herself with the marketing dashboard. The data had already been sorted within the operating system, with the active ads organized and listed from best to worst in a spreadsheet. One column listed the daily cost per advertisement, and another column, titled Conversion Rate, showed green arrows pointing upward and red arrows pointing downward, a designation that clearly corresponded with the advertisement's performance from the previous week.

She highlighted the top seven advertisements and emailed them to the advertising team she'd never meet, instructing them to increase the budget. In the same email, she highlighted the bottom five ads and instructed the team to try improving their performance. The entire task, having taken roughly five minutes, comprised the entirety of her assigned responsibilities.

The week before, during her interview for the position, the hiring partners had smiled and winked and assured her the position was hers, that the interview was just a formality and she was fortunate to have first dibs at this opportunity to take on such an important role within the firm. They'd presented her with a compensation package that included some perks like flexible hours and a company-funded retirement plan. She was told her pay would increase incrementally as the program grew in size.

Afterward, in the team lounge, she'd had an off-the-record conversation with her only female superior, Tina, who had sat in on the interview. "Sounds like you got the position."

"I'm hopeful," Julene said. "I feel as though the interview went smoothly and Bruce gave me the thumbs up on his way out."

Julene liked Tina right away. Perhaps it was the wild hair and the kind eyes. Maybe it was her warm and unpretentious demeanor. She couldn't pinpoint it exactly, but she was still cautious about how much she confided in her, unsure about how much she could trust her.

"You're an intelligent girl. You're over-qualified for this position," Tina whispered.

Julene, uncertain of what her father had purported her credentials to be, offered an altruistic reply. "I know, but I'm looking forward to helping people get legal assistance. I mean, you help them with the legal stuff after their loved one dies, right? That's got to be hard on some families, I bet. Plus, my increases and bonuses will be nice once it takes off."

Tina held up two crossed fingers. "Good luck then. I hope the program succeeds. You know, with your college degree, poise, and skill set, you should be sitting in the boardroom with us. What's the deal?"

Julene smiled at her new colleague and tried to quiet the thumping of her pulse within her ears. If anyone dug deeply enough, they'd see that she didn't have a college degree, and having only a high school diploma was preventing her from bidding for a higher-level position, here or anywhere else. They'd see she couldn't post for any position requiring more than a basic background check. She was lucky to have her foot in the door at all. She quelled her anxiety, reminding herself to relax and play along. She deflected the question with optimism. "Everyone has to start somewhere, right? I'm excited about the opportunity to get in on the ground floor of a program that has the potential to help a lot of people. It's an opportunity to serve."

Inside, she berated herself for being a liar. She was essentially a single mother of three living at home with her disgustingly fraudulent parents. She'd take whatever she could get.

The program was destined for failure, though, and within eight months, the project had completely fallen apart. There was no 'team', only Julene and an automated email program backed by an off-site help desk that targeted potential clients, offering a free self-help book to bait them into signing up for a monthly newsletter filled with important facts about estate planning. The advertising team had been eliminated, and Julene's role now consisted of little more than sending free ebooks to the clients who signed up for the newsletter.

Once each month, on the fifteenth, Tina placed a stack of invoices on Julene's desk. Although her task was simple—just scan each invoice and forward them to the accounting office for payment—it offered a reprieve from the mundane tasks she completed through the rest of the month. Julene savored the task of organizing and processing bills for payment with money that wasn't her own. It was satisfying, this act of wrestling this disheveled stack of invoices and dog-eared receipts into a tidy digital document before standing above the paper shredder to transform them into confetti.

Invoices from her department appeared to be a catchall of miscellaneous charges. There were receipts for lunches, hotel stays, sundries, office supplies, and advertising fees. She peeked at some of the charges, astounded at the amount of money spent and written off without explanation. Business lunches were paid to the tune of $1,500. Gas station receipts totaled more than $250 each. There were mobile phone bills, gifts, and entertainment charges.

For the remainder of the month, Julene pretended to look busy and professional at her desk, but she'd begun spending most of her day surfing the internet for celebrity gossip and watching shows on Netflix. She wasn't helping anyone, wasn't serving anyone, wasn't making any more money, and she was hating every moment of it. Every damn day. Still, she wore suits and shoes she couldn't afford, and she allowed her mother to brag about her at fundraisers and in front of the women in her social clubs.

Her daughter, the newest addition to The Law Offices of Russell, Russew, and Ramm, had become the youngest Senior Director of the Client Acquisitions and Development Program, a title Julene knew to be a joke, no matter how much it impressed everyone else. Her mother was pleased though, to have her daughter looking the part of an up-and-coming businesswoman, and she was eager to help with the children, babysitting them or dressing them up and parading them around the city at one charity event or another, to keep her beautiful family in the public eye.

"I'm taking the children to see *Finding Neverland* at Cadillac Palace today. Don't thank me—I can see you need a break. You look tired. Maybe you should go to lunch with your friends," Layla said casually as she moved around the kitchen where she'd been watching Martha Stewart on the flip-down TV while making waffles for the children. The upper-third of her body had disappeared into the fridge when she asked, "And when are you going to reel Tristan back in? He's been gone long enough, and you can't afford to let him get away."

Julene, having only walked into the kitchen for a cup of coffee, ignored her mother's critical assessment of her appearance. If she looked tired, it wasn't due to her maternal responsibilities. Her mother has assumed full control of her children. And it wasn't because of her work responsibilities, which were practically non-existent. Her fatigue, and the bags under her eyes with which she carried it, could have been the evidence of her late-night conversations with Tristan, who'd assured her he would come back to rescue her and the children from a life that wasn't their own—but only if she agreed to move down south with him.

He told her he'd found himself in Savannah, Georgia, that he could no longer survive the pressures of the city or the close proximity to his mother. He kept her awake at night, sometimes giggling about the fun they'd once shared, sometimes crying about the fun they'd once shared, always reminding her that they were still best friends. If only she'd pack up and come down south, they could reclaim the people they'd been when their eyes couldn't see further than the haze from their spliffs. Then, she'd remind him that she was still his best friend, too, but she was also a mother and he was also a father, and they couldn't live life inside a cloud of cannabis if they were to provide their children with the lives they deserved.

He'd challenge her to define these so-called *lives* their children deserved. Was it lives filled with material things, uncomfortable shoes, stiff manners, false personas, and drug-infested prep schools? Or might their children deserve happy parents, toes in sand, freedom of expression, and authenticity of character? She'd reply, occasionally to him and often to herself, both. They deserved a little bit of both.

In the kitchen now, a cup of steaming coffee under her nose, warming her face, she inhaled the earthy, caramel-coated aroma and exhaled slowly before acknowledging her mother. "Good morning to you, too."

CHAPTER FOURTEEN

After twenty-five years of learning to transform a husband into a puppet, Layla had perfected the craft. It was true that Brad controlled the money. He'd agreed to give Layla a generous allowance each month, not because he needed to be in control, and not because he resented her for thinking she had *made* him. It was simply the most prudent means for them to manage their finances, upon the advice of his financial advisor.

And so, Layla learned, by trial and error, to manipulate her husband, his social standing, and his bank account to her advantage. She accomplished this without threats, resentment, or confrontations other than a few missteps over the years. She'd mocked him once or twice and challenged him a few times, but ultimately took special care to reassure him her sometimes-tough love was only meant to support him.

She wore docility and submissiveness like full bodysuits, hiding all that lay beneath, cruising below his radar, making him none-the-wiser that their entire life—his, hers, and Julene's—was merely a chess match for which she would remain queen. She needed him, not as her husband in the Biblical sense, but as a pawn in the literal sense to move on her behalf so she could enjoy the life she'd built, from her seat on the throne he'd unknowingly built.

She'd been sick of him for years, her disdain magnified by his infidelities. Surely, he was cheating since he certainly wasn't interested in *her* anymore. He blamed his low testosterone for his absent libido and his decision to sleep in the guest room virtually every night for the past sixteen years, but she had invested far too much energy designing their lives to throw it all away now. She admired independent women like Tristan's mother, who could walk away victorious after squeezing a marriage of all its potential, eventually discarding the husband like spent pulp.

Layla, with much respect to the hustle, had chosen her own path. She had raised her daughter like a debutante, to be a woman of a particular stature, to be the better half of the power team she would form with a proper husband. The husband, in Layla's opinion, was an essential piece of the puzzle, not merely for the financial gain, but also for the *look*. Nothing, *nothing*, was more beautiful than a powerful woman on the arm of a powerful-looking man. She'd believed it since she'd been a young girl that she would become a trophy wife, the way some girls believed they'd grow up to be ballerinas.

Layla's story was that of an around-the-way girl who'd been lucky enough to catch the attention of a popular guy on her college campus. They had hung out with friends and then alone. They had a good chemistry, which made their relationship easy. He was from an upper-middle-class family and she wasn't, but she acquired an appreciation for the finer things in life and made it her mission to become his trophy wife. He was on his way to doing great things, to becoming a very successful attorney, and she wouldn't be so foolish as to let the promise of the good life slip away.

She began to upgrade him, to polish him until he shined, and she pushed him upward through society's ranks. When he succeeded, she reaped the benefits. She looked the part; she was flawless. She taught herself to consort with the wealthy and the influential, wedged her daughter into the right playgroups and clubs, and served on advisory boards and committees for fundraisers and galas. She had created a life every little girl from her old neighborhood would have envied.

Now, she'd do all she could to keep her daughter from letting this boy slip through her fingers when she was so close to being set for life. She'd already had the babies with him; all she needed now was the ring. Everyone knew how much money his family was worth.

Even now, as Layla's husband floundered financially and had become virtually uninterested in her company, she understood the rewards of their partnership. Keeping up appearances was a price worth paying. It was hard work, though, and it took a toll on her health, but she had a doctor in Sterling, a town just under two hours away, who freely wrote prescriptions for the antidepressants and antianxiety medications that kept her on an even keel.

She was strategic in creating enough distance between her beloved city and her doctor's office to protect her identity. No one knew about the prescriptions. She didn't need anyone thinking she was crazy; she was just doing what she needed to get by without jumping off a ledge.

She'd seen what happened when she went off her meds. The Brazilian bikini wax her husband had never seen. The secret tattoo on the inside of her thigh. The fits of depression that caused her to binge eat and then stick her finger deep into her throat afterwards. And there was the time she had woken up, gotten frustrated with the woman in the bathroom mirror and shaved her head completely bald. Then, in a panic because her husband hated short hair and the shape of her head freaked her out, she had run to the computer in her study and ordered a Wendy Williams wig with overnight shipping.

She had a standing commitment to visit a children's shelter in Sterling with her women's group every other month, but there was no children's shelter, no women's group trip, and the pills she kept in her medicine cabinet for her menopause weren't really estrogen.

When she found out Tristan had abandoned her daughter and his children, the shock prompted Layla to take an 'overnight' trip to the *children's shelter*. When she arrived at the hotel she frequented during her overnight trips, she mixed pills with wine and passed out in her car in the hotel's parking garage. She awoke at some point in the night, made a hazy attempt to freshen her face in her car's rear-view mirror, and steadied herself enough to walk into the hotel and check into her room. She changed into a robe, sucked the remaining drops of wine from the bottle she'd brought, and lay across the bed, replaying the phone call in her mind.

She had called Tristan to find out how the job was going, to see if he had plans to get home for the holidays, and was floored when he said that, since his mother had evicted Julene and the kids and he couldn't find a way to deal with his emotions whenever he was in close proximity to his mother, he had made the decision to move down south for a while. And now that he'd left and further embarrassed his mother, she'd restricted him to one credit card and one year to pull himself together, or she'd cut him off for good. He shared his truth with Layla, having known her for much of his life, unaware that this new information would cripple her momentarily in her emotionally precarious condition.

She hung up the phone but never let on that she knew the truth. Her daughter was clearly lying about her relationship, and maybe more, but Layla understood her reasoning. In fact, she felt a bit of pride. She'd taught her girl how to survive. However, it was clear Julene would need more guidance. Pulling Tristan out of his feelings, learning to manage his mother and her money, doing the hard work to be above average— these were lessons her baby girl would have to learn sooner than later. Tristan may not have reached the heights his family had positioned him for, but he still had assets. Something about him was still salvageable.

Very early in the morning, before the children were to awaken, Layla drove home, showered, and took her pills. She stood, watching herself through the fog of the bathroom mirror and gathered her thoughts. She would smile. She would carry on. She would find a way to get through to her daughter. She never intended to let anyone see her without her wig, but Julene walked into the bathroom unexpectedly.

CHAPTER FIFTEEN

"Mother! What happened to your hair?"

Layla stared at Julene in the mirror, frozen, embarrassed, pissed at herself for forgetting today was the day she'd promised to take the children to Gymboree, for not locking the door. Blinking slowly, she tried to get her brain moving faster, but she was still groggy from the pills.

"Mommy, is it cancer?" Julene asked. "Why didn't you tell me? I know we've had our issues, but I'm your daughter. Honestly, I hate when you act like everything is so perfect, like nothing is wrong and you don't need anyone's help!"

The word *mommy* hadn't been allowed to be used in reference to Layla since the day Julene had spoken her first words. Today, in this moment, it tumbled out of Julene's mouth as though it belonged here. Rather than correct herself or even acknowledge this Freudian slip, she stood her ground, staring into the back of her mother's head.

In the silence, both women knew they shared the same personality flaw. Both would die before anyone saw them down. The cancer diagnosis hung in the air as though it were the final answer. Layla inhaled sharply, released her breath slowly, and spoke firmly. "I can't do this with you right now, darling. I'm exhausted, and I do not answer to *you*. I am still the mother, here."

She turned around, stood up and walked to her lounge chair, where she propped herself up as though she were royalty. She clicked on the TV, waving her daughter away. "Let me rest. We'll talk about this later."

Though she hadn't anticipated it, she was grateful for the *cancer diagnosis*. It was better than admitting the truth—that she'd had one of many manic episodes and was just crazy as hell. Julene was absolutely correct—she'd keep right on acting like everything was perfect, even if it killed her.

Maybe it's true that mental health problems run in the family, at least if what they said about her son was true. It was a secret she'd kept buried so deeply that sometimes, especially when her meds hit just right, she almost forgot about him herself. Yet, sometimes when she thought about the sickly child she'd birthed, she wondered if he had inherited his disorders from her.

Layla had gotten pregnant by Mitchell, a white guy she'd befriended in her junior year of high school. She'd attended the Title I schools in her neighborhood since kindergarten, but had been identified as academically gifted by third grade. In high school, she'd become a dually enrolled student, taking most of her classes at her neighborhood high school and commuting across town on Mondays, Wednesdays, and Fridays to take classes at the prestigious Lederman Science and Mathematics Academy, where she met Mitchell. He was from a *good* family, but he was friendly toward her, not treating her differently because she was Black and from the hood. He was well dressed, an athlete, drove a modest car. They'd flirted with one another since they were freshmen.

His parents were well off, and his mother was the head of the Booster Club. She devoted herself to helping at the school tutoring, planning Teacher Appreciation celebrations, and organizing fundraisers. She was at every football and basketball game. So, when Layla found out she was pregnant with Mitchell's child, she was both frightened and relieved all at once.

Her mother had forbidden Layla, her two sisters, and her brother to bring any more babies into her house. Layla couldn't count the number of times she'd heard her mother say, *I have raised my own children and I'm not about to raise any of y'alls.*

Both of Layla's older sisters had been teenaged mothers, and her brother always had one baby mama or another dropping off a hollering child. The babies were never actually hollering, but her mother didn't want to wait until they started. And here was Layla, pregnant now, too.

At least her future child's father came from a good family. They were financially secure, and his mom was so much nicer than Layla's—until she found out Layla had 'trapped' her son. That's when the very warm classroom mother developed a particularly cold shoulder.

Then the baby was born, a baby boy, thin and practically albino. He wasn't chunky and caramel-colored like the ethnically ambiguous child she'd dreamed of. He had health problems and developmental concerns that were confusing to the doctors, and even more confusing to his frightened teenaged mother.

As a young mother, Layla didn't know how to care for him. She didn't know how to bond with her baby, and her mother maintained her resolve to withhold support of any kind where it pertained to grandchildren.

She begged for support from Mitchell's family, but she received only regrets and meager handouts until his mother proposed a final solution. "We'll raise the baby. You will never ask us for a dime or try to contact my son again for any reason. We've got to think about his future, and we can't risk letting you or anyone else ruin it."

Layla sat at the kitchen island, staring across at a lady who could have very well been baking cookies for an after-school snack, not serving legal documents to acquire a sick baby. She had not come here intending to give her child away. She just needed help with medical bills, finding specialists, paying for medications and special formulas, and transportation and emotional support. She needed to know how to parent, how to love a baby who couldn't love her back.

She had believed, foolishly, in the kind and generous woman whom she had come to trust at school. All the kids at school loved her. She had believed this woman would be as helpful and understanding and giving to this baby who shared her very DNA as she was to the children at school with whom she'd only come to know in passing.

Layla waited for an explanation, a summary of her options, maybe an apology, but there was only the sound of some dog barking out back and some kid shrieking out front and Mitchell's mother shuffling papers in her direction. She pushed a form across the countertop and marked an X where Layla was to sign. She tapped the spot with her finger and Layla signed it, quickly, in the full and bubbly cursive script of a high school girl, without reading it, without consulting her mother.

With the signed document between them, knowing the issue of her son's illegitimate child was just too complicated for any outsider to understand, Mitchell's mother sighed heavily and did her best to make Layla comprehend the divinity of their agreement. It wasn't that she was ruthlessly ripping a baby from its mother's arms. No one knew about the pressures and expectations Mitchell shouldered as the first-born son in her family. The male child who would keep the family name alive was a precious part of the family tree.

This child just didn't fit the mold. Not because he was Black, no she wasn't ashamed of the fact that her son had had a baby with a Black girl. She wasn't a racist. Definitely not. Look, she was the PTA Mom, the Classroom Mom, the head of the Booster Club, and the Team Mom at the high school. She had treated each and every football player like a son, most of them Black. They were always welcome for dinner, she helped to make sure they were ready for college, that they had help with their scholarship applications. She was often able to do more for the kids at the school than their parents could, whether they were Black or not.

She had a heart for serving others. In fact, at church, she volunteered for as many missions as possible to help and serve the less fortunate in Africa. It warmed her heart to go over there and just hold the babies. In fact, she and her husband had been on the waiting list for years—since her first mission there—to adopt an African baby. She had almost given up hope. And now, here was a baby who needed her love. She wondered if God had prepared this baby just for her. Everyone knew she was awaiting an African adoption, which meant no one would blink an eye when she suddenly appeared with a baby in her arms. She wouldn't have to explain why her son couldn't keep it in his pants. The family's legacy would be preserved without scandal. She would finally have the baby she'd been praying for.

She had her attorney to draw up the documents that very afternoon.

Layla, having signed her baby away, left the house, stunned, but not crying. She knew Mitchell's family could get her baby the medical care he needed. She hadn't expected them to shut her out, but maybe Mitchell's mom was right. Maybe this way would be best. What could Layla have offered to the baby or her family?

While her dream of being welcomed into Mitchell's family hadn't worked out the way she had hoped, it did offer her an opportunity for a fresh start. She was afraid to admit her relief even to herself, but that's when she learned to celebrate her strengths rather than her weaknesses. That's when she learned how to maximize every opportunity presented to her without dwelling on past missteps.

Layla's mother never even asked about her grandbaby's sudden disappearance, maybe never noticed. Her disinterest entitled Layla to distance herself from the baby's existence as well. In college, she reinvented herself. She wasn't a teen mom. She hadn't been cruel enough to sign her baby away and never look back. She was just another PYT on campus, looking for the right guy, searching for a second chance. She found her husband, Brad.

Years later, after the Internet made it easy to stalk people, she Googled Mitchell, his mom, and her son, and found out her baby had been institutionalized for much of his life. He was a special needs child, and his paternal grandmother had become an activist for children like him. She championed tirelessly for children who were mentally or developmentally disabled. She had launched a foundation to raise awareness, with Layla's son's picture on the website, and they had changed his name to Femi, meaning *adored* in the Nigerian culture.

She studied his picture with a clear remembrance of the baby she'd failed to mother. She fought to push down any feeling that might show up now. Guilt, fear, pain, sadness, *joy*. She wasn't certain of which feeling might bubble up from her gut and sit at the base of her throat, but she braced herself for the battle.

When his picture finally appeared, her stomach clutched only for a second before relaxing, and she found that she could face her baby after all. He was just a kid, one she could have easily seen on a St. Jude's or Shriners Hospital commercial. Obviously he was older now, but it was probably better for publicity's sake to have a youthful face on the website. His smile was wide and toothy; his mouth didn't accuse Layla or blame her for her choices. His eyes were hers, almond-shaped and widely spaced. The thin nose matched his father's. His face was still babyish and round, as though time had held him hostage.

He didn't look Nigerian or anything suggestive of Africa, but they'd given him a Nigerian name and had, no doubt, told their friends that God had finally blessed their family with an African baby. Layla could imagine, without effort, that people would look at her son and see a child from Nigeria if that's what they wanted to believe. She knew this because she had convinced so many people to believe things that were far more outlandish, simply because she knew they *wanted* to believe.

Beneath his picture, a description of his conditions: Atypical Rett Syndrome, bipolar disorder, and schizophrenia, and the foundation's mission statement, "Pediatric mental illnesses shouldn't be a secret."

For Layla, now with the binding legal document and so many years between them, meeting her son was an impossibility, and telling anyone about him would be equally pointless. After all these years, there would be too much to explain.

CHAPTER SIXTEEN

Julene's father deemed himself a man's man. Brad's notoriety as a big man on campus during his college years and an All-American athlete in high school had prepared him for life as a leader. Having a wife who complemented his stature in college and in the business world, helped to define him. He was a powerful and influential man who got what he wanted, provided an admirable life for his family, and enjoyed a relatively privileged life.

He regretted his financial standing, wishing he could rewind time and choose one investment over another, but he couldn't. The money wasn't flowing, but he wouldn't drown. He wasn't alone. In the upper echelon, who *wasn't* constantly moving money from one place to another? Who *wasn't* skirting the IRS if they could? Who *hadn't* invested their retirement, or their kids' college fund, or their third mortgage on one endeavor or another? Sometimes it worked, sometimes it didn't, but a real man would keep trying.

That's why he was pleased when his daughter began dating a boy who played sports. He believed sports added masculinity to a man's character. Although he'd never had a son of his own, he loved Tristan like a son, and couldn't have been more pleased to finally welcome his very own grandson, Jamison, into the family. He couldn't fault Tristan for taking a business opportunity overseas. Instead, Brad assumed the responsibility of making sure the little boy received the proper male influence in his father's absence, using every opportunity to get the stuffed animals out of his grandson's hands and replace them with basketballs. He didn't want his boy to look weak or gay—he couldn't stand a flimsy, feminine boy.

Even now, as the IRS breathed down his back and his daughter whined about the bankruptcy he'd regrettably saddled her with, Brad's connection to sports was still his lifeline. And when he couldn't figure things out on his own, his fitness club became his refuge. He played racquetball and golf with friends and associates who granted him favors—legal or otherwise—if he asked. They'd make contributions and investments into anything he proposed without so much as a question about the reason or the return. It was a welcome escape from his wife's demands and his daughter's judgment.

Sometimes he'd stay for a shower and then sit with his buddies in the sauna for a while. He was never in a rush to get home where he was often greeted by his wife struggling to look sexy. She knew it annoyed him, and he'd made it clear he hated when she flirted with him. It was as though she took pleasure in pressuring him when she knew full well that he was dealing with a medical problem. After telling her how the low testosterone had destroyed his sex drive, her sexual advances only emasculated and irritated him.

Back in college, when he had bumped into Layla at a recruiting event for the Young Adult Leadership Initiative, he had seen her as a fresh-faced, natural beauty whose magnetic energy drew him to her on the first day. His student advisor had encouraged him to attend the event to support a worthy cause and add some much-needed depth to his resume. He would be required to recruit future thought-leaders, law students, and young politicians who were passionate about transforming Chicago's most endangered communities.

During the event, the volunteers broke into groups to plan social mixers and fundraisers. Brad's group, a fair mix of male and female students, devolved quite rapidly from a think tank to a pissing contest. The group, tasked with electing a president, bickered over one another's qualifications, their strong personalities and strong voices challenging one another for control. Candidates were proposed and negated before they could be properly weighed until Layla offered her own quietly powerful voice. Within the group, she used her voice, not to promote her own agenda, but to support Brad's, touting his well-rounded personality, his record of voluntary community service, his soundness of character, and his uncompromising integrity.

"I'd use the term *compromising* loosely when it comes to Brad," interrupted a chuckling, rusty-haired kid from the swim team. "When we were away at a swim meet last semester, someone found a nude photo of some guy in Brad's locker. Coach confiscated the picture after the guys ribbed him about being gay. Sounds pretty *compromising* to me."

The kid laughed harder, recalling the nude man's photo inside their team captain's locker. The laughter lodged in his throat like an accidentally swallowed bit of chewing gum when he looked up to find Brad standing inches from his face, fists clenched at his sides.

He spoke between clenched teeth. "I told you guys it wasn't my picture. It was—"

"It was mine," Layla interjected as she slid her petite frame between the two athletes. She lay her gentle hand on Brad's chest, easing him backward. "Some guy's been harassing me—stalking me, really—because I won't date him, and he put a nude photo of himself inside my dorm. I don't know how he got inside, but I was frightened and I called Brad. I was too afraid to go to the dean about it, but he said he'd take care of it for me."

She beamed at Brad and his hands relaxed. "A true gentleman and a protector of the powerless—exactly what we need in a leader."

The two, the non-intimidating beauty and the future attorney, formed an unofficial alliance that day, neither addressing the fact that they hadn't known each other last semester. Neither discussing the story of the nude photo's origin or the allegations of homosexuality. Their bond was natural and unforced, and he couldn't tear away from her if he'd wanted. It was of no matter—he felt strongest when she was at his side. Her presence, her quiet encouragement, her support of his ideas, and her belief in his strength made him feel more masculine than any accomplishment on the football field.

She was beautiful without makeup and sexy without tight pants and push-up bras, but she didn't pressure him physically the way the other girls on campus did. *It's not that I don't find you attractive*, Layla had confessed to him one night after they had tumbled from one end of his couch to the other, kissing and pawing at each other's buttons and belt buckles and private parts. *It's just that I've never done it before, and I want to wait until the time is right.*

He fell in love with her then, because she was his small, but mighty rock, because she held him up and made him feel invincible, because she never competed with him for clout— she only championed his success, never neglecting his victories in search of her own. And her virginity—the idea that she'd never given herself to another man—made him an Adonis in the bedroom when the time was finally right: the night they'd said *I do*.

Those college years were of another lifetime though, and he'd learned, year after year, that he wasn't his wife's hero; he was her workhorse. She'd pushed him into jobs he hated, pressured him to form partnerships he would have rejected, and manipulated him into taking questionable financial risks, even when he would have chosen otherwise. When he resisted, when they began sinking in their self-made pool of financial distress, when he recognized his increasing unhappiness—those were the times she'd look at him with resentful, disappointed eyes, shake her head, and murmur, *I thought you were a real man.*

She challenged his masculinity privately, even as she exalted it publicly, and the low T manifested practically overnight, as though she had spoken creole voodoo over the essence of his manhood.

He was embarrassed that his body no longer responded in a manly way when it really mattered. It was like the sleeping bear only awoke when he was in the sauna at the club. When he'd have to adjust himself or pretend to need more time in there so as not to have to walk across the roomful of guys without being able to hide it.

He wasn't gay. There had been that time in college when he and his roommate stayed up all night drinking and daring each other to do college-boyish stunts, but as far as he could recall, nothing serious had happened. He. Was. Not. Gay.

CHAPTER SEVENTEEN

The Thursday morning after Julene's twenty-second birthday, she rubbed her eyes and walked into the children's room before her mother woke up. The children had become Layla's new reason for existing, but Julene still enjoyed watching her children wake up in the mornings.

She loved their sleepy eyes, their questions, their warm body odors—and she loved watching them chat with their daddy. It had become Julene, Tristan and the children's routine to start and end the day with FaceTime.

When you coming to get us, Daddy?

Are you at the beach, Daddy?

Julene had been pissed with him for leaving them. He'd gone down south and fallen in love with the freedom of his anonymous life. She'd refused his calls and requests to FaceTime with his children at first, but he wore her down with their late-night chats, his tears, and his incessant promises to bring their family back together again.

"I'm trying to set some things up for you and the kids down here in Savannah," he'd told her. "You'd love it! The beaches, the weather…"

"There's no way in hell we're up and moving to Georgia!" she protested. "We've been through this a million times. How would we support ourselves? I have a job here. We have a support system here."

"I know. I just…." Tristan exhaled softly, and Julene watched him nibble at his cuticles, as he often did when he was frustrated. "I just miss you and I miss my kids, and I cannot be in Chicago anymore. I'm not healthy when I'm there."

He was right, of course. Home was unendingly toxic for him; she'd witnessed it since they were kids.

"Hey, I get it. Sometimes I wish I could just pick up and run away—start over as someone else. Start over as the real *me*. But I have responsibilities here. I have children who deserve a certain quality of life. So this is what's best for us."

And then, because she didn't hate him—he was still her best friend, and maybe because she envied him a little—she added, "But you can send some money and maybe we'll come down for a visit."

He chuckled lightly. "Alright. Bet. I'm working on that as we speak. So put my kids back on the phone. Turn it around so I can see them. I know it's time for you to go to work, and I gotta get some things done, too."

After much kissing of the phone screen and *I love yous* and *I love you mores* between Tristan and the children, Julene ended the call, hustled the children into her mother's bed to snuggle, and headed off to the office.

At work, Julene stood in the parking lot, peering under the front end of the well-worn Range Rover, hoping the dripping oil would just effing quit dripping. A new car would have been ideal, but even with a year of steady employment under her belt, her minimum wage salary and the ever-present bankruptcy continued to render her ineligible for a car loan or lease. To keep the Range Rover alive, she'd been feeding oil into the reservoir every few days, staving off the huge bill she would amass if she took it to the dealership for a proper repair. She knew there would surely come a day when a bottle of oil would no longer postpone the inevitable.

"Car trouble, huh? These things turn into money guzzlers real quick, don't they?"

She straightened her back and stood to face Preston Tiller, her father's associate at the firm. His name had been mentioned between her parents once or twice, but not in the friendliest of tones. Julene traveled in the same social circle as his daughter, but, in her recollection, she never interacted with him directly. She nodded at him. "What gives it away? Me, standing out here like a shade tree mechanic?"

She didn't laugh, but he did. "I've seen a lot of mechanics, but never one dressed in Gucci."

This time, she laughed a little. "Everyone has a side hustle, right?"

Tiller squatted down to peer under the car and looked up at Julene. "Why don't you just drop it off at the dealer? They'll put you in a loaner and have this leak fixed in no time. Is it still under warranty?"

"It's my mother-in-law's truck, not mine, so I don't know and I'm not putting any money into this thing if I don't have to." She shifted her voice downward, hoping it sounded nonchalant.

Tiller raised his eyebrows. "Mother-in-law? I don't see a ring on your finger."

"Well, *future* mother-in-law." She shoved her hand into her jacket pocket.

"Still don't see any ring on that finger." Tiller grinned.

"Don't worry about me. You can just mind your own damn business!" Julene snapped, but offered her hand to pull him to standing. "The car will be fine."

They walked into the building. Tiller used his key fob to access the elevator and stood aside to let Julene in first. Inside, he spoke to Julene's reflection in the elevator door. "You can get a company vehicle, you know?"

Julene lifted her eyes to meet his reflection.

He lowered his voice, although they were alone. "You've worked here over a year now. Your father is a partner. Why don't you have an expense account yet? Get a car. Hell, put your cell phone on it, your rent.... Everything's a write-off around here if you word it properly."

She shrugged her shoulders. "Nobody told me. Why didn't Dad tell me?"

"I can't speak for your dad. Maybe he's worried about nepotism or something. Who knows? Plus, the culture around here isn't what you'd call *inclusive*—especially when there aren't many of *us* in the building."

He paused for emphasis and then continued, assuming she understood who *us* was. "Most things around here are on a need-to-know status. People won't volunteer much information. I'm not like that, though. I'll get you the expense account info later this afternoon. Do you have plans for lunch?"

The elevator stopped, and Tiller held the door so Julene could step out first.

"You can just email me. I'm having lunch with my friends today. Isn't Candace your *daughter*?" Julene asked, emphasizing the word *daughter* to put Tiller on notice. "She'll be there."

He chuckled. "Yup. That's my girl."

His last comment and all of its innuendo reached her ears before the elevator door slid closed, but she didn't glance back or dignify it with a response.

With no lack of care for her children and at her mother's request, Julene made an effort to socialize with her friends more often. Her puny paycheck created a bit of an obstacle, though, and she'd listened to her parents speak passionately about money—sometimes arguing, sometimes conspiring together—enough to know they hadn't any cash or charge cards to lend her. However, she'd become an expert at finding more creative ways to finance her lifestyle.

She splurged on retail therapy with her friends on the weekends, but was practical enough to return her purchases on her lunch breaks during the work week.

There had been a time when, attempting to make a return once, she had panicked at the customer service desk and became sick to her stomach after her $4,995 Brunello Cucinelli purse—the one she'd purchased with the one charge card Tristan's mother still permitted her to use for the children's incidental needs—was not accepted for a refund. The card, with a credit limit of $7,500, had made it possible for her to shop freely with her friends, swiping without abandon, then swiping again a few days later for the refund.

The sales associate, a mature, well-groomed woman who'd likely taken the retail job to avoid the boredom that often comes with retirement, had given her a well-rehearsed speech: "Here at Neiman Marcus, we respect and value every customer. Because your trust is important to us, we want you to be completely happy with every purchase, but we can only accept merchandise in its original condition. And here, there's a mark of some sort. Make-up, maybe?"

The powdery saleswoman whose stained fingers bore evidence of her sloppily applied self-tanner pointed into the purse at the silky lining. Julene peered into the purse, leaning in close enough to smell the woman's Chanel perfume.

"That must have been stained when I purchased it," Julene protested. "I've never even used this bag. I bought it to go with a certain outfit, but it doesn't work with it."

The saleswoman chuckled lightly. "Don't you hate when that happens? You think you've got it perfectly coordinated, but you put it all together and," she paused, mid-chuckle, "—there's no security tag. It's got to have all the tags on it for the return. I'd be happy to complete the transaction for you, but it's got to have the tag."

Unable to convince the sales associate to bend the rules, and furious with herself for making such a rookie mistake, Julene's only alternative was to sell the purse on consignment for a loss. She learned to think more strategically and practice greater caution about her future purchases.

Today, sitting at lunch with Candace, Daryl, Madison, and Brooke, the sick-to-the-stomach feeling returned like Deja vu. She could tell from the way the server walked right up to her at the table that something was wrong.

Attempting to maintain an appropriate level of discretion, the server stooped to speak into Julene's ear, her bistro-length white apron dusting the floor.

CHAPTER EIGHTEEN

I'm sorry, but there seems to be a problem with this card. I swiped it twice, but it wouldn't go through."

Embarrassment churned in Julene's gut from the moment she realized the server was approaching her, and now, as the table's conversation simmered down to silence, she became acutely aware of her friends' stares. She chose dismissive arrogance with a hint of annoyance as her preferred defense mechanism in that moment.

"I just got this card, and I've had nothing but trouble with it," she said. "The money's there, though. Hang on and I'll get it straightened out."

She pulled her banking app up on her phone and logged into her account. After a moment, she informed the waitress and her girlfriends with a dismissive laugh, "It's my fraud protection. It says I need to verify that I'm the one using my own card."

She selected 'transfer funds' and waited for the money to move from her anemic savings account to her emaciated checking account.

Attempting to fill the awkward silence, the waitress chattered to no one in particular. "I hate these new fraud protection programs. Everyone's having problems with their cards—especially the ones with the chip in them, but hey, I understand. The banks are trying to keep the bad guys out."

Julene's friends laughed politely while they clicked their purses and clutches opened and closed, shuffling charge cards and cash to settle their own tabs.

As Julene worked to complete her online transaction, a message appeared on the screen of her smartphone: '*Maximum transfers exceeded. Unable to complete request.*' She racked her mind, though it had gone completely blank, trying to buy enough time to figure out how to produce $83.71, plus tip out of thin air. Pressure pulsed along her temples and she briefly wondered if she might pass out. She considered excusing herself to the restroom, but the pressure in her head made it impossible for her to think of an appropriate segue between her current situation and a believable escape.

Instead, she remembered a last-minute lifeline. She pulled a credit card from the back of her billfold. It was the card Tristan's mother had given her to pay for incidental maintenance expenses at the rental property last year. She'd never returned it. "I meant to give you this card." She passed the card to the server and tapped flippantly at her phone's screen. In minute the server returned. "I'm so sorry to interrupt you, but this card didn't work either."

Sitting there amongst friends with no money and no means of paying for her own lunch, Julene died a thousand quiet deaths, never taking her eyes from her phone.

"Ma'am, if you're unable to settle the tab, I'll have to get my manager." The server nodded toward the open kitchen where a young, crisply dressed woman stood chatting with the chef.

While Julene sat with her eyes fixated on the manager, her brain oscillating between panic and disbelief, her friend Candace's voice rose above her internal dialogue, "You'll have to get your manager? How dare you imply she is unable to settle her bill?"

As if on cue, Madison, Brooke, and Daryl took turns chastising the server:

Do you have any idea who we are? We spend a lot of money in this establishment!

How dare you embarrass a guest in this manner? She's got enough money to cover your entire paycheck!

Are you assuming she can't pay because she's Black? The audacity!

Go ahead and bring your manager. Why are we even talking to you?

Who's in charge here?

Julene glanced around the restaurant, ashamed to be the center of attention right now, but when her eyes returned to the corner where the restaurant manager stood, she rose from her seat and moved toward her, as though in a dream.

"Lori?" Julene mouthed the words although her voice was drowned out by her friends, still berating the server, still demanding respect despite the unpaid bill.

That Lori could have heard her cousin's voice above the restaurant's din, when they hadn't spoken since the baby shower nearly eight years ago, was an impossibility, but she looked up instinctually and a brilliant smile eclipsed her face. Before Julene could wind her way between the tables to reach her, Lori ended her chat with the chef and rushed across the restaurant to meet her halfway.

When they were within arm's reach of one another, Lori grabbed Julene by the shoulders and drew her into a warm embrace. "Cousin! How are you? I haven't seen you in so long!"

Julene stepped back and returned Lori's bright smile. "I've been okay. How about you? How's Aunt Lucille?"

Lori's smile faltered. "Aunt Lucille had a…"

"Excuse me, Ms. Davis?" The server appeared between the girls, interrupting their reunion, and the both paused at the mention of their shared surname. The server paused too, looking from one to the other before focusing her attention on Lori. "Ms. Davis, this is the guest whose credit card was unable to be processed. I've made multiple attempts but it won't go through." She placed a stack of credit card receipts into Lori's hand and waited.

When Lori read the receipts, she tucked them into her pocket and dismissed the server. "I see what the problem is. Go ahead and get back to your tables and I'll handle this one."

Julene's toes clenched inside her Jimmy Choos and she remembered she needed to return these shoes to the department store, so she forced her feet to relax, and she nibbled at the inside of her cheek instead.

Lori and Julene stood quietly, watching the server walk away, and when she was out of earshot, Lori grabbed her cousin's arm and led her to a quiet corner near the restrooms. In an instant, they picked up right where they'd left off so many years ago.

Lori was giddy, breathless. "What's been up, cousin? I just graduated from Johnson & Wales. Bachelor's. Food service admin and management. Had to go all the way to Providence, Rhode Island! Got a few scholarships and Aunt Lucille paid the rest with some investments she made a long time ago. I didn't take a single student loan! I got picked for this restaurant management internship. If they like me, which of course they do, then they're sending me to Dubai to open and manage a new concept restaurant." She paused to catch her breath, then bumped Julene's shoulder. "What about you? Did you graduate this year, too? Where'd Uncle Brad send you? Are you working?"

Her questions were rapid-fire and Julene's thoughts were ablaze. When she opened her mouth, still undecided as to what version of her reality she'd share with Lori, especially in light of Lori's impressive accomplishments, the server appeared again. They both paused to look at her.

"Um, Ms. Davis, sorry to interrupt again, but the ladies at Ms. Davis' table have become--" she lowered her voice a bit and whispered, "*antsy.*"

Lori peeked around the corner, took note of Julene's friends, and gave the server an assignment. "Let them know I've taken care of their bill and offer them desserts on me." She wrapped her arm around Julene's shoulder. "This is my favorite cousin and those are her friends, so they're my guests today."

When the server walked away, Lori pulled the receipts from her pocket and waved Julene towards a nearby computer. She chatted with Julene while she entered her password and searched for the transaction. "So, you're living here? Did you say you're working? How's my uncle? Haven't seen him since..." Her words ran dry as she studied the words on the screen.

She turned to meet Julene's eyes. "Are you in trouble, cousin? Talk to me."

Julene shoved her hands into her skirt pockets and swung them forwards and back until the hem fluttered like butterfly wings. "Everything's fine. I told the server I just gave her the wrong card. It's a new card and the bank has put a ridiculously low spending limit on it. I just need to call and have it increased. It's nothing."

Skepticism pulled Lori's lip to one side and she waved Julene closer, tilting the screen to give her a better view. She pointed at the alerts highlighted next to each transaction. "See this? This means insufficient funds. No money on that card. We get a different alert if the issue is related to a simple bank hold or limitation." Her finger trailed down the computer screen as she continued explaining, "And these alerts mean the card has been frozen by the cardholder due to possible theft or identity fraud. This last alert is for me. It means I'm supposed to contact the police and hold you here until they arrive."

She turned to face Julene. "So tell me, is something wrong?"

Julene shook her head slowly, her vision swirling in a vertigo fog, and her voice was feeble when she answered. "I don't know much about the software you use in this restaurant. Every business is different. But it's not what you think. Everything is fine. I'm actually headed to the bank to straighten the whole thing out right now." She hugged Lori and backed away. "It was so good to see you! We should get together before you leave."

Lori grabbed Julene's hand, tethering her while she pulled three twenty-dollar bills from her pocket. She shoved the money into Julene's purse and hugged her tightly. She whispered into Julene's ear, "Take this money, cousin, and don't be too proud to let me know if you need help. We're family, I love you. Call me tonight." When she released her grasp, Lori used an ink pen to write her phone number on the inside of Julene's wrist.

Pride begged Julene to return the crumpled cash in her purse, but desperation wouldn't let her give it back. She embraced Lori again, fighting hot tears, and whispered, "I love you, too," before turning away and rushing back to her friends.

Madison and Candace were laughing over coffee and picking at the remnants of their shared Bananas Foster, but paused when they noticed Julene approaching. They watched, bemused and then confused as she passed their table without speaking and continued out the door.

When she had buckled herself safely into the driver's seat of her oil-hemorrhaging Range Rover, she placed her forehead on the steering wheel and cried softly for a minute. She'd been so shaken by the fiasco inside the restaurant, she hadn't even let Lori finish telling her about Aunt Lucille. Was she okay? Julene studied her cousin's phone number written on her wrist before rubbing it away. She'd never have the courage to call.

After another moment, as though the river of warm tears had been the valve to release the stress and anxiety of the last two hours, she was able to sit up and exhale. She wiped her face, exhaled again, and exited the parking lot.

CHAPTER NINETEEN

When she returned to work, the Audi key fob and brand-new iPhone lying on her desk momentarily confused her. The key fob was attached to a plain metal key ring and paper tag. A sticky note lay curled on top of the iPhone box. Next to them, a note written in block-shaped capital letters suggested male penmanship.

Check your email for the link to sign off on your expense account inventory. Just enter the item numbers from the key fob and cell phone, sign off, and return to me.

Even without his signature, she was certain who had left these items. Although she'd done nothing wrong, she cautiously logged into her email and clicked the new message from Tiller. Inside, she found an attachment, which proved to be an expense account inventory acceptance form.

The fine hairs on her arms were pushed to standing as Julene settled into her seat. The mere thought of the lunch fiasco, still fresh in her mind, triggered a sickening bout of recurrent embarrassment. This special brand of embarrassment had attached itself to every precarious aspect of her life, making every day a fresh, new Hell. Every day could be the day Tristan's mother disabled the cellphone Julene still used or repossessed her rickety Range Rover. Every day could be the day the bank closed her account, or the firm discovered the bold lies on her resume. Now, at least, here was a step toward asserting her independence.

In the seconds before the attachment opened, the anxiety in her belly subsided for a few seconds before it returned, this time in a wave, rising to the base of her throat. There were still other personal issues to juggle, other rivers to cross, before she'd be able to live life as her true self, rather than the carefully crafted persona.

Pressure wrapped itself around her skull for the umpteenth time today. She closed her eyes until it released its grip. She considered confiding in a friend, perhaps Candace, the one who'd been first to speak up in her defense at lunch, or maybe Madison, the one whose husband booked monthly spa days at the InterContinental Hotel for their entire friend group. She picked up her phone and put it down again, unable to imagine making herself nakedly transparent in the eyes of any one of her friends. What kind of support could any of them provide—especially when they all lived in houses made of glass and cardboard themselves?

In their own opinions, they were the Windy City's Elite: beautiful, successful, well-kept by their husbands or parents. Except for Daryl, the proverbial ugly-duckling-turned-swan who'd somehow—there were conflicting stories as to how, exactly, she'd done it—managed to snag and marry a young skills coach who had been hired and relocated to the area by the Chicago Bulls franchise. Daryl was home-grown and well-known in the area, the daughter of influential politicians. When anyone made reference to her, they'd choose adjectives like *smart or sweet*, but never *pretty*.

In time, with the assistance of her parents' financial resources and her husband's, she had enhanced every physical part of herself, from her hair texture, to her eye color, to the curvature of her hips. The eventual result was a new and improved Daryl, barely recognizable compared to the original Daryl. The most notable difference was the absence of her wedding ring. Just four and a half years after the fairytale wedding, she was now divorced and collecting an impressive alimony payment each month.

She was resourceful, however, despite anyone's opinions regarding her appearance, and used the young coach's money and status to open a boutique that specialized in luxury stationery and gifts—PapierLuxe. Daryl enjoyed substantial success with her boutique, expanding it from Hyde Park to a secondary location in River North. However, her main priority was basking in the limelight of her local celebrity stature.

Daryl, like Candace, Madison and Brooke, loved to see and be seen. They documented every moment of their lives on Twitter and Instagram.

They strove to distance themselves from anything that might be considered basic. They overtly dressed in the top labels and popped bottles in the VIP sections of exclusive clubs and restaurants. They'd meet for late lunches on Saturdays and spend the rest of the afternoon in boutiques and salons, spending money, laughing, and getting drunk from the attention they commanded wherever they went.

Yet, while they knew everybody who was anybody, they didn't really know each other. It was odd, Julene often observed about the system within which she operated with her friends, the way they put on a carefully cultivated façade for one another. Their friendships, having been so superficial from the start, left no one comfortable enough to let down her guard in front of the other. They couldn't trust or confide in each other privately, but together, they were a tight-knit outfit, living the lives they'd engineered for the appropriation of everyone else's envy.

Julene sat at her desk, staring at, but not focusing, on Tiller's email, and thought about her friends' Botoxed, contoured, painted faces. Designer brows, lash extensions, hair extensions, nail extensions, boob jobs, butt jobs, tummy tucks, waist trainers, jewelry, bags, clothes, shoes—their lifestyles had become their careers.

They joked about the way they shopped—checking the labels before checking the price tags. Julene had done well to assimilate with them on the surface, carrying rented or consignment handbags and wearing knockoff shades when she needed to stretch her budget. She had purchased a real pair of red bottomed Christian Louboutins for the

Beyoncé concert, however. Some things just couldn't be faked.

They were the friends who had been chosen for her, but not the friends she would have chosen for herself. They'd been thrown together back when they were young girls being groomed by their parents. Julene, having always been drawn to friends older than herself, was the youngest of the group, but was of the same pedigree, had the same fake-fancy parents, and had been in the same Girls Scouts troops, dance classes, and etiquette clubs.

They'd played Never-Have-I-Ever at sleepovers, gone to dances and homecomings, and hosted baby showers and bridal showers. They'd stuck together, however loosely, for most of their lives. They certainly didn't confide in each other the way real friends would, but, thanks to the streets, they still managed to accumulate plenty of scandalous and intimate information about one another—things they would never discuss openly. And there was one thing they all knew about the streets: there was always a little misinformation thrown in, but you could best believe there was also some truth to every rumor. The streets were reckless in that way.

For example, when Madison had told her friends she would be away for a few weeks getting a tummy tuck at a spiritual and health retreat in Arizona that had been vetted by one of the Real Housewives of Orange County, the streets said she was going out there to get her vagina done. They said she needed vaginal reconstruction surgery to compete with her husband's newest sugar baby—the one who didn't have any kids or the loose cootch that the birthing process created.

The truth was, she was having a hysterectomy after suffering silently for years with uterine fibroids. The early hysterectomy meant she would also experience premature menopause.

She was also considering the idea of vaginal reconstruction. According to her gynecologist, motherhood had resulted in the excessive loss of elasticity in that area, a problem many mothers experienced, but it was a condition that could be surgically corrected. With a procedure called a Mommy Makeover, the surgeons were confident they could put everything back in place. Her husband hadn't strayed away yet, but she didn't intend to give him a reason to, either.

Brooke, on the other hand, had informed the girls that she had a weekly standing appointment at Touché with the most sought-after male masseuse in the city. He listed, among his credentials, that he was a certified positive-sex provider—a therapist with extensive experience in the art of therapeutic, sensual massage, and one of the few in the city who provided happy endings for his female clients, when necessary, based upon his professional judgement. It was almost impossible to get an appointment with him unless you booked it at least a year in advance, but she had connections. For her, he had cleared his schedule and made an exception. His techniques, she was pleased to report, had worked wonders for her insomnia.

The streets were saying she wasn't even on the books at Touché. They said her son was a stoner who was on academic probation at his private school, and she was driving him to a weekly appointment with a private hypnotherapist who could ween him off the marijuana and manage his ADHD.

The truth was, he *was* a stoner, and he *was* on the verge of being kicked out of school, not for his academic struggles or ADHD, but for getting caught selling illegally obtained vape cartridges and Adderall in the school's cafeteria. She was taking him to a teen and youth support group every week as part of a mandatory alcohol and drug abuse program.

Candace's husband was enjoying success as a young real estate tycoon. She amplified her own social relevance with his merit, dazzling her friends with stories about how he was in talks to purchase a mixed-used development that would feature residential, commercial, and entertainment spaces to bring the city's tech and arts cultures together. Of course, his business meetings were consuming all of his time, but it would be worth it when they finally launched the project.

The streets were saying he was having an affair with one of the cute new associates in his investment group. Multiple sources had seen them around town meeting at lunches and dinners together on several occasions.

The truth was he was fooling around with his longtime business partner, Marc, and had moved into Marc's Gold Coast condominium for a few weeks after she had found their sext messages on his phone. Although he had sworn their partnership was strictly business, she knew what she'd seen on his phone. Still, she had allowed him to come back home and agreed to give him another chance, mainly because a foolishly signed, airtight prenuptial agreement held her in bondage. She signed it under the duress of his heady charm and Swarovski-encrusted promises, but it couldn't be undone.

Whenever anyone asked, Julene would tell the girls that Tristan was down South brokering a massive real estate deal for his mother. She'd tell them he was having a home built for her on the Inter-coastal Waterway, that she already had the twins on the waiting list at Savannah Country Day School, and that the weather and his busy schedule had caused continual delays in the construction process.

She'd explain his plan to send for her and the children as soon as they finished the house and that she would spend half of the year down South and half of the year back home in Chicago. Sometimes she'd throw in a little braggery, all dressed up to look like complaints, about the difficulties of importing countertops, about configuring the floor plan to create more closet space, about the need for additional hurricane insurance coverage, or the pattern of the school uniforms her children would wear.

The streets were saying Tristan was getting a home ready down there, but it wasn't for Julene. According to Facebook, he was spending quite a bit of time with a low country beauty and an angelic little munchkin with whom he bore an uncanny resemblance. They said the baby had his nose.

The streets were 100% wrong about the baby, but not about the girl. Tristan *was* down South, living in an apartment with a girl and her baby, along with the girl's male cousin, her two brothers, and the baby's actual father, who was a friend of Tristan's. Tristan had been residing on her couch while he searched for his own apartment. He and Julene had spoken of his trouble finding a place of his own. Without his own established credit history or his mother's backing, no landlord had been willing to give him a chance thus far. He assured her he was saving money and didn't mind the company of his housemates. They kept his mind occupied on the days he missed Julene and the children too much.

The friend-girls in Julene's circle often whispered amongst themselves about the rumors, but not in an *OMG-can-you BELIEVE-it* kind of way because they weren't completely without compassion. They whispered to the tune of *somebody-should-tell-her-but-it's-none-of-my-business*. After they whispered, they prayed because they weren't soulless heathens. They prayed and asked God to protect them from falling victim to the struggles and suffering their friends were enduring.

For as long as they'd known each other, for the magnitude of the battles they were all fighting, they didn't trust one another enough to admit their individual truths. Perhaps, if they were honest, each woman would admit she didn't trust herself enough to be vulnerable amongst friends.

The dripping, gas guzzler in the parking lot and the domineering ball-buster who owned it infiltrated Julene's thoughts, forcing her to confront her immediate circumstances. She stared at the cellphone, which would be turned off, almost predictably, in direct relation to any subtle change in her attitude or a flux in Tristan's mother's mood.

As instructed, she clicked the blue button in the top right corner of the screen, acknowledging her access to the document, entered the item numbers from her keys and new phone, electronically signed the bottom, and clicked submit. She might have been able to read all of the small print at the lower edge of the screen if her fingers hadn't been clicking faster than her eyes could move, but she briefly noticed the business name Legacy Builders Real Estate, not The Law Offices of Russell, Russew, and Ramm, at the bottom of the form just before the image on the screen disappeared.

Her trepidation vanished more quickly than it appeared when, after walking around the parking lot, chirp-chirping with the remote, she finally found the buttery, creamy Audi parked on the far side of the building. Once she located the car, she walked around it, looked in the front and back seats, and even looked underneath to see if it was leaking oil before jumping in the driver's seat and pushing the ignition button.

CHAPTER TWENTY

The car hummed so quietly, she wasn't immediately sure she had started it. But the engine was running, the heat and air blew on demand, the pavement was clean underneath, and she knew she'd never drive that shoddy Range Rover again.

She sat there a few minutes longer to transfer the data from her old cellphone to her new cellphone, and then called Triple A, instructing them to deliver the Rover with the old cellphone packed inside, to the Scott residence.

At her parents' home that evening, over dinner, she remained purposely closed-lipped about her new car and phone number, but it didn't stop her parents from asking questions.

Her mother was the first to broach the subject. "Are you sure all three baby seats will fit in there? At the same time?"

"What made Old Lady Scott decide to trade in the Range Rover?" Her father was snide when he mentioned Tristan's mother, selecting the moniker *Old Lady* in reference to the well-known fact that Tristan's mother was a full fifteen years older than her now ex-husband.

Julene ignored her parents' questions, exchanging them for questions of her own. "How well do you know Tiller?"

"Well, he's been my partner for, oh, two, three years now. Your mother actually introduced him to the firm. She's known him for…" He hesitated and looked toward his wife, allowing her time to insert the length of time she'd been acquainted with Tiller.

Layla, uninterested in this topic, waved her hand with mild annoyance, offering no additional information.

Brad continued with his answer, showing no hint of concern or malice at the mention of Tiller's name. "Years. It's been quite a while. He's been a standup guy for the most part—a great addition to our team. Why?"

"I see him around the office a lot and he's become something of a mentor to me since I've been at the firm, but I've never heard you mention his name," Julene replied. "Just thought I'd ask." Julene's answer was evasive, and her father left it unchallenged.

To her mother, she answered two questions, one asked aloud, one not. "It has a third-row seat just like the Range Rover. They're happy with the work I'm doing at the firm, and Tiller has shown me how to leverage their resources to my benefit. Isn't that what you've always..."

The doorbell rang, interrupting their conversation, and Julene excused herself from the table to answer it.

She opened the door, shocked to find herself face to face with Ramona Scott, who spat words through a heated smile as soon as Julene appeared. "You had the gall to have that truck dumped onto my front lawn by a tow truck? You didn't even have the decency to say *Thank you, Ms. Scott. I don't know what I would have done without your help, Ms. Scott.* If I didn't feel so sorry for you, I'd sue you for the cost of having the oil cleaned from my driveway."

While Julene stood, mouth agape and unable to respond to this hostile ambush, Layla pushed past her to face Ramona. "You don't need to feel sorry for my daughter. You've got enough to manage with your deadbeat son. How dare he abandon the mother of his children? Your son took advantage of my daughter and you stand on my property, berating her?"

Ramona stepped forward, assessed Laya and then disregarded her as she addressed Julene again. "Your mother is right. My son is a deadbeat. I tried to set him on the right path, just as I'm sure your mother tried with you. But we can only do so much. You children just think you have it all figured out, but you don't. One day, when your children are old enough, you'll see how it feels to be disrespected by the people who depend on you for food, clothing, and shelter."

Stepping back again, Ramona finally acknowledged Layla. "Shame on you for allowing your daughter to exploit my generosity for all these years, but I guess that's your modus operandi. You haven't even had the decency to thank me for what I've done for *you* and your pathetic husband over the years."

Julene found her voice and stepped out to defend her mother. "You can leave my mother out of this. Your issue is with me. I do owe you my appreciation for the way you've supported me and the kids the last few years, even though you were determined to make it as unbearable and as humiliating as possible. But you didn't do my mother any favors. She would have preferred to have us here, but I chose to leave--"

Ramona raised a hand to interrupt. "Wake up, little girl. Do you honestly believe you made that decision on your own? Your mother called me as soon as you stomped out of the house in a tantrum that day. She begged me to take you in. She cried about how she and your father squandered every penny they had and she asked me for a personal loan. I knew I'd never see that $11,000 again but I felt sorry for her. She was afraid you'd never--"

"Leave! Get off our property, you liar!" Layla erupted, screaming at the top of her lungs, seemingly oblivious to what the neighbors might see or hear. "I want out of here immediately or I'll call the authorities! You're a liar!"

Ramona laughed as she backed slowly toward her car. "I think I've said enough. Layla, it was a pleasure chatting with you after all this time. Julene, I wish you the best. I believe life will teach you more than your mother or I ever could. Please give the children my love."

When Ramona's car disappeared from the driveway, Julene closed her eyes and massaged her temples as she addressed Layla. "She's not lying, is she, Mother? What did you do?"

Weariness clouded Laya's voice when she answered. "Darling, who knows what that woman was saying? I can't believe she had the audacity to show up at our home unannounced. Honestly, I have such a headache now, I can't think clearly. I'll be in my study resting for the rest of the evening."

Julene returned to the dining room, battling a headache of her own, but mustered enough energy to usher the children upstairs for their bath. She passed the door to Brad's office and considered stepping inside to find out what knowledge he'd had of the transaction between Ramona and Layla. When the familiar sound of ice rattling in a whiskey tumbler could be heard through the door, she decided against it and continued up the stairs.

CHAPTER TWENTY-ONE

Small doses of freedom are incredible rejuvenators for the spirit. The freedom of living life beyond Mrs. Scott's grip was proof. Julene breathed a little easier every time she pushed the button that made her car purr. She appreciated it each time she succeeded in making an outbound phone call without interruption. It made her a better mother, a more motivated employee, a more driven woman. The taste of freedom was sweet on her lips, only bittered when she pulled into her parents' driveway each evening. That's when she was reminded that she wasn't legitimately independent. She would have to take a deep breath before she walked in the door, dig deep to find a pleasant expression for her face, pretend not to see her mother's craving for her father's attention, ignore the pile of bills and collections notices on her dad's desk.

To a degree, she could manage her personal feelings about her life, but she couldn't overlook the way life in this house had affected her children, whom her mother dressed every day in stiff, logo-laden outfits that couldn't be wrinkled or scuffed or sullied in any way. She watched her children's smiles fade while her mother trained them not to be children: *don't crawl around on the floor, place your hands in your lap during dinner, don't laugh too loud, don't wear shoes and shirts with Elmo on them, don't fidget, don't...don't...*

Julene had been raised under the same sterile, pretentious, unnatural expectations when all she'd wanted as a child was to be regular in the comfort of her own home when no one was watching. Her children deserved to be regular, too, at least when no one was watching, at least in the comfort of their own home.

So, after a month with her new car, new phone, and new attitude, when Tiller stopped by her office to ask a favor, she was open to it.

"Alright, now! That new car looks good on you! You like it?" he asked, appearing in her doorway, chatting as though they were old friends.

Julene looked up, shrugged just one shoulder, and smiled. "Do I like it? If it looks good on me, does it matter?"

Her eyes returned to the shoes she was ordering online and exhaled. "No, I love it. It's nice to drive something that works and doesn't leak. No lights blinking on the dash. It's such a relief. Thanks for making it happen."

He waved a hand toward her, pushing the appreciation away. "No thanks needed. You work hard around here, and this job comes with perks." He slid a few steps closer to her desk and pushed her door closed. "Let me ask you something, though."

He held both hands up, anticipating her objections. "Forgive me if I'm speaking out of place, but I would have expected your father to tell you how to navigate around here. I mean, hey, I look at you like my daughter, and if my daughter was working here with me, I'd make sure she had the inside edge from the start."

Julene sat back in her chair and studied Tiller's face. At first glance, he was sharp—a bright smile, freshly edged hair, warm, brown skin, and hazelnut-colored eyes. But she'd been trained to spot flaws—to check for the details—and she suspected Tiller was an extremely polished man with some barely-concealed rough edges. His bright smile was composed of very obvious, ill-fitting dental veneers. His freshly edged hairline was the powdery texture of the spray-on hair used by balding men. The white part of his eyeballs was the blotchy, brownish color of a much older man. She'd been suspicious of him at first, but saw in him today the face of a father figure and allowed her suspicions to fall away.

She sighed heavily. "We don't talk very much. I mean, I live with my parents, and they help with the kids, but we're not as close as you'd think."

She sat up straighter, finding a brighter point to focus on. "It'll be fine though. I'll get my own place soon and I can take care of myself around here."

She smiled, pointing past Tiller's shoulder toward the hallway. "This job? This is a piece of cake."

He laughed with her, pointing his finger at her playfully. "You're right. You're a smart young lady, I can see, but you don't have to do everything alone. If you need something, don't be too proud to let me know."

She smiled and nodded, thankful for this small alliance, and watched him move toward the door before a thought stopped him.

"You said you're planning to get your own place soon? Coincidentally, I have a property that needs a tenant if you're interested."

Before she could tell him she probably couldn't afford it, he was showing her a picture of the property on his phone while simultaneously explaining the details. "Here's the deal: The firm recently represented a client in a foreclosure proceeding. She and her husband are fighting over this gorgeous lakefront estate. Per the divorce settlement, she must sell the estate and split the proceeds with her husband or retain the property and buy him out. The problem is, she can't afford to keep it and she doesn't want him to have it, either. My team is working to prolong the foreclosure proceedings and buy her some time to work things out."

"Why doesn't she just sell it?" Julene's mind raced, trying to guess who was about to lose their home, who'd recently finalized a nasty divorce.

"There's a pile of tax liens on the place, so it's not very attractive to potential buyers," he explained. "We're working with the bank to do a short sale and I'm representing her as her real estate agent and property manager. She owned the property before they were married, but there was no prenup in place. It was a second home for her—a vacation home, really—because her permanent residence is in Florida. It turns out her new husband had been sneaking around with his mistress and using the vacation home as a love nest. When she found out, she filed for divorce, and he promptly laid claim to half of all she owns—including this property. Neither of them can live there unless or until the estate is settled, and she'd rather allow it to fall into foreclosure than let him enjoy one penny from it, so it's my job to sell it."

"But you said it won't sell," Julene pointed out, her curiosity piqued.

"Well, it will. It'll just take some time," he said. "I've been showing the place. It's stunning, but it's empty, and it's much harder to sell an empty home. No one has lived there for a few years. Potential buyers need to see themselves living in the home. It needs to *feel* like a home. It needs to *smell* like a home."

She nodded, interested in the psychology behind real estate sales.

"What I like to do is have someone living in the homes I sell—make the home feel warm and welcoming. It makes it a lot easier to sell a complicated property like this one. Plus, I don't charge rent. Basically, I let you live there rent-free in exchange for your help. You'll keep it clean, burn lots of candles, bake cookies, anything to make it feel like a home."

Julene sat forward in her chair to make sure she'd heard correctly. "I can live in this, this mansion for *free* if I help you sell it?"

She sat back, more her mother's child than her father's. "I should get a commission for helping you sell it."

He smiled and tapped his temple with his finger. "I knew you were a smart girl! So, here's the thing, there's no *commission* per se, but there are perks with the job. And I've never let you down when it comes to perks, right?"

"So, you basically need a house sitter? That won't work for me. I have children. I'm not going to drag them, with all their stuff, into that house for a few weeks just to move back to my parents' house again. Doesn't make sense to me."

It was the mature response, though it cut deeply on its way out of her mouth. If she'd been single with no children, this arrangement would have been a Godfather deal—an offer she couldn't refuse.

Tiller smiled again, with pride, much in the same way her father had when she'd challenged him beyond his expectations as a little girl. "Now, don't forget, our firm is handling the foreclosure proceedings. That's a process that could take a *very long time*, especially since my client is only half-interested in truly selling it. I've seen these things drag on for years."

He winked at her. "Think it over, but don't take too long. I'll email a lease agreement, which will be zero dollars monthly as long as you uphold your responsibilities in the home. You can sign it if you so choose."

A moment later, alone in her office, Julene pulled up the email and signed the offer she couldn't refuse.

CHAPTER TWENTY-TWO

From the moment she read his email, which included the Zillow listing for the home, she was in love with the two-floor penthouse. It was an entertainer's dream. The entire top floor was dedicated to it, with a full-sized basketball and racquetball court, a huge Jacuzzi and steam room, and a wraparound porch with endless, unparalleled views of the lake and city.

Located on one of the most coveted streets in Streeterville, it was a rare solace in the middle of the city—one she'd never be able to afford, even if she actually lived the life she advertised to her friends.

The home afforded incredible panoramic views of Lake Michigan, the Chicago River, the iconic Lake Shore Drive, and the city skyline from its private 1,000-square-foot wraparound balcony. The imported marble from Italy, three 500-gallon saltwater fish tanks, and incredible glass and marble spiral staircase were exquisite. Each bedroom had its own private balcony and en suite bathrooms, and the master suite featured a huge walk-in closet with custom storage and incredible southern views.

It wasn't necessarily a family-friendly home, but it would provide her children with a respite from their grandmother's scrutinous eyes. Plus, it was an opportunity Julene would likely never be offered again.

True to his word, Triller provided her with perks, funded by the fees his client paid him for property management: a parking pass, monthly grocery deliveries, and fresh flowers every Thursday. The Thursday flowers, he explained, were for the weekend showings—window-shoppers who made appointments to view high-end properties on the weekends. They weren't likely to be serious inquiries, but they would be impressed enough to tell other people about this amazing listing. Word of mouth is an invaluable piece of the real estate puzzle, he'd said.

He was spot on about the power of word-of-mouth advertising. Julene's faux ownership of a luxury home was a priceless tool in her efforts to perpetuate the lie of her perfect family life. Friends and even loose acquaintances in her social circle complimented her on her beautiful home, making up reasons to stop by, persuading her to host one event after another just to come up and see the view from the forty-first floor for themselves. Privately, they whispered amongst themselves about what Tristan must *really* be doing to have catapulted Julene and the children to the top of the food chain in such an impressive fashion.

The glory, she immediately learned, comes not to she who has no grit. Even with *perks*, this higher level of living was exhausting and expensive. She leaned on her mother more than she would have liked for help with the children, for support when she hosted gatherings, and advice on social etiquette, knowing full well, her mother operated under the power of her own motives. Her daughter's elevation in social status created enhanced optics for the entire family.

And there were moments when, much like the declined debit card at lunch, the entire sham buckled under the weight of the lie. Times when her dressed-up, fabricated life threatened to fall away, exposing the naked truth hidden beneath.

That time came on a blustery February evening when, after a late day at work, the parking pass for the penthouse garage refused to work. She sat in her car, her children in the back seats chirping like baby chicks about whatever they'd done at Grandma Layla's that day, while she tried over and over to wave her parking pass in front of the sensor. She tried punching the code in manually. She tried the guest code. Traffic mounted behind her, held up by her inability to open the gate to the parking garage, and stress churned inside her stomach with a growing ferocity. Finally, a gentleman emerged from the car in line behind hers, walked up and waved his own parking pass in front of the meter. She pulled the window down to thank him as he passed, but he only pulled the lapels of his coat up to shield his red cheeks from the lake-effect snow flurries and hustled back to his car.

Inside the building, annoyed by the malfunctioning parking pass, she hustled her three lively children toward the elevator.

"Who can press the number four and the number one for Mommy?" she quizzed Jada and Jacinta, watching them scramble to be the first to press the buttons with their tiny fingers.

The girls pressed the buttons at the same time, shouting, *I win!* at the same time, followed by *jinx!* at the same time.

Julene stood watching, enjoying moments like this, when the girls were more like best friends than sisters. They were identical twins, but their personalities were vastly different, so much so that they sometimes *looked* different. On most days, Jacinta looked more like Julene and Jada looked more like Tristan, and some days the girls only looked like each other.

"Mommy! My shoe!" Jamison's husky little voice broke through her wonderings, making her aware that the elevator still hadn't arrived.

She stooped down to retrieve her son's dropped shoe and punched the elevator buttons again, holding her key fob closer to the keypad. When the elevator failed to respond, she headed to the Resident Relations office for help. "My parking pass and elevator keys aren't working."

Ms. Marlene, the Resident Relations manager, looked up from her desk and smiled when she saw Julene and the children.

"What's that, sweetheart? Your keys don't work? We can't leave you and these precious babies in the lobby all night, can we? The code probably needs to be reset. Didn't you get the email? I can do it for you right now. Don't worry."

Ms. Marlene's voice was soothing tone as she logged into her computer. "Do you have your license on you, baby?"

"Yes, Ma'am." Julene flipped open her wallet, showing Ms. Marlene her identification, but her heart quickened as she watched the older woman tap and tap again on the keyboard.

"It's the penthouse, right?" Ms. Marlene asked. "I know I've walked up there with maintenance and deliveries a few times."

The woman paused and studied Julene's face more closely. "Are you—is Layla Davis your mother?"

Julene smiled, pleased to know her mother's name carried some weight. "That's right. Layla is my mother. How do you know her?"

Ms. Marlene stood and took a closer look at Julene. "We went to high school together. We didn't run in the same circles, but we knew each other very well. You're a beautiful girl. The spitting image of your mother. How is she, by the way? Is the penthouse in her name? Or your father's? What's his name? I'll try both. Maybe that's the reason I can't find you. I'll try searching again."

She sat again, typing new letters into the keyboard. Her face twisted slightly, stumped.

Julene stopped her. "The penthouse isn't in my parents' names. The lease is in my name. Maybe you spelled my name wrong."

She presented her license again, allowing the woman to check the spelling.

After two more failed attempts, Ms. Marlene held her hands up. "Your name's not listed on the lease."

She looked over the rim of her glasses, waiting for Julene to clear the confusion.

"I live there. *We* live there!" Julene exclaimed. "You've seen us coming and going for months now. Can't you just reset my passes? I mean, what's the problem?"

Julene noted Ms. Marlene's expression to be that of a woman who wasn't about to sacrifice her job over a technicality. She tried a different approach. "I'll just need to make a phone call to get this all cleared up."

Twenty minutes later, Tiller walked into the office and Julene stood to meet him. "She's saying I'm not on the lease. I don't understand."

He moved toward Julene as though to hug her, and she turned sideways to deflect it, offering her hand for a shake instead. Tiller's expression was a mixture of embarrassment and apology as he reached across the desk to shake Ms. Marlene's hand. "Ladies, I'm sorry for the confusion."

To Ms. Marlene, he said, "I'm here on behalf of Legacy Builders Real Estate Group. I have power of attorney granted by the owner."

He fished his driver's license from his wallet and waited for Ms. Marlene to find his name in her computer system. When she located it, she smiled. "Thank you! That's all we needed. Now, we can reset those codes."

She clicked a button, checked Julene's key fob and parking pass to confirm the serial numbers, and turned to Tiller to offer a suggestion: "You can add Julene to the lease and you won't have to run down here every time something like this happens. All we would need is a copy of the lease agreement and her ID."

Tiller cleared his throat, glanced at Julene, and then at Ms. Marlene. "She's not technically a leaseholder. She works for me, and she manages this property for me. Her responsibilities require her to live in the unit full time."

He noticed the children sleeping on the plush sofa. "And she has permission to maintain the residence with her children."

Julene's jaw clenched and unclenched as Tiller spoke, but Ms. Marlene only waved his words away with a smile and returned to her computer screen. "That explains it! Okay, that's easy. Let me see your license again, baby. I can add you as a permanent guest. Mr. Tiller, you can change this at any time. Now, you can access the property, handle minor access issues and such, and Mr. Tiller won't have to drive over here every time there's a little hiccup."

She clicked her mouse twice, waited for confirmation, and then stood to shake hands with Tiller and Julene.

"Thank you for your help," Tiller said. "I'm sorry for the inconvenience."

He turned to Julene and said, "Let me help you get these sleepyheads upstairs, and then I'll head home."

The journey to the forty-first floor was excruciatingly slow. Tiller held a sleeping Jada in one arm and a sleeping Jamison in the other. Julene carried Jacinta, along with everyone's coats, scarves, and mittens. Inside her own coat, the heat of her embarrassment forced a furious river of sweat to run down the small of her back. She chewed the inside of her cheek to bide her time until she could tell Tiller exactly what was on her mind.

CHAPTER TWENTY-THREE

U pstairs, with the babies tucked warmly in their beds, Tiller pushed an overfilled glass of Prosecco into Julene's hand and ushered her toward a seat in front of the fireplace. He poured himself a cold beer and joined her.

"What the hell, Tiller? I *work* for you? I *do not* work for *you*. You are not my landlord! I work for Russell, Russew, and Ramm. I don't know what you think—"

He sipped his beer slowly and raised his eyebrows. "Are you finished?"

"Don't you treat me like some child throwing a tantrum! I signed a lease! Don't you think I saved a copy? You misled me and you *humiliated* me! What the hell were you thinking?"

Her hands trembled as she placed her glass on the table. Tiller exhaled and sat back, crossing one leg over the other, his knee brushing against Julene's leg without regard for her personal space. She slid away, as far as the small sofa would allow, and reached for her glass again, waiting for him to speak.

"First, you do technically work for me. I am part owner of Legacy Builders Real Estate Group, and you have a signed contract with *me*, not Russell, Russew, and Ramm. You signed it when you moved into this gorgeous penthouse."

He looked around himself, taking in the opulent accommodations, and continued. "Relax. It's just on paper. In order for me to create write-offs for tax purposes, I had to list you as an employee and document your perks. I'm not charging you anything, so there's no income for you to report, but it helps me out on the back end."

Julene shook her head. "I don't get it. You should have told me."

Tiller stood up and placed his glass on the table. "What does it matter? I told you—it's paperwork. That's the way business goes. Besides, look around yourself. You've got it made! I'm the one pushing papers and keeping this place available to you and your kids! All you have to do is live here, keep the place clean, and keep your mouth shut. Is that too much to ask? Because if it is, you can move out and I'll find someone else."

He stood there, glaring at her. It was the first time she'd seen him so agitated. She couldn't describe him as a father-figure right now. His energy was quite the opposite. His threatening, intimidating cold heat nullified Julene's tirade almost instantly.

She nodded finally and looked up at him. "It's cool. It's fine. I would have felt better if I had known the whole story before I went into Ms. Marlene's office and embarrassed myself. You should have told me."

His shoulders relaxed and he smiled when he pointed at the glass he'd left on the table, and then strode to the front door. "Get that cleaned up. You play your part and I'll play mine. Okay?"

When Tiller left, Julene sat staring into the fake embers of the gaslit fire logs and thought about his words. *Keep your mouth shut. Play your part.* He'd been harsh, but had he been wrong? Hadn't she been raised under this dogma her whole life? Resistance burned in her chest, begging to be acknowledged, and she pushed it down, as she had always done, and she thought of the old, leaking Range Rover. How long could she stave off the real problem before she'd have to deal with the inevitable?

Though the key card incident had been an embarrassment to Julene, it had also been the start of a friendly relationship between her and Ms. Marlene.

Ms. Marlene's choices in clothing and accessories were the perfect reflection of her personality. Neat, clean, warm, no fuss, and very nice. Dependable. She carried the same black pocketbook made of soft, high-quality leather and wore the same comfortable-looking, sensible shoes with the thick, wedge soles every day, but they always looked brand new. What you saw was what you got. To do otherwise was to put on airs to impress other people, and she didn't care to put on anything that wasn't necessary. She reminded Julene, too often to be coincidental, that God had made us all equal and He hadn't put anyone ahead of anyone else.

On most days, Julene stopped and chatted with Ms. Marlene about everything from the building's social events to the weather, but the day she dashed into the first-level restroom behind the recreation room because she didn't trust her unsettled stomach to hold steady for the forty-one-story ride to her own bathroom, she prayed for privacy. She had found this particular restroom, though it was for public use, to be clean, new, and almost always empty. Perfect because recently her smoothies moved through her system and made her stomach bubble in a way that felt more urgent than normal. To be honest, she couldn't be sure if her stomach was unsettled because of the smoothies or the unending precariousness of her life.

Sitting on the toilet, happy to be alone, she relaxed in the stall, and when the door opened, she cussed to herself. The presence of someone else in the bathroom washing their hands or fixing their makeup disturbed her peace. She relished this quiet time when she could do her business without the concern of someone hearing it or smelling it.

She watched the nondescript shoes with the thick soles stroll across the floor in front of the stall door and stop at the paper towel dispenser mounted on the wall outside her stall, if she had to guess. She knew those shoes well. They belonged to Ms. Marlene.

Julene sucked in her breath and held it just as she held her feet inches off the floor, praying for Ms. Marlene's departure, desperate to finish her business in solitude. The feet moved over to the supply closet, and then the sink.

"Ain't nobody got no home training? Leaving fingerprints on the mirror and not refilling the paper towel dispenser?" she heard Ms. Marlene mumble.

She wasn't the janitor. She had been the resident relations manager for nearly twenty years—since the building was first built—and she took great pride in her job. She didn't take no mess. She was a sweet woman who never said as much with her words, but her presence commanded respect in a way that reminded Julene of Aunt Lucille.

Ms. Marlene rambled on, "No one ever replaces the roll when they take the last one. They act like we have maids around here. People don't want to clean up after themselves!"

There were, in fact, janitors who were responsible for these things, but Ms. Marlene was old-school. She was perhaps the last of a generation who believed in leaving things better than you found them, rather than expecting someone else to clean up after you.

Realizing Ms. Marlene could continue dawdling for a while, fussing and straightening the spotless restroom, Julene sighed and ventured across a previously unbroached boundary. "How are you doing today, Ms. Marlene?"

"Julene, that you? Umph! I'm just here mumbling. Didn't know you were in here!" the older woman said as she laughed, freely, easily, undaunted by whatever Julene was doing on the other side of the stall door. She launched into one of her daily stories. "Well, my oldest grandbaby got her nursing degree because she wanted to be a baby nurse. She got hired at the hospital, but they put her on the third shift in the ER and she hates it. They're always understaffed down there, and the supervisor isn't the easiest person to communicate with, but what can you do about that?"

Ms. Marlene giggled. "So, she called me this morning to tell me she's going to quit because she deserves better than that."

She giggled again with the maturity of a grandmother who has seen too much to sweat the small stuff, before continuing, "I said to her, look here: You don't just quit a good hospital job just because one person isn't nice to you. Don't you know how hard it is to get your foot in the door in a place like that? And anyway, I don't know where you're going with no job, because you're a grown woman and no one is going to take care of you."

Julene seized the pause in the story to finish in the stall and step up to the sink. She waved her hands under the faucet until a warm stream of water poured over her fingers. Looking into the mirror above the sink, she studied her own reflection as she offered a rebuttal to Ms. Marlene's argument. "If she's unhappy at work, don't you think life is too short to stay stuck in a life that makes you unhappy?"

Ms. Marlene's voice was as solid and comforting as her thick-soled shoes. "No, you just bide your time. Wait until you can see your way to get into the passing lane. That's what I told her—life is like a highway. Once you get yourself into the passing lane, you just put your foot on the gas and you don't let up! Move forward if you aren't where you want to be, but you have got to wait for your opportunity. And in the meantime, be patient, learn what you can, apply for other positions, get your ducks in a row, because when it's time to make that move, you've got to be ready."

Julene stood at the sink, absorbing Ms. Marlene's words, curious about how the granddaughter had received this message, forgetting for the moment, about the water rushing through her fingers.

Ms. Marlene waved a paper towel in Julene's direction and continued her story. "I always say, stay ready so you don't have to *get* ready. And that's exactly what I told her. I said, 'Baby, God has placed you in that position for a reason. Late at night, in the Emergency Room with some of the worst things you'd ever want to see. He's got something for you there, and he has *never* made a mistake. He's never had bad timing. He'll let you know when it's time to move into that passing lane. I told her something I heard Oprah say once, *Do what you have to do until you can do what you want to do.*'"

Ms. Marlene was out of the bathroom and moving down the hallway before the word 'do' was out of her mouth, while Julene stood, gripping the paper towel, clutching the remnants of the older woman's wisdom.

CHAPTER TWENTY-FOUR

A day without Ms. Marlene's warm hug or enlightening conversation was an underwhelming one, and the windows of her darkened office were sad, massive eyes that captivated Julene just as much as they antagonized her. The gaping absence stretched on for ten days, coming to an abrupt end when Julene ran, nearly headfirst, into the older woman as she rounded the corner near the elevators.

"I was worried about you, Ms. Marlene! I thought something happened to you. Where have you been?"

The daily conversations, no matter the brevity, had become as necessary to Julene as the butterfly kisses she shared with her children every day, the glass of Prosecco she sipped every night, and the sun she watched rise every morning in the quiet hours before the children awoke. She blinked away the spontaneous tears the surprise reunion had called up.

"Hey, baby! Did you miss me?" The older woman's energy was so contagious. "I took myself on a Mediterranean cruise! By myself! My old man wanted to go, but I said, 'look, I need to do this on my own.'"

She leaned in and lowered her voice, letting Julene in on her true motives. "I didn't want to compromise my time, wanted to see what I wanted to see, sleep when I wanted to sleep, eat what I wanted to eat. Because I can enjoy my own company, you know? I signed up for every tour and excursion available, met some new people—really enjoyed myself."

She grabbed Julene's hand and patted it gently, a hint of gold glinting off the tooth at the edge of her smile. "Here's the thing: I have saved and budgeted for this trip for so long! I organized my affairs way in advance so I could relax and not worry about any debt. Since I paid my house off a few years ago, I thought it was finally time to treat myself to something special."

Julene fought to stop her mouth from dropping open and her eyes from bulging, repressing any facial expression that would convey her surprise. Ms. Marlene hadn't struck her as someone who was wealthy. She wore unidentifiable clothes, shoes and purses. She was still working—past the age of retirement, Julene supposed—in an apartment building. Her salary couldn't have amounted to much more than Julene's, plus she had raised children *and* grandchildren.

Despite her own assumptions, she was happy for the woman of whom she'd become so fond. She found a smile. "I'm impressed! That's a huge trip to take alone, but it's beautiful, isn't it? We traveled to Barcelona, Naples, and Venice when I was in sixth grade. It was expensive, though. What I remember most is my parents arguing about money the entire time."

The last bit, about the money and the arguing, had slipped out inadvertently. When had she last mentioned a money problem to anyone except Tristan?

"Baby, I can't tell you enough how important it is to pay yourself first. Handle your expenses and don't carry any debt—but don't forget to pay yourself, too. When you pay your bills, slide a certain amount into your savings, too. If I hadn't done that, there's no way I could have afforded this vacation or to have paid off my home. That's why you don't see me carrying expensive pocketbooks and paying a whole bunch of money for things that don't matter. I'd rather have a cheap purse with *all* my money in it, than a high-priced bag with *no* money in it! You get me?"

She winked at Julene and smiled again before she continued. "No disrespect to you. I know your parents put you on the right track. You're able to pay for the things you want. These are things I try to teach my granddaughter—things *her* parents should have instilled in her."

She shrugged her shoulders.

Julene shrugged her own shoulders, imagining having Ms. Marlene for a grandmother. "She's lucky to have you—your wisdom."

The older woman stepped back a bit to show off her outfit, displaying her satisfaction with herself. "I don't try to make myself out to know everything, but I have learned a lot in my years on this Earth. I buy for quality, not names, and I cut corners where I can, whenever it makes sense, because I always knew if the Lord blessed me to reach an elderly age, it would be up to me to take care of myself. Not my old man, bless his soul. He is a sweet man—loves me to pieces."

She leaned closer, smelling of Ivory soap and cocoa butter lotion. "But baby, he's just a man. Only human. I had to make my own preparations and be responsible for *me*. I'm not trying to take it with me, either. I'm going to live and enjoy myself while I'm here on Earth and do what I can to make sure I'm not stressed about money or worried about someone coming to take my stuff."

She paused and glanced down the hallway, realizing perhaps, they'd been chatting for too long. "Look at me lecturing you about finances and living the frugal life! I know your mama and daddy taught you well. I sure wish my kids could take a lesson from you! You're doing so well for yourself as far as I can see, and I'm so proud of you! I'll have to talk to you later, though. There's a bunch of work waiting for me in that office!"

Julene tried to imagine what Ms. Marlene would think about the smoldering mess that was her life—the stolen identity, the dishonest parents, the debt, her children's absent father. She toyed with the idea of inviting Ms. Marlene upstairs just to listen to the older woman talk. Just to let her guard down and relax with a real person, without pretensions, without judgment, without pressure.

There was no time for daydreaming today, however, and the women hugged again as one walked across the hallway to bring light back to the window's somber eyes, and the other eased a questionably obtained Audi from the parking garage, pointing it toward her questionably obtained job.

After a full two weeks of minimal contact with Tiller, Julene looked up from her desk to find him standing in the doorway of her office, smiling. She answered his smile with a blank stare, unwilling to extend even a cordial acknowledgment.

"You're still mad at me. I don't know why, but it's okay." He stepped inside the threshold of her office and leaned against the doorframe.

"It's just—," Julene patted the itching spot on the crown of her head and straightened her freshly sewn-in ponytail. "It's just that you embarrassed me, number one, and number two, you falsified documents with my name on them. I'm not comfortable with that."

He crossed his arms and legs before tilting his head to peer at her across the rim of his glasses. "You're cute when you're mad. You're feisty. I like that. Now, a few corrections. Number one, I *did not* falsify any documents. You signed them of your own free will. You were not misled, nor were you under duress. Number two," he started, mocking Julene. She considered throwing him out of her office, but the cellphone and keys that lay on her desk begged her to keep calm. "Number two, I need to ask you a huge favor, if you can quit being stubborn for two seconds."

He tossed an envelope on her desk. She peeked inside and pulled out the contents, read silently for a moment, and laid the envelope back on the desk, awaiting more information.

"Tickets to the ribbon-cutting at the Bronzeville Artists' Lofts this weekend. There's an all-white party at Gallery Guichard," he explained. His smile, youthful and a shade mischievous, drew attention to his eyes and away from the gray hairs threatening to overtake his goatee.

She pushed the tickets toward him and shook her head with admonition. "Tiller, you're old enough to be my *father*. I'm not going on a date with you."

His laugh was healthy and full-bodied when he explained, "I promised to take my daughter to this event. There will be lots of celebrities and influencers there, but I have a prior engagement. I want you to go with her in my absence. Have fun, of course, but do something else for me. Try to find out as much as you can about the Bronzeville revitalization project. I want in on those deals and I need to know who to get close to. It'll be an outstanding opportunity for my real estate portfolio to take off."

"You want me to go to the social event of the year as a spy?" she asked, eying him. She scrutinized his relaxed posture, the self-assurance in his expression. His suit was custom-tailored, but a dark line rimmed the edges of his nails, and the space between his thumb and index finger bore resemblance to Martha Stewart's lightly floured baking pans— a distinct contrast to his rich brown skin and posh demeanor.

Momentarily distracted, Tiller pulled his phone from his breast pocket and answered her without looking up. "I like to call it reconnaissance, but yes, get the info and get back to me."

He stepped out of her office without waiting for her to accept or decline and tossed one last directive over his shoulder. "You can thank me later."

The tickets lay on Julene's desk for the rest of the day. Two thick rectangles trimmed in gold foil—a PapierLuxe signature feature—promising exclusive access to a magnificent extravaganza. And it *would* be grandiose, as purported, but it would require *work* on Julene's behalf— hair, nails, shoes, bag. She'd have to dance, not because a live band would be there to encourage everyone to make it a night to remember, but because the city's insider secrets weren't going to spill themselves. Everyone knows you've got to be proficient in the art of tap-dancing if you expect to get the tea flowing.

By the day's end, having resigned herself to Tiller's request, though she'd much prefer to stay at home making pillow pallets on the bedroom floor with her children,

Julene tucked the tickets into her purse and logged off her computer.

At home that evening, as she hustled her children toward the elevator, juggling their scarves and mittens and a takeout box filled with chicken tenders and French fries, she nearly walked headfirst into Tristan.

Chapter Twenty-Five

S he looked up just in time to avoid colliding with him, and when her eyes finally convinced her brain that he was really there, she held her arms out for a hug.

He grabbed her, holding her close as though she were a baby doll, her toes skimming the floor, while their children clammored around them, sqeezing their tiny bodies between their parents, tugging at Tristan's coat and pants, eager for their turn to be in their daddy's arms. When he relaxed his grip and settled her feet firmly on the ground, she pinched the soft tissue on the inside of his bicep, squeezing until he whimpered for mercy.

"What was that for?" he asked. There was pain in his voice, even as his dimples and smiling eyes compelled her to reach out and hug him again.

"I'm sorry," said. "You surprised me, big head! You could have let me know you were coming! We missed you, fool!"

She ushered the children into the elevator and grabbed the front of Tristan's shirt, pulling him inside, too.

On the trek to floor number forty-one, she stood back, savoring the sight of Tristan and the children dissolving into a pile of hugs and giggles in the center of the elevator floor. Their laughter blended together until she could no longer discern the children from their father. And it continued upstairs, at the dinner table, in the bathtub, while he helped everyone into their jammies, on their knees saying their little kid, nighty-night prayers, and as he tucked them into their beds and smothered them with powerful kisses. He'd burst right into their lives on what would have otherwise been a mundane Wednesday night, with his brilliant smile and intrinsic warmth to love on his children and reconnect with his best friend. The lingering resentment Julene had harbored in his absence made a graceful and immediate exit.

They sat together on the floor outside the children's room, well after the last request for water, a story, and another trip to the potty. They sat with outstretched feet, playing toe-tag, occasionally bumping shoulders and peeking at each other sideways.

Julene was the first to speak. "You look really good. Like, refreshed. Are you tan?"

He laughed quietly, not wanting to wake the children. "I'm a Black man. I can't get *a tan.*"

"Aw, stop it. You're a light-skinned brother with freckles. You can *definitely* get a tan. You definitely *do* have a tan. Life down South must be good to you."

She looked over at him critically. "To what do we owe this surprise visit?"

Tristan wrapped his arm around her shoulder, and she nestled her head in the space just above his collarbone. He smelled of patchouli. As he spoke, the vibration from his words were soothing against her face. "I missed y'all. I hate being away from you, but I couldn't be *here* anymore. This city—this life—was killing me. Mom was killing me. And yeah, the South has been good to me. I can be myself down there. No one judges me. The cost of living is cheap. I wasn't lying when I said I was trying to get things in place to bring you and the kids down. I hate being away from my kids."

In the dimly lit hallway, Julene could see the shimmering tears pooling in his eyes. Even after so much time apart, she still knew him as well as she knew herself. She waited for the rest of the story.

He exhaled for a long while, and then the words all rushed out at once. "A business opportunity fell into my lap, and Mom's going to loan me some money to fund it."

"You came all the way up here to hit your mother up for money? What kind of business opportunity is it?" She turned her body toward him to watch his eyes for the truth.

His mouth opened and closed, unprepared to back up his story with facts. He laughed and lay down to rest his head in her lap. "Okay, you're right. There's no business opportunity. I just missed you and the kids like hell, and I didn't have the money to fly you down, so I decided to hustle a few dollars out of Mom to come up here and chill with y'all for a while. She was a terrible mother. I consider this to be reparations."

Julene traced the hairline at the nape of his neck with her fingertips, and then twirled her fingers in the thickening curls that began in the middle and traveled up the back of his head toward his forehead to form a low-profile Mohawk.

"This haircut looks cute on you. I'm glad you're here—*we're* glad you're here—but you better get your story straight before you approach your mother."

Her fingers left his curls and traveled over to pinch his ear softly.

"I can handle that woman. Don't worry about it." He stood up and grabbed her hand, pulling her to standing as well, and led her to the expansive window in the master suite.

"You're really living here. It's cool," he said. He stood for a moment, taking in the contrast between the serenity of the city's twinkling lights and the pandemonium of the whirling snow flurries. Julene stood behind him, watching quietly, until he whipped around to face her. "We should take the kids ice skating at Maggie Daley. Remember when we used to smoke a fat one and go hang out there? Or we can take them to the South Shore and see if there's anything happening at the cultural center."

She nodded slowly, feeling guilty for not sharing his enthusiasm. "I have a work thing Saturday. One of the partners gave me tickets to some big event at Gallery Guichard, so—"

"That's in the evening, right?" He tilted his head, unwilling to let her off the hook without a better excuse.

She shrugged her shoulders. "Technically, yes, but I need the day to get ready. I have a mani-pedi appointment, a facial, a hair appointment, and then I booked the One-

Woman Glam Squad to come and do my makeup. You can take the kids yourself, though. They'll love it."

He looked at her for a long while, studying her eyes as though he might find his old friend hidden in them. "You hate that stuff. You can't tell me you *want* to go to that thing. Blow it off and hang with us for the day."

"I *can't*." She walked to the bed and stretched out on her back, studying the pattern of the coffered ceiling. "Do you remember my friend Candace? Sometimes I help her dad with things at work. He wants me to report back to him about the plans for the Bronzeville revitalization."

Tristan was quiet for a second. "Sell your ticket. Ditch the thing, sell the ticket—I know it's worth a grip—and chill with us. Come on! We used to be experts at blowing these things off."

She parted her lips to protest, but he shushed her with a single finger to her mouth. "Just tell the daughter something came up with the kids. Who can argue with that? I can sell the ticket to some wannabe who actually cares about being seen at the event on my way to talk to Mom. She probably has the inside track on the Bronzeville thing, anyway. All I have to do is ask her."

He lay down beside her, studying the ceiling and initiating a momentary foot fight with her before drifting off to sleep.

Julene lay awake a while longer, happy to have her best friend at her side, happy her babies had their daddy for as long as he would stay.

In the morning, she called her mother. "I just wanted to let you know you don't have to keep the kids today. Tristan is here for a while working on a deal with his mother, and he wants to spend as much time as possible with the babies."

Layla was silent for a beat, before finding the silver lining. "He's here? That's great! I knew you'd be able to reel him in and bring him back to his senses! And he's working on a deal with his mother? Hopefully it will be very lucrative. What am I saying? She's no slouch with her money! I'm sure it will be great for the family—for *your* family. He's like the prodigal son, returning to take his family's empire to the next level!"

Julene closed her eyes and rubbed her temples while her mother tried to guess how much money would be involved in this *deal*. No matter the situation, money and status were still the only currency she recognized.

"Listen, Jules," Her mother's voice was warm honey flowing thorough the phone line. She hadn't referred to her daughter with this level of affection since she'd been a very small child. "Jules, darling, do you have a credit card I can borrow for a few weeks? Or maybe Tristan can get one from his mother? I'm sure she would give him anything he asks for just to keep him around for as long as possible. It doesn't matter if the card is yours, his, or hers. I'm just in a pinch right now and need to move some cash around."

Through teeth clenched tightly enough to trigger a migraine headache, Julene reminded her mother of her own dire circumstances. "It'd be pretty hard for me to get a credit card with a stolen identity and a bankruptcy on my record, mother. Obviously, I can't give you something I don't have. I only have the emergency charge card Tristan asked me to hide for him and the business card I was given to use for work."

She paused, regretting her decision to call her mother this morning, torn between hanging up and asking a question. She chose to ask the question. "If you're in such a bind and if you were able to borrow someone else's charge card, how would you pay it back?"

Her mother spoke excitedly now, her voice echoing inside her soulless home. "Darling, it's your father who is in a bind. I'm just trying to help. He's got a new business venture in the works and we've dumped a ton of money into it, but we'll get it all back soon enough. I've maxed out all my cards just to hold us over until the new venture pays off, but that's okay, too. I have an idea. It came to me just this morning! I just need a credit card to purchase a few gift cards. I'll use the gift cards to buy some money orders and I'll sign the money orders over to myself! Brilliant, right?"

"Gift cards? Money orders? What are you trying to purchase, mother? Why not just pay for whatever it is with the charge card from the beginning?" Annoyance filtered through Julene's voice and her mother matched her energy through the phone.

"Listen to me. I need cash and I can't take a cash advance from someone else's credit card. And I can't use a credit card to purchase a money order. However, I can buy the gift cards, use them to buy the money orders, and deposit the cash directly into my bank account before ComEd shuts off our lights. They've given us forty-eight hours."

Layla was quiet again, and Julene imagined her mother draped across her chaise lounge, weak from the burden of concocting this new scheme.

"I don't have a card, mother, at least not one that isn't nearly maxed out," Julene said. "Plus, I'm pretty sure they can't cut your electricity during the winter, anyway. Tristan's mom threatened to let ours get cut off when we were living in her duplex once, but I contacted ComEd and I was told they cannot disconnect during winter months."

Julene used her fingertips to rub the tension away from her temples. She measured her breath and straightened her shoulders. "Listen, mother, the kids are up. I've got to run but I'm sure you'll figure this out as you always do."

"Oh, yes they can! And they will!" Layla's voice was shrill. "If the forecast calls for temperatures above 32 degrees, they can do it! They've shut it off before, but we were able to borrow money from a business partner to get it restored. That isn't an option this time. If we can't pay the bill this time, we'll have to come and stay with you."

When the phone call ended, Julene sat at the foot of her bed for a long while. She hadn't lied to her mother. She *was* managing as best as she could with what little money she'd been able to shuffle around on her own. The idea of using credit cards to acquire cash was pretty brilliant, she had to admit. She considered trying it, not to save her parents from having their utilities disconnected, but to save herself from having them spend even one night under her roof.

She pushed the entire issue to the back of her mind and returned to the plan Tristan had proposed. She called to cancel all of her beauty appointments and texted Candace with an excuse for missing the event, promising to leave her ticket at the door.

Almost immediately, she, Tristan, and the kids settled into a comfortable, new routine. She worked steadily at the law firm, doing her best to make her position appear valuable to the team, avoiding her father, whom she hadn't yet found the capacity to forgive, and appeasing Tiller by keeping her mouth shut about the work she'd been handling for him on the side. Tristan kept the kids clean, fed, and entertained, never making excuses to hang out with friends, never complaining of boredom or fatigue.

On the weekends, they were a genuine family—children's museums, restaurants, movies, skating—comfortable and happy in the private paradise they'd created for themselves.

Tristan hadn't even told anyone he was home, except for his mother and Julene's. Ms. Marlene had quickly grown accustomed to seeing him shepherding the children in and out of the building, and she had daily stories for him, just like the ones she shared with Julene.

At work, Tiller, all grins and winks, appeared on the threshold of her office week after week with tickets to VIP functions, private parties, and limited engagements, never noticing that she wasn't actually attending these events as long as she supplied the information he instructed her to glean from the city's elite. Who was planning what, with whom, where, and when?

She and Tristan had developed quite the system—selling the gratis tickets to the highest bidder and milking Tristan's mother for insider info on the local real estate market to keep Tiller satiated. The money, flowing freely and easily, funded their family excursions and loosened the strain on Julene's skimpy paycheck.

CHAPTER TWENTY-SIX

O n a bright Thursday afternoon, when there was cake in the conference room and a company-sponsored happy hour planned for the evening, Tiller stopped by Julene's office offering information rather than requesting it.

"The firm is celebrating record growth and a huge merger, hence the conference room cake and the social hour this evening," he said. "All the higher-ups are getting huge bonuses and promotions. If I were you, I'd be asking for a raise, too."

She clicked *send* on an email and swiveled her chair to face him directly. "And what else? What's the catch?"

He feigned innocence and clutched his heart as though her skepticism had pained him deeply. "There's no *what else*. That's it. You work hard. These people have more money than they can count, and if you don't ask for it, you won't get it. A closed mouth doesn't get fed."

He shrugged and moved toward the hallway. "I'm just saying…"

He hesitated at the doorway, and then turned to face Julene again. "Who processes invoices for payment in this department? I noticed you and Tina are the only ones on this side. Who's the admin assistant?"

Julene pushed away from her desk and held her hands up. "I guess that would be me. I've been processing invoices, handling marketing, getting her coffee, and any other tasks I can find to keep busy. Why do you ask?"

She scooted closer to her desk and picked up her cellphone. There was a text message from Tristan, a selfie of him laying across the bed on his belly with the children piled onto his back like a stack of pancakes, their tiny arms wrapped around one another. She smiled at the picture and began texting a row of hearts to her small family while Tiller assigned her a new, simple task.

He placed his briefcase on the edge of her desk and unlatched it as he explained, "Take these invoices—there are only a few—and include them in your monthly report. You don't need to mention it to Tina, just add them in."

He placed the invoices near her keyboard. Julene dropped her phone in her lap and pushed the invoices back toward Tiller. "That's extra work for me. Why would I do that? If they're from your department, give them to *your* admin assistant."

He shoved the pile toward her again, this time with enough intensity to force some of them under the keyboard and some of them onto the floor. His smiling face was a poor match for his stern voice. "Just do it, please. These invoices don't belong to my department. They're just extras, and as I said, the firm can cover it. They've got so much money coming in, they can barely keep tabs on how much is going out. It's fine. I'm just making sure I get what's owed to me."

The tone of his voice was more relaxed, more assuring, when he placed his hand near his heart and stepped backward toward the door. "I told you, there's enough money to go around here. You should make sure you get yours, too. Closed mouths don't get fed."

He smiled and tapped his temple with his finger. "Remember that."

When he disappeared down the hall, Julene sat at her desk, giving Tiller's comments more consideration than she had permitted him to believe, wondering how much money she'd need to pack up and move her family out of the penthouse. How long would it be before Tiller found a buyer for the place or the current owner discovered, and objected to, her living there?

Right then, before she could find a reason not to, she decided to ask for a raise. She made a list of her talking points, running reports of her accomplishments and production numbers and inflating them to pump up her own worthiness. She became her own devil's advocate, listing potentially negative issues, should they arise, and preparing comebacks to any of her boss' possible objections. Then, she emailed Tina Dyer and requested a review. Almost immediately, a response appeared in her inbox, confirming a lunch meeting the next day for the review, reminding her that, per protocol, there would be two other superiors in on the meeting as well. As if triggered by the rapid response, adrenaline flooded her limbs, her head, and her chest. The steady thumping of a song she'd constantly pushed to the recesses of her mind began a slow crawl to the forefront.

According to an expert on the *Today Show*, negotiating for a raise meant knowing what others in your field are earning, knowing your own worth, and being prepared to walk out if necessary. Tiller was right: the firm was handing out money during reviews like it was—well—a bank, but she also knew what she was worth. Nothing.

Her stomach muscles contracted with an involuntary sharpness that caused her to draw in her breath almost from the second she'd clicked *send* on the email confirming the meeting. The message couldn't be retracted. And, even if she could retrieve it, she'd be foolish to do so. As Tiller had said, a closed mouth doesn't get fed.

To soothe her jittery stomach, she forced herself to confront the worst-case scenario: they could deny her request and she'd remain trapped, squatting in a home she couldn't afford, unable to trust her own parents for support, unable to support her family independently. Their saying no would mean nothing would change. She had nothing to lose. This simple truth, meant to mitigate her anxiety, only made it worse. She emailed her team with her regrets, explaining that she was feeling a little under the weather and would have to pass on the company happy hour that evening. Then she logged off and headed home.

An hour later, while waiting for the elevator to open and hurtle her to the forty-first floor, Julene looked up to see Ms. Marlene.

"Hey, Ms. Marlene! How's your day been?"

Ms. Marlene smiled a little devilishly, walking closer before whispering, "Well, you know I'm not the gossiping type because the Book of Proverbs says whoever restrains his lips is prudent. So, keep this information to yourself. But, pray for your friend up there on the fifty-third floor. You know, the one who had that big wedding last year? Today, she came to me in tears, asking me to let a process server go up to her floor to present her husband with divorce documents. And she *never* speaks to me! But I guess when you're going through something, you're looking for any shoulder you can find to lean on."

She shook her head with gentle concern, stepped just a little closer to Julene, and lowered her voice while she shared the rest of the story. "Well, I said, wayminute baby, what do you mean? Didn't you *just* get married not too long ago? She said yes, but she didn't know he had been gambling all of their money away on some kind of Ecstasy football."

Julene, confused, repeated the words. "*Ecstasy football?*"

Ms. Marlene paused for a second, a quizzical expression on her face, before snapping her fingers. "No, that wasn't it. Fantasy. Right. *Fantasy* Football gambling ring and lost EVERYTHING! EVER-Y-THING. You know, she had that big old wedding ring and that $7,000 pocketbook? Well, baby, she had to let all that expensive stuff go back. She said he had ruined their entire future and she was moving back home to work at her daddy's business out there in Kentucky or somewheres. I told her—not that she asked for my advice, but I've reached an age where I just have to say what's on my mind—no one can tell you what to do about your marriage. I don't know your husband from Adam, but I will tell you that running back home to Mommy and Daddy every time the going gets rough won't solve anything. Maybe you can make the marriage work, maybe you can't, but no marriage is easy, and that's a fact."

Julene bobbed her head, devouring the older woman's words, not for the sake of gossip, but for the access to her wisdom.

Ms. Marlene planted one hand on her hip and gestured outward toward the world with the other. "If you look around you at any marriage that has lasted, I'm talking thirty, forty years, you better know you're witnessing two people who went through something tough. You need to understand they've been through some unimaginable things, but by the grace of God, they didn't give up on it. You just have to stick in there and see if you can make it work, because I'll tell you, there's nothing good out there in those streets. Some of these mens are momma's boys, doing drugs, doing other mens—you just don't know what you might run across out there. When you find a good one—Julene I know you've got a good one—you'd better try to hold on to him. That's what I told her and that's why I'm telling you this. Not to gossip, but because you and your husband might want to pray for her and her man when you say your prayers tonight."

Julene nodded respectfully, but shifted from one foot to the other, shamed by the innocuous request. Ms. Marlene had not only assumed Julene and Tristan were married, but also that they were a praying couple. Sure, they prayed with their children—childish pleas about protecting tiny souls as they lay down to sleep and appealing to the Lord to whisk them away to Heaven should they not make it through the night—but they'd never prayed for their own relationship, had never invited God's presence or requested His protection or thanked Him for his omnipotence. She wondered if anyone had ever prayed for them before, as Ms. Marlene was requesting she do for someone else. It was doubtful.

Julene was quiet with introspection and Ms. Marlene concluded her story. "Okay, well, baby, I probably said too much. You go on and have a good night. Kiss those babies for me, and I'll see you later."

CHAPTER TWENTY-SEVEN

Y ou need to show me a badge or some kind of identification or you're not coming in here!" Tristan's voice echoed down the hall, distant at first, mingled with her dream, perhaps, until it forced her into wakefulness, rousing Julene from her sleep. She peeled her eyes open, measuring the light creeping in around the windowsill to gauge the time. It was morning.

"I don't need to show you a damned thing! You're on *my* property! I should be asking for *your* ID! Where's Julene?" Tiller's voice challenged Tristan's, and Julene tumbled out of bed toward the front door, not even grabbing her robe on the way.

When she burst into the foyer, clad only in a T-shirt and panties, the tussle between Tristan and Tiller had spilled into the hallway outside the front door of the penthouse. The younger man's strength, quicker and more agile, was evenly yoked with the older man's strength, which was slower, but more certain.

Julene pressed herself into the center of the melee, struggling to keep her voice hushed, even as she hollered at the men.

"What the hell are you doing? What happened?" Her eyes boomeranged from one man to the other, looking for an answer.

Tiller was the first to speak. "Julene, he can't be here. How stupid can you be? To have another man—"

"What do you mean, *another man?* Julene, are you sleeping with this old dude?" Tristan pushed away from Julene, leaving her standing exposed in the hallway.

"Are you serious? I'm not—" she stopped speaking, tried to collect her breath and turned to Tiller. "You need to leave. We need to calm down. Just leave and let me speak to my children's father."

Tiller was incensed. "You don't get to tell *me* to *leave*. You're lucky I don't throw your asses out right now! *I'm* in charge around here! I stopped by to bring you a cup of coffee."

He pointed at a box tossed onto its side near the front door. The coffee, in a bright orange and white travel mug, was tipped over, spilling into the plush carpet. Giant cookies, decorated with the same bright orange design, lay scattered amongst the mess. "How was I to know you'd be stupid enough to have your baby daddy living here? I mean, what were you thinking?"

His voice had increased to shouting again. Maybe they'd all been shouting. Their commotion, enough to prompt a concerned neighbor to call building security, echoed along the plush hallway. When the security guard rounded the corner from the elevator, a middle-aged gentleman with whom Julene had exchanged daily smiles on her trips from the parking garage to the building, she was immediately aware of her scant attire.

She gripped the lower hem of her t-shirt and pulled it taut across her thighs and backside, before quick-stepping backward, moving inside her doorway, pausing only to make sure the disturbance hadn't woken the children.

Satisfied with the peaceful silence inside the penthouse, she whispered a prayer of thanks that the children weren't awake to witness the developing altercation, She pulled on the sweatpants Tristan had left lying on the floor near the bed and trotted back to the front door.

When she returned, the security guard was standing between the two men, doing his best to diffuse the confrontation, unsure of who had ultimate dominion over the property and who was technically trespassing.

"I'm managing this property. I have power of attorney and I want this punk removed *immediately*." Tiller locked eyes with the security guard, reinforcing his position as the higher level of authority in the scenario.

"I want this punk removed immediately?" Tristan repeated as he pierced Julene's eyes with his own, pleading for clarification. "Who does he think he is? Is he *crazy?* Does he know who I am? My *children* are in there!"

He tried pushing past Tiller and the security guard, intent on getting back inside the penthouse. The two older men formed an unyielding blockade. The three men scuffled, and Julene inserted herself into the huddle again, fighting to create space between the men while holding Tristan back from a potential assault and battery charge.

In seconds, two police officers arrived, instructing everyone to take a step back. They determined it was best for Tristan to leave until tempers could be diffused, allowing him a few moments inside to gather his belongings. Without another word, he kissed his sleeping children goodbye, hoisted his duffel bag onto his shoulder, and headed toward the elevator. Tiller stood behind the security guard and the police officers, nodding, glaring, his eyes challenging the younger man to another power contest if he was still feeling tough. Julene, jogging to catch up, grabbed Tristan's arm, hoping to make peace before the elevator arrived.

"Hey, what the hell happened?" she asked. "You know what? It doesn't matter. I'm sorry. You didn't deserve that. I should have introduced you to Tiller before today, but I'll straighten everything out. Just go cool off, I'll handle things here, and then you can come back."

She was breathless, watching the hall lantern above the elevator illuminate each floor number on its way to forty-one.

"I'm not coming back. This is why I left. This life, this control everyone has over us. It's bullshit. And why? For an address? For car keys? For money? This isn't me. This isn't *you.* But I can't wait around for you to figure it out. I'm going back to Savannah. One day, when you finally realize what matters in your life—what matters in our *children's* lives—you can come down and join me."

She hadn't even seen the number forty-one light up. She stood, feet and mouth frozen, as the door opened and Tristan stepped inside. Before her or his tears fell, she turned and walked away.

The police officer raised his eyebrows at the security guard, no doubt signaling his intent to leave the rest of the mess in the guard's hands. Tiller busied himself, cleaning up the ruined continental breakfast, before bringing the whole mess inside and dumping it on the kitchen counter.

Julene stood at the door, arms crossed, until he finished. "You can leave now."

She placed one hand on the doorknob, ready to slam it behind him as he walked out, but he stopped, inches from her face and breathed a hot warning. "You don't know what you've done."

She waited, unintimidated, eyes bucking, reminding him the door was waiting to close behind him. He strode out, finally, and Julene punctuated his departure with a door slam that woke the children and knocked a small mirror from a nearby wall.

The clock on the microwave said 7:13. The sun had barely taken its rightful place, and already, so much had happened. Time wouldn't stand still for her, though, no matter how badly her emotionally drained body was craving her bed, blankets, and drawn shades. It didn't matter how desperately she needed a best friend to call or a mother from whom to seek advice.

Her children were already wandering about, calling out for their daddy. Her performance interview was still scheduled for lunchtime and Tristan would be halfway to Georgia by then. He wouldn't be able to watch the children, but cancelling the meeting was out of the question if it meant the possibility of receiving a bonus.

She was slipping, weighed down by the strain of it all, and having reached the end of her rope, she did her best to tie a knot and hang on. She grabbed her phone and dialed her mother.

CHAPTER TWENTY-EIGHT

L ayla was groggy, barely intelligible, when she muttered *hello* into the phone.

Julene's words tumbled out, a heap of lies and half-truths, with no known endpoint. "Hello, Mother. Sorry to wake you, but I need to drop the kids off with you today. Tristan had a thing and I can't rearrange my work schedule, so…"

"Darling, say no more." The sound of her mother getting out of bed, stretching, and pulling on her robe traveled through the phone line. "I'm up. I'll put some oatmeal on for them. Have they eaten?"

With her mother having planned the children's breakfast and a string of activities for the day, Julene murmured a distracted *be there in a minute* and forced herself to shift gears, helping the children into the bathroom to wash up and get dressed. When they were ready, they piled onto the elevator and began their descent to the bottom. Somewhere between the ninth and seventh floors, Julene noticed the bright orange cookie clutched in Jamison's hand.

"Did you bring that from the house? Do we eat cookies for breakfast?" Without waiting for him to reply, she reached down to take the cookie away. "This one is yucky, anyway. It was on the floor, baby. Let's throw this one away and Mommy will bring you a cookie after work today, okay?"

Jamison, disappointed but too sleepy to protest, relinquished the cookie and buried his face in the shearling lining of Julene's coat.

She looked at the distressed cookie, intricately detailed with Tiller's Legacy Builders Real Estate Group logo, and tossed it into the garbage can as soon as the elevator door opened. When they rounded the corner from the elevator to the parking garage, Ms. Marlene was walking toward them, concern and relief intermingled on her face.

"Hey, baby! Are y'all okay? I heard about what happened this morning. You know I worry about y'all up there with these sweet little babies of yours."

Julene produced a faint smile. "We're fine. Everything's okay. We just had a small misunderstanding."

"I figured that's all it was." Ms. Marlene reached into her pocket, pulled out a folded slip of paper, and pressed it into Julene's hand. The warmth of the older woman's hands, as soft and as comfortable as buttery leather, provided Julene with a moment of peace that ended too soon. "I know you have to get to work, but I just wanted to give you my address and tell you today is my last day. I'm finally retiring, thank you Jesus, and my grandson will be coming to visit soon. I'm looking forward to spending some time with him. I'd love it if you and those precious babies could stop by to see me sometime."

"Ms. Marlene! You're leaving us?" Julene exclaimed. "Congratulations on your retirement, but I wish I could be selfish and keep you here with us. Where's your grandson coming from?"

She fidgeted with Jacinta's hair bow and tried to hide the tears that kept swelling and receding in her eyes.

"He's riding his bike somewhere in South America," Ms. Marlene replied. "He can't carry a bunch of stuff, so he tells me where he plans to stop and I try to send him a little care package when I can. He comes home every so often to work a little bit before his next adventure. God has blessed him with a good job delivering packages for the parcel system—been working with them for years, They love him down there and he does a good job, so they always hire him back. But he loves to bike and camp, so him and his buddies will take off on a trip for months at a time, just shipping their bikes and riding and camping all over the world. They've been to Alaska, all up and down the west coast, across Canada…you name it, they've biked it."

Julene listened intently, wrapping her mind around the idea of the unconventional and nomadic lifestyle chosen by someone related to Ms. Marlene. The tidy, sensible, unassuming elderly woman could have easily passed for a retired grade-school teacher rather than an employee in an apartment building. She brought to mind words like reasonable and rational with the outside potential to be as stern as necessary. She most certainly would have expected her grandson to live a more stable, predictable, and respectable life. Wouldn't she?

Ms. Marlene, however, was only barely able to contain her pride in her grandson and his choices. "I'm not mad at him, baby! I don't understand it, but I told him, you've got to design a life that *you* can live with—not anyone else. Whether or not you enjoy your life, that's up to you. As long as you can pay your own way and you aren't hurting yourself or anyone else, why not? It really doesn't matter if anyone else likes it or understands it."

She pulled out her phone, thumbing through pictures until she found a picture of her grandson, a grinning, pecan-skinned young man standing next to a bike beneath a canopy of lush green trees, helmet nested under his arm. His hair was coarse and unedged, his t-shirt and shorts spattered with mud. Wet leaves and fallen trees littered the path in the distance behind him.

Julene smiled, taken aback by the boy's shaggy appearance. Ms. Marlene studied the picture herself, beaming as though he were wearing a tuxedo, speaking to his picture as much as she was speaking to Julene. "I told him, if you like it, I love it. And he's smart, too. That's why I'm so proud of him. You know he had a degree in biomechanical engineering? He was good in science and math, but he just knew in his heart he couldn't be happy in a factory or laboratory. He could have made a lot of money, I'm sure about that, but that wasn't important to him. He needed to make his own way and find true joy in his life. And you know, most people can't say that. Most people waste their whole lives away trying to do things to impress other people or trying to fit into molds that other people create. And baby, I'll tell you because I've lived long enough to realize most people can't even figure out what they want for *themselves*, so why let them tell you what *you* should want for *yourself*? When my grandson—his name is Duncan—said this was his choice, I said to him: 'take an honest look into your own heart. Go to the Master and tap into the Holy Spirit and see what the Lord really has for your life. He gives you everything you need. It's up to you what you wanna do with it.'"

She slipped the phone back into her pocket and shifted her purse from one shoulder to the other. "I told Duncan, I said, 'I'm happy for you. I love you and want you to be safe, and Lord knows I wish you were closer to home sometimes, but I know you need to do things your own way.' I love to hear about his adventures when he comes home, but mostly, it blesses my spirit to know he's doing what his heart drives him to do. He's not miserable and he's not making no one else miserable, either. Isn't that really what life's all about? Don't harm yourself and don't harm anyone else. Other than that, have at it!"

She smiled down at the sleepy children, who had woven themselves around Julene's legs, captivated by Ms. Marlene's storytelling, and then checked her watch. "Look at me, keeping you from getting on with your morning. I have a bunch of things to do, too. Gotta clean out my office."

Ms. Marlene stretched her arms out and hugged Julene. When she kneeled to hug and kiss each of the children, admonishing them to be good babies and always listen to Mommy, Julene used the edge of her coat sleeve to blot her tears.

In the car, on the way to her parents' home, Julene tried to figure out who had designed the life she was living. She certainly didn't love it. The thought of the freedom Ms. Marlene's grandson enjoyed seemed both uncomfortably complicated and invitingly simplistic at the same time. Not the rugged outdoor living and the absence of simple comforts like sheets and walls and cooked food, but the peace of mind. The absence of scrutiny and judgment and endless, unspoken expectations.

She had to consider her children, of course, but how much do children really need? Hadn't they been their happiest when they were playing peekaboo with their daddy? Did they care if they arrived at the park in a Range Rover, an Audi, or on foot? Weren't they thrilled when they got to eat alphabet-shaped noodles from a tin can rather than hand-breaded chicken nuggets and pommes frites without ketchup at the Waldorf Astoria?

She tried Tristan's phone only once before she pulled into her parents' driveway, and wasn't surprised in the least when he didn't answer. He'd need time to calm down, just as he'd always needed, and she'd give him his space, just as she always had. When the time was right—once she'd secured her raise— she'd get him to come back. She'd give Tiller his keys and his phone, and she'd create a fresh beginning for her small family. The statute of limitations on the bankruptcy would expire in a few months and she had maintained steady employment. She would qualify for a lease on an apartment and a small loan on a reliable and affordable car. She could convince Tristan to come back. Once she'd trimmed away the things that didn't matter, he'd have to come back. He was her best friend.

Inside the house, Layla had arranged a highchair and booster seats in the breakfast nook for the children. While Julene fastened her children into their seats, Layla started a Mickey Mouse Clubhouse DVD on the kitchen TV. Julene stood back, watching as her mother slipped small bowls of oatmeal, fruit, and milk in front of the children, reminding them to sit with their hands in their laps until they were served.

They were so happy, these little babies, as their eyes followed their grandmother's every move, waiting for her approval. But they received, as they always would, limited kisses and unlimited corrections, instructions, and lessons. She tapped their elbows when they rested on the tabletop, raised her eyebrows with disapproval when the girls stuffed sideways cantaloupe slices into their mouths, creating bulging, comical smiles, and wiped Jamison's fingers again and again as he used his hands to push the oatmeal back into his mouth because he hadn't yet mastered complete control over his spoon.

It had only taken a few moments, according to Julene's observation, for the sparkly, vibrant children to become dull and subdued under their grandmother's oppression. Layla, satisfied at having brought the children to order so quickly, drifted to the coffeemaker, filled a bright orange travel mug for herself, and held a matching mug out toward Julene. "Shall I pour, or do you want to pour your own?" The mug screamed Legacy Builders Real Estate Group, a realization so disarming, Julene half-expected to see Tiller walk in at any moment.

CHAPTER TWENTY-NINE

"Where did you get this coffee mug? Where's dad?" Julene asked. She walked toward the rear stairs and yelled, "Dad! Daddy!"

Layla walked into the sitting room and sat on the ottoman near the fireplace. "Darling, please don't yell. Your father left very early this morning to catch a flight. He'll be back late Monday evening."

She snapped her fingers. "Which reminds me... I RSVP'd for you and I to attend the baby shower at the Parkway Ballroom on Sunday at three. I knew you'd forget, so I did it for you." Julene, her mind a tangle of concerns that were in direct contrast to the jubilance of a baby shower, vaguely recalled the celebration's details. The three-dimensional baby rattle, which she had looked at only briefly when it had arrived by courier a few months ago, still lay where she had discarded it in the mail basket on the kitchen counter.

Were it not for the mother-to-be, Arlen, the girl Julene had befriended in middle school, who'd shown up at every one of Julene's baby showers with genuine hugs and handwritten well-wishes, she would have rescinded her RSVP without regret.

She often reflected on how they taken separate paths but had remained supportive of one another. By the time the girls graduated from middle school to high school and Arlen grew strong enough to stand on her own amongst the elitists, she formed her own group of friends— a somewhat motley crew of good-natured artsy kids who were brave enough to toy with the fringes of rebellion.

They were wealthy, yes. Privileged, yes. But they were more fun, more *real*, than the circle of friends Layla and Brad had selected for Julene.

Had it not been for their propensity for encouraging their daughter to associate with *these* kids and not *those* kids, Julene might have enjoyed spending more time with Arlen and her friends. As it were, by high school, the two girls drifted apart, though their fondness for one another remained strong.

Begging off just because her own life happened to be in a state of continual detonation was impolite, particularly toward someone whom she'd always considered a genuine friend. She still had the capacity, be it miniscule, to shelve her own problems for an afternoon in order to be happy for someone else. She'd attend, not to please her mother, though Layla would undoubtedly enjoy the fringe benefits of Julene's participation. She would do this one thing, show up for this one event, only to repay the kindness Arlen had always shown to her.

Her mother pointed at a silvery oversized Neiman Marcus shopping bag near the entrance of the room. "I bought new outfits for my babies. It's a family-friendly event. Take that bag with you and don't forget."

Julene glanced at the bag and then looked away quickly, as though the bag held the power to reduce her to a pile of stone. She studied her mother's smiling face for a moment before pulling the emergency charge card she'd been saving for Tristan and holding it up for her mother to see. "I brought this for you. You said you were in a bind, but I guess you don't need it anymore."

Julene was already out of the door and down the driveway when Layla began explaining that her financial issues had improved, that cash was flowing again, and that everything was perfectly fine now. Her words pelted off Julene's back, unable to penetrate her daughter's understanding. Julene buckled herself into the driver's seat, busying herself with adjusting the rearview mirror, checking over her right and left shoulders, easing her car out of the driveway, and ignoring the words spilling from her mother's mouth.

Driving to work, the image of the coffee mug with Tiller's logo parked itself at the forefront of her mind. She couldn't shake it loose.

When she walked into her office, she'd planned to prepare herself for her review—to be at the top of her game in front of the bosses and get the raise she needed to care for her children—but first she needed to check one thing online.

She'd only typed the words *legacy builders* when the search engine filled in the blanks, and a website with a PDF of the business's corporate structure, as filed with the Secretary of State, popped up. She scanned the page for the names of the business's officers, steadying herself for whatever feelings she'd be flooded with when she saw her father's name.

She'd been foolish to think he wouldn't deceive her—that she could work in a law firm alongside her father and expect him to concern himself with her welfare, that he would feel regret for stealing her identity and abusing her financial status. But to place her at the mercy of a man like Tiller—one who looked as though he would just as soon lick your face as he would represent your interests in court—was disgusting. To not even warn her, advise her—these were not the actions of a loving, remorseful father, and, though she had done her best to fortify the wall she'd built to protect herself from her parents' trespasses, she still found herself vulnerable. There was still the capacity for more disappointment, and therefore a new incentive for her to distance herself from them. It was true, she'd worked in the same office with him and hadn't parted her lips to say so much as good morning, but she still expected him to tell her if he owned the company that furnished her lifestyle. To tell her she worked for him just as much as she worked for the Law Offices of Russell, Russew, and Ramm.

What she didn't expect to see—listed above Tiller's name as the business's primary officer—was her mother's name. The discovery blindsided her in a way for which she hadn't been able to prepare. Her mind raced, searching for the clues she must have missed, leaving her light-headed and disoriented. Then, because the mind has a way of insulating itself against trauma, the thumping began, far away at first, and then coming in closer, filling her head with a familiar rhythm, until she could no longer feel the pain of her mother's deceit, until she could hear the voice of the young Chicago rapper narrating the story of a young girl who struggled to keep a grip on a world intent on falling apart. This morning, the song taunted her, goaded her, chased her down a path she no longer wished to travel, challenged her to choose her own ending or let the ending choose her first.

She exited the screen filled with her mother's lies and opened the document where she'd saved a list of her strengths, weaknesses, and professional goals. Her phone buzzed and she glanced at it, lying next to her mouse. It was Tiller calling.

Her ringtone, the very song that played over and over in her head, rang from her phone softly, and she let it play, ignoring him while she studied the talking points she'd prepared for her meeting. The rapper's lyrics, streaming from her phone, verbalized the internal conflicts of a person battling an unseen enemy, wearing confidence like a costume, a nervous wreck on the inside, unable to differentiate her own self-imposed expectations from the expectations of those around her, distracted by the ever-growing sense of distrust regarding her parents. The rapper, partially shaming and partially empathizing, used his song to acknowledge the fact that, no matter how convincing the façade, it all eventually falls down.

She sat quietly for a moment, examining her circumstances, considering what lay behind her, envisioning what lay ahead, and decided she would not lose.

By lunchtime, she sat in the conference room, taking notice of everyone's faces curved into easy smiles. These were people with whom she rarely interacted, some she'd never seen at all. Yet here they were, prepared to exert their authority, poised to determine her future. Her phone buzzed periodically, with a call or text from Tiller, but she ignored each one. She focused instead on the people seated around her, on the task at hand.

One guy looked like he could be a young grandfather, mid sixties if she had to guess. He looked friendly and mature, but not ostentatious, like he had planned well for his retirement and would probably spend his golden years traveling around the country in an RV with his wife, visiting the National Parks. He might even take his grandchildren with him during the summer months, sharing stories of his youth and teaching them the wonders of the great outdoors.

In reality, he looked forward to his future retirement, but suppressed lingering regret that he hadn't taken these trips forty years ago, when he and his wife had been young enough to hike without pain and fit enough to eat without concern for their blood pressures or glucose levels.

Back then, they had been on the fast tracks in their careers, raising their children and not taking time off to explore the country. He was of a generation that saved and planned. They had stronger work ethics than today's generations, and he had been rewarded with a very nice life. It just wasn't the life he had wanted as a college kid.

He had loved nature, history and the back country. He'd wanted to work for the National Parks Services, making trails and taking groups out on guided hikes. He'd been an Eagle Scout up until the moment his dad forced him to quit those activities in favor of a summer internship at a law firm.

To please his father, he accepted that internship, but had fully expected to return to his outdoor activities at the end of the summer. That was thirty-six years ago. Sometimes he laughed to himself at the irony of his life. Now that he could afford to do the things that he loved, whether it was a cross country adventure or a meal in a fine restaurant, he was just about too old to enjoy it. He got winded too fast, his back hurt too much, he had to pee too often, and he had to avoid the foods that would give him heartburn or gas.

The other partner in the room was a younger man closer to Julene's age. He sat behind the expansive conference table as though he'd been there his whole life, like he was born to hold a position of stature even though, up until three years ago, he'd been a pot-smoking frat boy who hadn't even been required to email a resume to secure his current position.

In Julene's snapshot opinion, he was likely a privileged schmoozer, but not a jerk. He probably played basketball with his buddies on Saturday afternoons, a few of them Black she guessed. He probably called them *bro* while they traded friendly insults over craft beer and hot wings. He would clean up his act, shaving his face and tucking his shirt on Sundays, though, before he met his parents at The Bristol for brunch.

In truth, when it all boiled down, he knew his place. He knew he'd been fortunate and had been given more than he had earned in life, were he to be remotely honest with himself. If he could be wholly honest, he would admit that he loved golf more than the practice of law, that he'd always wanted to be a golf pro and maybe even teach golf to kids on the weekends. But he'd taken the job because his friend's dad had literally given it to him without so much as the formality of an interview.

He accepted the job because it offered the status and position his parents expected of him and he knew better than to disappoint his family. He knew better than to settle for a career as a golf coach when his sisters were both so successful in their careers, one the Senior Director of Global Management at Cornell, the other, a consultant to the Office of Domestic Finance for the U.S. Department of the Treasury.

This morning, he'd struggled to shake off the remains of the hangover he'd earned from staying out too late watching the game last night. Now he sat, feeling a little better, cuffing his mid-day coffee with one hand and booking a tee time on his phone with the other as Julene entered the room.

Tina Dyer, the only woman in the room, was the one who'd almost warned her not to take the job in the first place. The one who'd suggested maybe she was overqualified for this low-level position. Tina smiled as easily as the men in the room, but she locked eyes with Julene as though she sought to send her a message without words. Her smile and eyes sent mixed signals that, blended together, conveyed a conversation which could not happen out loud.

When the meeting began, Julene jumped right in, listing the key points she'd written. She wanted to appear confident and prepared, expecting them to grant her request, hoping it wouldn't be perceived as too aggressive or presumptuous.

Before she could fully summarize her strengths, the older gentleman interrupted. "Le-lemme stop you right here. We've been more than happy with your performance. You're a gem. However, it's come to our attention you were involved in a pretty serious altercation this morning involving a member of our firm and that's put us all in a serious predicament."

Julene struggled to insert an explanation, to reframe the morning's conflict. "It wasn't exactly an altercation. It was more of a mis-"

He continued, as though Julene hadn't uttered a word. "In light of the merger, we've been advised to distance ourselves from any unsavory business dealings or unscrupulous behavior regarding our associates. We think the world of you, despite your unfortunate involvement with Preston Tiller's ill-advised real estate debacle. Ultimately, we need to do what's best for the firm, and that is to part ways with anyone associated with that fiasco—including you, I'm sorry to say."

Julene shuffled her notes, scanning her words without reading them, desperately unprepared for *this* conversation—this, this *misunderstanding*. She'd pushed the morning's events out of her mind. She'd left her problems at the door. That's what a true professional does. Her superiors needed to know she could make the distinction between her personal life and her professional one. "I can assure you—"

He wouldn't allow her to finish. "When our client was notified by the police regarding your *incident* this morning, they reached out to us as well. The client was under the impression that Legacy Builders Real Estate Group was a subsidiary of ours, which it is not. We terminated Tiller's position with our firm based on a conflict of interest and, not to mention, a breach of trust. The Illinois Bar is preparing to file a complaint against the parties involved. It's a problem that won't go away easily."

"But I wasn't involved," Julene protested. "When he provided me with things, he—I thought it was on behalf of the firm. I thought Legacy Builders was a subsidiary of this firm. He—"

Julene searched the table for an understanding face, for anyone who would support her. She locked eyes with the man seated across from her.

He leaned closer to the table and offered her a smile. "It's easy to see how you could have been an unintentional accomplice in all of this. Tiller has claimed you acted illegally, without his knowledge, but our IT guys gained access to his emails and obtained copies of the contracts you signed. Not one of them was legally binding. No one has considered taking any action against you, though you may be called to testify during the hearings. Regarding Tiller's involvement, we're looking at a slew of infractions: scope of representation, conflict of interest with current clients, conflict of interest regarding former clients, responsibilities regarding nonlawyer assistants…. The Bar is throwing the book at him. He's been reprimded for misconduct inthe past so he was already on our radar, but when your name came up this morning, I was floored. I think we all were."

He gestured around the table. Heads nodded sympathetically before he concluded the meeting. "The firm is offering you a very generous severance package. Your position in this capacity will officially end today. Personally, I believe in finding the silver lining during times like these, and, if I were you," he said, sliding a folder across the table, "I'd maybe take this opportunity to travel around the country for a little while. You're young. Get out there and find yourself!"

His smile was only partially sympathetic. Julene couldn't have known it, but he imagined himself in her shoes and allowed himself to explore, just for a *second*, what he could have made of such an opportunity when he was her age.

CHAPTER THIRTY

Julene watched, as though from above, becoming an observer in the room as though she were witness to, and not the main attraction of the circus that had become her life. The papers lay before her, untouched by her hands, unacknowledged by her mouth. A document appeared in front of her, placed there by a gentle, feminine hand that lingered long enough to point at a line intended for Julene's signature.

Tears pooled along her lower eyelids, but she kept her eyes lifted toward the room's crown molding to keep them from falling. Only when a weighty, rhodium-coated ink pen found its way into her hand, did she tilt her face toward the form and signed her separation agreement while fat tears splattered the paper, forming small puddles that smeared the ink.

She sat alone in the conference room after the meeting ended. The men had left the room casually, teasing each other about Fantasy Football picks and poor draft prospects. Finally. *Finally,* she opened the folder she'd been given, tried to scan past all the bullshit verbiage specifying the basis for her termination, and found her way down to the numbers.

One month's pay. One month's pay. Her regular, sorry ass salary for a month. The old guy's words echoed in her head: *travel the country, take some time off, find yourself. What the fuck was he saying? Who could afford to do something like that at a time like this?*

Her debt-to-income ratio was in the negative, if that were possible. The severance wouldn't even make a dent in her current situation, much less help her find a new home. She damn sure couldn't go back to her parents.

The thumping in her ears reverberated throughout her body. She sat a while longer replaying the failed meeting in her mind, too stunned to make a move. She'd never really had control of the situation—never had the chance to pitch herself to them. Her opportunity to save herself had been stripped away before she had ever taken her seat at the table.

Her fake fancy world was coming undone. Perhaps it wasn't coming *undone*. Perhaps it had never been *done* at all. Nothing— not her parents, her address or her job— were real, and these things were tumbling down as though they'd been left in the hands of an inexperienced juggler. Unable to keep all of her balls in the air, she sat helpless as they fell down around her. Now, Kanye, the rapper who'd penned the song that taunted her so often, invaded her consciousness again with his lyrics about how, when things start falling down, they tend to fall down in a major way. She willed herself to recall just one optimistic bar from his anthem, something to drive her toward the light at the end of the tunnel. Instead, she sat, under the glaring spotlight of Kanye's words, forced to acknowledge the gravity of her current situation.

With tremendous effort, she willed her feet to move toward the door, when she noticed Tina Dyer was still in the room using her laptop at the other end of the table— or watching her. She couldn't be sure. She didn't know how long she had been frozen there having a silent meltdown, or if her meltdown had even been silent at all. Had she been talking to herself, or crying, or what?

Tina's voice broke the silence. "I begged them not to do this. I know you. I trained you. I believe you were the unfortunate victim of manipulation by a man who had us all fooled. Honestly, the partners felt the same way but they weren't willing to risk any issues with the governing board, so they made the decision to let you go."

Tina snapped her laptop shut and shoved it into her briefcase. She paused and studied Julene's face. "I think you're a great girl. Very bright. Super intelligent. You have my number. If I can do anything for you in terms of a future recommendation or just some professional advice, please don't hesitate to call me, okay?"

Julene nodded, exhausted and deflated. On any other day, she would have chosen certain death before accepting the continual public humiliation she'd suffered since her eyes had opened this morning. Today, it no longer mattered. Her house of cardboard and glass, of smoke and mirrors, now lay in shambles around her feet.

Late in the evening, after she'd spent the balance of the day crying, gathering herself, and then crying again in the Graceland Cemetery, she pulled her coat and scarf closer to her neck and cheeks and wandered back to her car. This place, as much a park and tourist attraction as it was a place for reflection and solitude, seemed, given the day's events, to be the perfect place to cry openly without drawing unwanted attention to herself.

She half-expected the vehicle to be towed or booted by the time she made the slow walk back to where she'd parked, but it sat, unrestrained, stationed along a row of hedges on Main Avenue. She sat inside the car, just now feeling the skin on her cheeks tightening, burning, dry from the stream of tears she'd been wiping away for hours. She tossed her coat into the backseat. She hadn't really needed it, as the weather was unseasonably warm lately, but she reached back for it, searching the pockets for her phone.

Inside her right pocket, along with her phone, was the scrap of paper with Ms. Marlene's address, written in the shaky, careful cursive of a woman whose generation valued the quality of penmanship. Her fingers, even though the temperature outside had felt more like June than April, were numb when they moved across her phone, ignoring missed calls and text messages from her mother, Tiller and Tristan, to type the address to Ms. Marlene's home.

CHAPTER THIRTY-ONE

S tanding in front of the modest home with impeccable landscaping, her head threatened to explode without notice. The pressure was almost constant now, and the stress of merely putting one foot in front of the other had left her exhausted.

The door swung open, and Ms. Marlene stood looking at Julene, surprise and relief, and then concern, registering across her face in rapid succession.

"Well, hey Julene!" she greeted. "I didn't expect to see you standing at my door, but I'm sure glad you're here! I had been thinking about you and wondering how you were doing since that mess this morning. Are you alright, baby?"

"I, I…," she literally couldn't think. She didn't remember knocking on Ms. Marlene's door and couldn't explain why she'd just appeared on her doorstep.

"Wayminute, why are you crying, baby? Come in here, come in." Ms. Marlene pulled her into the house, leading her through a cozy den, and out onto a small patio that overlooked an equally small backyard.

Was she crying? She had no idea. She tried to compose herself. She had so much experience in faking it. She was used to pulling herself together when she felt like falling apart.

She tried to distract herself by focusing on the tiny yard. Gardenia bushes in various stages of bloom and flowering hibiscus bushes filled every corner. Various-sized, wild-looking succulents accented the yard in unexpected places in no obvious order. Some in colorful planters of all sizes, some with flowers, some without. There were bird-feeders, fountains and wind-chimes, all of random colors, styles, shapes and sizes. There was no theme, no color scheme, no centerpiece—just a beautifully eclectic, peaceful space, a safe haven Julene hadn't known she needed.

Her eyes settled on a small garden plaque propped under a nearby gardenia bush. It said, *'Everything is absolutely alright.'* There was another plaque painted with the words, *'Just breathe.'* And she did, as though it were a mandate.

The pressure in her ears lessened gradually with that intentional breath. Her eyes searched the tiny garden for more signs, more inspiration, more assurance:

The quieter you become, the more you can hear.

Thank you, God, for blessing me with much more than I deserve.

Be brave with your life.

I am fabulous.

Count your blessings.

They were everywhere, yet they didn't seem to come into view until she sat still and looked for them. She wanted to stand up and move around the little yard, looking for more treasures, more encouraging words, but she was aware of Ms. Marlene sitting and watching her with a slight grin. "Don't worry about me, honey. Sit out here as long as you want. I created it for times like this. It's my little sanctuary. You know, it's small, but it's mine and I can do what I want, think what I want here. You look like that's what you need right now."

Julene looked up at the older woman, making no effort to stop the flow of fresh tears. "I'm sorry, Ms. Marlene, to just drop in on you like this. I just didn't know where else to go. My husband, Tristan, left me."

Julene caught the words as they spilled from her mouth, shaking her head gently, and reframing her statement with the truth. "He's not my husband. He's only the father of my children, but he left us after the altercation this morning."

The corners of Ms. Marlene's mouth turned downward, but she didn't raise a brow in response to this news. Julene continued. "He left me this morning, I got fired today, can't afford my bills…. It's like the stress is just building. Every day there's something else. I've been lying about my life, fooling everyone into believing it's perfect. I can't talk to my mother, can't confide in my friends. I'm so tired of this life."

There. She'd said it. All of it. She hadn't come there intending to unload her baggage on Ms. Marlene, but here, in the safety of the garden, sitting with a woman who exuded consistency and trustworthiness, the words flowed without restraint.

Ms. Marlene sat in silence for a moment, perhaps waiting to be sure Julene had gotten it all out. Finally, calmly and evenly, she said, "Baby, you can't walk around living a lie for too long. Lord knows most people try, but it just doesn't work. Eventually, it all comes out, and you tear yourself up. Now, I'm sorry for the mess you're in. If I had to guess, I'd say you had some bad luck, but you've also made some poor decisions. Again, we've all done that at some point. So, you do your best. You make better choices, you *move on* with your life. You pray and you listen for the answers. And then, be honest with people. You let them know you're human and you don't spend any energy trying to impress them or fool them. They've got their eyes on their own problems, anyways.

"Now, your friends and your family may want to be there for you, but it doesn't always work out like that. They may be fighting their own battles, and you just don't know what's on their plate. Your mother, she seems like she hasn't been the same since she gave that baby up for adoption when we were in high school. She tried to keep it hush-hush, but of course that sort of news travels fast. I found out about it and I only had one class with her. I imagine she never got over it. Some people said she was depressed, and some said she was bi-polar. It wasn't for me to say, but I could always tell she was troubled. Still is to this day, it seems.

"But that's why I don't judge! I stay in prayer. I ask God to give people what they need or show them what they need to see. Because I don't know how it feels to give up a child or what she's struggled with since then. That's *her* road to travel. Just like you've got *your* road to travel. Take inventory of your situation. Take it to the Lord, get your head together, and figure out what you need to do. There's no need in walking around here talking about how you hate your life. It's yours! Own it! Fix it!"

She smiled and rubbed Julene's back gently. "Iyanla isn't going to show up and fix your life for you. That's just a TV show. It doesn't work that way in the real world."

"Ms. Marlene, my mother never told me she'd had another child," Julene said, barely able to absorb this new information. She wondered if Ms. Marlene had mistaken her mother for someone else but something in the older woman's expression verified the truth.

"Baby, that's no surprise. It was a little boy, if I recall, and he may have been born with some issues. I never knew if that was fact or fiction. She's been running from that part of her life since we were in high school. I told you everybody is dealing with their own demons. Pray for your mom. And pray for your friends. I've heard some curious things about the people who claim to be part of the upper crust. I'm not one to gossip, but I've lived in this city all my life and you'd be shocked at how much information finds its way to me."

Given Ms. Marlene's naked assessment of everyone's lives, there was no such thing as privacy or secrets—only the false narratives spread by all and believed by none. She had heard what she needed to hear—the hard truths she'd known all along. She'd have to salvage her own life all by herself.

CHAPTER THIRTY-TWO

Julene stood up, butt numb, unable to gauge how long she'd been sitting in the same spot. "Thank you."

She grabbed the older woman's hands for a long moment, not knowing what to thank her for—the temporary refuge, the tough love, or her gentle wisdom. Instead, she stood there crying again like a giant baby, hoping Ms. Marlene understood.

"It's okay, baby. You can come by or call me anytime. I'm pulling for you, praying for you. I believe you're going to be alright. I don't know how it'll all work out, but I have to believe God. He never fails."

They were standing at Julene's car now, where Julene played with the door handle, not really wanting to leave. She turned toward her confidante and whispered, "I wish there was something I could do for you, Ms. Marlene. To repay you for the way you've treated me. You don't know how much I'm going to miss talking to you and hearing your stories every day."

Ms. Marlene tsked and gripped Julene's hands a little tighter. "You don't owe me anything. I'm going to support you and cheer you on endlessly and unconditionally. I don't have any agenda or expectation of being repaid. This is just what my heart tells me to do."

Julene sat in her car before driving to her parents' home to collect her children. She thanked God for Ms. Marlene, although she wasn't accustomed to speaking to Him directly. As she drove, a string of immediate worries grew in the pit of her stomach. *Would she be able to get into the penthouse tonight? Would her children's belongings be tossed out?*

Would she have to sleep at her parents' home tonight? Or in her car? Would she even have a car?

Her phone rang, interrupting her worries, and she answered quickly. Tiller's voice was hurried on the other end, rushing to convey important information before Julene could say a word. "Listen, everything is okay. Trust me. I'm sorry about what happened today, but this is just as much your fault as it is mine. You shouldn't have brought anyone into the penthouse without informing me, but we can't do anything about that now."

For a moment, the road, the traffic lights and the other cars became a blur. Her head throbbed again. "This is *my* fault? Are you insane? I lost my job today because of you. I'm homeless because of you. And now I find out you and my mother and God knows who else are working together to do what? What is happening?"

More tears flowed. Fresh hot ones that tickled her chin when they reached it, infuriating her.

Tiller's voice was subdued, tired. "Will you just listen for a second? I'm sorry. Your mother assured me she would explain everything to you, but she kept stalling. She kept changing the plan. She's all over the place. I was never supposed to partner with her in the first place. She was only to connect me with your father, but—"

He stopped, mid-sentence, and began again. "There's no time to get into that right now. You're safe for now. The car, the penthouse…it will take a while for the authorities to sort it all out and even longer for any eviction proceedings or repossessions to be finalized. I just need time to move some things around. We're going to be okay. In the meantime, don't say anything to anyone. Trust no one!"

A laugh burst through Julene's lips. A deep, low-pitched, hysterical laugh that pushed the last of her tears away. "Trust no one? That's the best advice you've given me so far."

She ended the call just as she pulled into her parents' driveway. The house was dark, its windows hooded and despondent. She thought for a second that her mother and the children might not be inside, but the front door swung open, and her three children stood at the threshold, huddled together in a way that pulled Julene, running across the lawn to sweep them all into a hug. She did her best to sound cheery, light, trying to push the panic away. "Hi, you guys! What are you doing opening the door? What if I had been a stranger?"

She was disturbed by the darkness inside her parents' home, but relieved the children couldn't see she'd been crying. "Go get your things. We need to leave right away."

She patted their bottoms and waited near the door while they gathered their small tote bags and jackets. She fumbled in the dark, feeling for the lamp switch. "Where's your grandmother? And why is it so dark in here?"

When she succeeded in getting a soft light to shine across the foyer, she noticed her mother, wig disheveled, struggling to make her way toward the front door. "Julene? Darling, is that you? I must have fallen asleep. What took you so long to get here?"

Layla rubbed her eyes and gathered her robe against her body. The unmistakable sound of pills in a bottle rattled from her pocket. Julene resisted her initial impulse to confront her mother about Tiller, the real estate business, and the secret baby. She chose instead to breathe, as the sign in Ms. Marlene's garden had suggested, to pray and wait and listen for guidance before making her next move. "Mother, what did you take?"

Layla's hand fluttered up and away as though she were shooing a gnat. "We need to talk, darling. I need to explain some things to you. I'll put some coffee on for us."

Her face brightened as though she'd flipped a switch, and she snapped her fingers. "No! How about tea? I've got a great tea for you to try—balloon flower and ginger. They only serve it during the afternoon tea service at the InterContinental, but I was able to get some extras directly from the woman who imports it. We have the same manicurist."

The children had gathered around Julene's legs, pulling at her hands, chattering in their little kid voices. Julene shepherded them out of the door. "I can't stay, Mother. The children are tired and I…"

She allowed her voice to drop off, too tired to offer her mother any additional explanation.

Inside the car, with the children buckled in and singing the seatbelt song, Julene eased the car from the driveway, hands gripping the steering wheel to keep them from shaking. She watched her mother tighten her robe again in the doorway.

On her way back to the penthouse, she fought the urge to pull over and vomit. Her phone pinged with the sound of incoming text messages, each chime bringing a new wave of nausea, but she wouldn't allow herself to look at them. She focused on driving, on her children's voices, on getting them all home safe. She checked the phone only when they were sequestered together on the forty-first floor.

Multiple messages from Ms. Marlene were waiting on her phone when she finally checked it. They popped up, one after the other, into the evening, continuing throughout the next day. They came via text message, email, Facebook and Twitter. They were encouraging, funny, insightful, motivational:

You don't find a happy life, you make it.
What you imagine, you create.
The best time for new beginnings is now.
Ambition without action is fantasy.
Mistakes are the stepping stones to wisdom.
Live more from intention and less from habit.
Life begins at the end of your comfort zone.
If your compassion does not include yourself, then it is incomplete.
If God is all you have, then you have all you need.
Even a bad day ends at midnight.
It isn't the mountain ahead to climb that wears you down; it's the pebble in your shoe.

There were also scriptures and quotes. They were perfect, each one. Julene found herself searching for messages everywhere that evening, from the television shows she watched while the children played in their room, to the books she read to them before bed. Just as she had realized in Ms. Marlene's tiny garden, when she stilled herself enough, she could find positive affirmations hidden in plain view all around her.

In the morning, her bedroom door slid open just enough to allow three small angels to slip through. She'd been lying, motionless, half her face smothered in the bedsheets, staring at the hinges that held the door to its frame for hours. She'd watched the pale blue light of Saturday's earliest hours slide through the window shades, trickle onto the floor, and creep across the room until it found the far wall.

But the angels, when they pried the door open and slipped into the room, assuming their mommy was asleep, weren't nearly as stealthy in making their way from one side to the other. She lay there, unmoving, watching them tiptoe across the floor, feet padding, whispering to one another, like cat burglars, until they reached her side of the bed. Jada, the brave one, leaned in close to peer into her mommy's face, and seeing that her eyes were open, leapt back in surprise.

"Go! Go! She's awake!" The children turned to run, herded toward the door by Jada, giggling and tripping over each other, until they heard Julene's wafer-thin voice. "Hey, little babies."

They froze in place just at the door, and Julene peeled herself from the bed. She rubbed the eye that had been smashed into the bedsheets, loosening her stuck-together eyelashes and clearing the crust from the corners. She pulled her blanket up to her neck and beckoned the children closer. "What is it? You guys can come into my room. You don't have to sneak, but that was very kind of you to try and be quiet."

She patted the side of the bed where Tristan had once slept. "Wanna get in and snuggle with Mommy?"

Jamison took a tentative step toward the bed, but stopped when Jacinta spoke. "Can we have cereal, Mommy? If we are very, very, very careful, can we eat cereal with you in your bed?"

On any other day, the question would have been a joke. She'd never permitted her children to eat in her bed, on her Bellino duvet—especially three bowls of cereal—but today, she recognized the blessing of three children who could get their own cereal when she wasn't sure if she could muster the strength to do it for them. She nodded slowly, watching their expressions dawn with understanding and then excitement at the thought of piling into her bed to eat and watch movies.

Just twenty minutes into Finding Nemo, when Julene had drifted off into a light nap and the children had settled into their places on the bed, Jamison began to cry, and Jada's warm morning breath was brave as it steamed the side of Julene's face. "Mommy, he spilled it."

"Hey, hey, bud. It's okay. Everything's fine." She pushed herself up onto one elbow and shushed her son. Jada and Jacinta were already hopping to the floor with their own bowls, panicked and unsure of the threat level now.

Julene was tired. So deathly, profoundly, achingly tired. The duvet, the spilled milk—there was no way the children could have understood the sheer insignificance of these things today. She pulled Jamison close, tucking him into the warm space she'd carved for herself at the edge of the bed. Then she gathered the bedding and tossed the entire heap onto the floor while Jada and Jacinta stood watching, frozen by the uncertainty of it all.

"Hey, girls." Her voice shocked her daughters out of their trance and they took a step backward. "Hey! It's okay, I promise." She attempted to sweeten her voice, to push aside the weariness and become the bright light her children deserved. "Are you finished with your cereal? Did you get enough?"

They nodded in unison without needing to look at one another, and Julene lay down again, curving herself around Jamison like the big spoon. "Alright, then. Go and put your bowls away. Take Jamison's, too, and bring us another blanket when you come back."

The girls raced from the room, on a mission to find the softest blanket, relieved they hadn't ruined this rare opportunity to snuggle in bed with Mommy all day. When they returned, Julene was sleeping again, Jamison tucked under her arm like a living teddy bear, and the girls worked together, tossing the blanket onto the bed, making sure it covered all the corners, and tucking it around their mother as she had done so many times for them.

She awoke again some three hours later, to the sound of someone knocking at the front door. The weight of her own head seemed to have multiplied, and lifting it from the pillow required significant effort. Extracting her body from the tangle of sleeping children warranted just as much effort, and by the time she'd reached her bedroom door, the phone was ringing. She raced, head still wrapped in the fog of slumber, to retrieve the chiming phone before it woke the children. "Hello?"

Her mother's voice, smooth and non-negotiable, came through the phone and echoed from the hallway at the same time. "I know you're home. I've been out here knocking for ten minutes, and I know you're angry with me, but Darling, you've got to open the door and let me explain."

When Julene opened the door, her mother stepped across the threshold offering kisses, which Julene declined with a deft sidestep and a turned cheek. Layla moved into the kitchen, laid a folded piece of paper on the counter, and rummaged through the refrigerator until she found a bottle of Prosecco and a carton of orange juice. "Let's have a drink."

She said this to her daughter, not in the form of a question, while she busied herself finding wine glasses.

"It's ten-thirty in the morning. I don't want to drink with you. I don't even want to *speak* to you. Please, just—" Tension and annoyance rose in Julene's voice, and she stopped herself. She hadn't yet prepared herself to be in her mother's presence. She'd worked so hard to channel the peace she had found in Ms. Marlene's garden to tamp down the frustration and disappointment and pain she'd been born into. And she wasn't ready yet— not this morning— to confront her mother. She also hadn't the energy to sip mimosas and pretend everything was okay.

"Well, you're being evicted." Layla pointed at the letter laying folded on the counter. "That was taped to your front door when I got here."

She walked over and pressed the heavily poured mimosa into Julene's hand. "Take this. Take it now and come sit with me."

Julene did as she was told, following her mother into the living room, where she clicked the switch to ignite the gas fireplace and wrapped herself in the faux fur throw she kept at the edge of the couch.

Layla breathed deeply, sipped her drink, and clung to the glass as though it held the meaning of life before she chose her first words. "First of all—"

"I know about Legacy Builders." Julene tossed the truth right out into the open to spare herself the agony of watching her mother wrestle to get it out for herself. "I'd assumed Daddy put your name on it to protect himself, just like he used my name on his previous business, but now I'm not so sure."

"*Your* daddy?" Sarcasm and pity sparked a fire in Layla's eyes. "He has nothing to do with this. He knows nothing beyond what I allow him to know. Legacy Builders is mine."

"But Tiller?" Julene pushed her brain to move faster than her lips to make sense of the big picture before her mother could tell another lie.

"Tiller, too." Layla nodded slowly. "He does what I tell him. He does the heavy lifting. He thinks he makes his own decisions, but he doesn't."

Her laughter was bitter, though it wasn't directed toward her daughter. She reached for Julene's hand and squeezed it warmly. "Listen. Darling, you have to hear me. When I found out he was representing the client who needed help with this property, I convinced him to let Legacy Builders manage it and rent it to you at no charge. You needed help. I needed to protect you and the children. I did that for *you*. You are still my heart."

Julene shook her head, unwilling to believe the words tumbling out of her mother's mouth. "You're a liar. It doesn't make sense, Mom. How would you know who his clients are? He lost his job because of that! I lost *my* job because of that! Why would he take such a foolish risk?"

Layla shrugged, "He loves me. He's such an idiot—so full of himself. He'd do anything for me. He's spent years risking his license, his money, his marriage for me."

She finished her mimosa, stood and smoothed her blouse, and held her empty glass toward Julene. "Want another?"

Julene nodded, stunned silent, and stared at the changing, flickering rhythm of the flames in the fireplace, wondering how a fake fire could mimic a real one so perfectly. The way it licked the air, high in one spot, low in another, crackling and popping to sound exactly like real fire. Who could control the pattern of a burning flame?

In the kitchen, Layla poured herself another Prosecco with a splash of orange juice and offered her daughter a MasterClass. "The thing is this, you're a woman now. You're a grown woman, and it's my job as your mother to teach you how to hustle and grind like a real boss."

She stopped pouring to pull her daughter's eyes across the room. "You may not understand this, but you were born to be a boss, darling. I assumed you knew it, and I assumed you'd know how to capitalize on the opportunities Tristan could offer you. He was your ticket. Every girl needs one. Clearly, you needed more guidance in that department, and I should have recognized it."

She returned to her seat by the fire and sipped quietly for a spell. "I was born to be a boss, too, but I didn't have anyone to teach me these things. I had to figure everything out for myself. I had to learn how to take control of my environment, of my circumstances, to make things work to my advantage."

A new, exhaustive rage tore through Julene. "Every time you claim to help me or teach me something, my life explodes! I don't trust you, Mother. You're a liar and an opportunist." Those words, once they'd forced themselves through her clenched teeth, didn't harm Layla nearly as much as Julene had intended.

"I've been called worse, and that's fine," Layla replied. She sipped again and placed her glass carefully on the stones at the edge of the fireplace.

"You cheated on Dad." Julene allowed her thoughts to flow out loud without taking the time to decide if they were questions or statements.

"Yes. I'm not proud of that, but your dad's not a real man, let's be honest. But he gave me *you*, my daughter, my only child, the love of my life, so and if I've got to lie a little, manipulate a little, spend a night or two with a man who can appreciate a woman like me just to make life comfortable for us, then I'm not ashamed in the least."

Layla reclaimed her glass again and sipped.

"Am I?" The mimosa trembled in Julene's hand and it matched her voice.

"Are you…what?" Layla prompted her daughter gently, understanding she needed time to process her thoughts. She hadn't wanted to force reality on her so harshly, but with Tiller's incompetence and the untimely eviction, they'd need to formulate an alternative plan sooner, rather than later.

"Am I your only child? Do you have another child?" She pierced her mother's eyes with her own.

Layla stood and walked to the kitchen. She placed her glass in the sink and then gathered her jacket, purse, and sunglasses. "My reality is what I've made it. Some of it may be painful. Some parts may be ugly. But I've learned not to cry once I've put my makeup on. I'm doing my best to teach you the same."

Tears rimmed Layla's eyes even as she spoke of controlling them, and true to her word, they did not fall. "So, yes, in this reality, you are my only child. Kiss my little angels for me. I'll see you at the baby shower tomorrow."

They walked to the door, the mother and the daughter, one standing in the hallway looking in, the other holding the door only slightly ajar.

"If you want, I can come over on Monday to help make arrangements to hire movers," Layla offered.

"You've done enough," Julene spat before slamming the door.

CHAPTER THIRTY-THREE

When, on Sunday, the time came to get dressed up and put on a happy face for the baby shower, she dressed the children in the outfits her mother had purchased, cloaked herself in as much peace as she could muster, and loaded them into the car.

She had considered foregoing the baby shower to spare herself the misery of smiling when she still had so many tears left to shed, but she was genuinely happy for Arlen. If she could muster the energy to celebrate a deserving person, Arlen certainly fit the bill, and she welcomed the opportunity to focus on something other than her own pain.

The sky was a cauldron of blue-black clouds, gusting winds, and retreating birds. It was a spring storm that signaled a transition away from winter. The bottom hadn't yet fallen out, but the threat was clear and present—a mirror to the turmoil in Julene's life.

The rain transitioned from a soft drizzle to a torrential flood in a matter of moments. She still drove slowly with the music turned down so as not to distract her from the road. The road ahead was barely visible, even with the windshield wipers beating at a maddening pace. Ahead, other drivers had decided against fighting the weather, pulling over and turning on their caution lights while they waited out the storm.

She continued to drive on, recognizing that the roads were becoming barely passable. Even if she drove as slowly as possible, she couldn't see well enough to stay within the lines. She considered pulling over as the other drivers had done, but she made a deal with herself instead: she would drive as slowly as she needed, but if it got much worse, she'd pull over.

As she moved past cars sitting stationary on the side of the road, she understood she was driving directly into the storm. She faced the raindrops head-on, looking past them while they pelted the windshield, blurring her vision until the windshield wipers could push them away.

The storm got worse, but she continued to push through the storm anyway. Creeping ever so slowly, but not stopping, she realized she could go a little further than she had thought just moments ago. It was scary. She doubted the depth of the water on the road and the other drivers. She struggled to make out the colors of the traffic signals, but she pushed forward, challenging herself. She wasn't interested in getting to the party any faster, and she didn't want to risk her children's safety. She simply realized she was able to keep going, so she did.

Just a minute later, when she turned the corner from Superior onto Hudson, the rain's intensity turned down a bit. *Could anyone honestly measure the intensity of the rain? Probably not,* she thought to herself. Even without metrics, the storm was different now. It continued to rain at a hard and steady pace, but with noticeably less vigor than a few moments ago. She relaxed her grip on the steering wheel a little and tried to release the tension in her shoulders. She'd been driving, tense with concentration, for too long.

"Mommy, I bet if anyone saw this rain right now, they would think it was really hard, unless they could see how hard it was raining back there, huh?" Jacinta asked, her small voice piercing the silence that remained when the pounding of the raindrops on the roof softened. Julene hadn't even realized her daughter was paying attention back there.

She looked into the rear-view mirror, where Jamison was asleep in his car seat, Jada was working feverishly on a coloring book, and Jacinta was staring out the window, tracing the raindrop paths with her fingers.

"Yes, baby, this rain is hard, but it's nothing like the rain we just came through, right?" she replied. "And you know what? If we had stopped back there when it was so hard, we might have been sitting in the rain all night. Who knows how long it would have stormed in that one spot? But we pushed through, we kept on moving forward, even if it was only a little bit, and we made it to a place that is still tough, but not as bad. Don't ever forget that, baby. We can always push through the hard stuff."

Jacinta didn't respond. She had, as small children are wont to do, moved on to another interesting discovery: if she pressed her warm hand against the window, condensation would create a steamy handprint. Julene watched her in the rearview mirror for a while, trying to imagine what else her little brain was thinking, whispering thanks to God for these beautiful children who were her only true joy, tattooing the lesson about the hard rain across her heart.

The rain ceased. Mild excitement rose in Julene's chest as she pulled into the valet line forming in front of the Parkway Ballroom. She recognized many of the luxury vehicles ahead of her and she knew well who the occupants were. Despite what she knew about each of them, despite her own life's ugly truths, she was looking forward to this baby shower.

There seemed to be fewer and fewer positive reasons to justify a gathering of the Range Rover Girls anymore. Such occasions were hotly anticipated from the moment an invitation arrived in the mail—or The Email, or The Facebook, or the Text Message. Baby showers, bridal showers, and birthday luncheons were the most common catalysts for get-togethers, but for Julene, baby showers were the best.

All generations of women coming together to extol blessings and well wishes on an expectant mother in celebration and anticipation of a brand-new life provided the perfect blend of mostly clean fun and low-key drama. Plus, it was a reason to enjoy blog-inspired decor, creatively themed foods, and the time-honored Baby Shower Punch. The punch, a blend of lime sherbet, lemonade and Sprite, was typically a delicate gender-neutral shade of green—

not pink or blue—if the expectant mother hadn't chosen to find out if her baby was a girl or a boy.

Those things aside, Julene loved the party games more than anything else. The trivial activities helped break the ice and assured each guest an equal opportunity for inclusion. Julene enjoyed the light-hearted competition and the momentary recognition when the prizes were awarded. Games of speed, concentration, and creativity were her favorites, though bittersweet in the way they reminded her of the games she once enjoyed with her father and the brief time she'd enjoyed with Aunt Lucille. She could breeze through word find challenges in seconds and had no difficulty making long lists of words using the letters from the names of the expectant parents. She could sniff out a smashed Snickers bar in a baby diaper and she could estimate a good length of ribbon to tie around the Baby Bump of Honor.

Though the city was enjoying an early spring, the interior of the ballroom had been transformed into a whimsical winter wonderland, all glitter and fur, with silver platters, mirrors and snow globes. One corner of the room was staged as a cozy sitting area with white leather ottomans, velvet benches, and overstuffed armchairs to encourage guests to mingle comfortably. Food and drink stations—charcuterie and mimosas here, mashed potatoes and toppings there, cookies, candy and cakes in the back— provided the backdrop for the eight-top round tables that filled the room. The tables, covered in crisp linens, held eight place settings each, with small notepads and ink pens for the games at each seat.

A play area was cordoned off in the far corner of the room, with building blocks, a playhouse, and coloring sheets to keep restless children entertained. Layla had whisked the children away from Julene the moment they'd entered the room, walking them to the play area, but not before stopping to display them to her friends and acquaintances at each table along the way.

Left alone, but not lonely, Julene signed the guest registry and placed the card she'd brought into the life-sized, antique baby stroller that had been converted into a gift depository, and then found an empty seat near the far side of the room.

She exchanged pleasantries with the women at her table, some she was more familiar with than others, until the hostess called for everyone's attention.

"Our mother-to-be is almost ready to make her entrance!" the hostess announced. "We'll start with a few games and enjoy these delicious treats, and when she's ready, we'll open gifts!"

To begin the festivities, she announced the first game (and it was one even the children could play), The Clothespin Game, and Julene's heart skipped a beat. This game, the one she'd first played at Aunt Lucille's house so many years ago, transported her back to a moment in time when she'd felt most like the person she was meant to be.

The hostess passed out three old-fashioned clothespins to each guest while the women of the older generation all chuckled at how much things have changed, how the younger generation couldn't remember a time when clothespins were once a staple in all households. The object of the game, she explained, was to avoid the three wrong that which could result in the loss of your clothespins:

1. Don't cross your legs, not even at the ankles.
2. Don't cross your arms.
3. Don't say the word *baby*.

To get caught violating one of these rules would grant another guest the right to steal your clothespin. The object of the game was to protect your own clothespins while collecting as many pins as possible from the rest of the party guests. They would play other games of course, but this one would continue throughout the day, during the gift-opening and cake-cutting, and the guest who had collected the most pins by the end of the afternoon would win the big prize. This game, a standard at most every baby shower to date, kindled the competitive spirit in the room, and the guests were eager to steal each other's clothespins as though they were lucky golden coins.

Julene sat forward, listening carefully as the instructions for the games were explained. She wondered what the big prize might be, certain she could win. Her strategy was to choose the easiest targets first—the guests who hadn't been paying attention, the ones who had only shown up for the optics, the ones who just weren't quick enough. No one, not Arlen's Grandma or someone's little niece, was off limits if it meant winning.

But right off the bat, settling down into the couch to chat with an old classmate, Julene crossed her legs and her clothespin was promptly confiscated. The loss was an early blow to her game plan, and she reasoned it would put her at a slight disadvantage. She would have to win one extra clothespin to make up the deficit.

Trying to guess the baby's name with a friend from the Rage Rover Girls, she uttered the forbidden word that would cost another clothespin. She was edgy after that loss, not in a way she could put her finger on. This was a game she'd won with ease that day at Aunt Lucille's house. It was a growing distraction that fought for her focus while she played other games and interacted with other guests. The responsibility of holding on to the clothespins lingered around her neck and shoulders, its weight indistinct and unnatural. It kept her from relaxing and she was forced—self-imposed, as it were—to preview every word and every movement in her mind's eye before actually carrying them out. Otherwise, she would be in danger of losing the last clothespin.

Sitting back and waiting for her letters and numbers to be called during Baby Bingo, she had to surrender her last pin as a penalty for crossing her arms, and subtle agitation nipped at her attitude, mainly with herself, though a little irritation was reserved for the person who smiled so kindly while robbing her of her only remaining pin. It was a meaningless game, she knew, but it had so occupied her thoughts and so limited her movements over the course of the celebration, she hadn't been able to enjoy the party at all.

Trying to protect her clothespins had driven her to distraction all afternoon. Her conversations and concentration had been interrupted over and over again by a sneaky guest who just wanted to reach in (ever so politely, even quietly), snatch her pin, and go lurking around in search of more loot. She'd spent the greater part of the party guarding her pins and an equal amount of time preoccupied with the idea of acquiring more.

As she glanced around the room, she noticed everyone sitting uncomfortably, lest they crossed some body part or accidently said the "B" word out loud. Leaning back, taking in the big picture, her arms fell across each other on her lap, and someone swooped in to grab her clothespin. There was no pin to capture—they had already been stolen—and Julene smiled quite pleasantly at the would-be thief.

"Sorry. I don't have anything left for you to take," she said. Thus, a new game began for Julene.

While she enjoyed a far more relaxed posture, she interacted freely with the party guests, crossing her arms and legs whenever she chose—sometimes on purpose, just to elicit a reaction from whomever lingered nearby. She watched their eyes take in her infraction and then scan her body for a clothespin. They'd lose track of their thoughts or change their posture as they mentally computed their own status in the game. She would smile, laugh, and disclose that all her pins had already been captured.

She afforded herself the right to give up on her former hopes of winning the game. Instead, she made an intentional decision to really live in this odd feeling of freedom, to truly breathe it in and recognize it for its full value. *This must be how the crazies feel—the ones who let it all hang out, never caring who notices.* The feeling was so refreshing, so feather light, it begged to be shared. If she noticed anyone's uneasiness, if they hovered around her checking for a clothespin, she would smile and tell them not to worry. She hadn't any clothespins for the taking, and she wasn't looking to steal their pins, either.

And so, while everyone was celebrating the blessing of a new life that day, she was in celebration of another new life. It was *her* new life, and it wouldn't include the burdens and limitations the world had handed out like clothespins at a baby shower. She tested the concept of letting things go—both literally and figuratively—and found it to her liking.

She visualized all the clothespins she'd been gripping so tightly, keeping them from being taken away by her friends, her neighbors, her former work associates, or her parents. Some of these pins weren't even hers to shield. She'd acquired them from the media, stolen them from the people she'd heard about from the Streets. These invisible clothespins added weight to her decisions about her religion, her hair, her finances, her clothing, her children's clothing, her address, her grammar, her dietary choices, her Facebook posts, her politics, her sexual orientation, her past, and her future.

She threw the damned invisible clothespins off just like that, which was much easier than she might have imagined once she realized she could simply choose not to carry them. She welcomed anyone else who chose to do the same.

Shedding the pins voluntarily meant she was no longer at risk of having them taken away. Honestly, the pins held no true value in the first place, not to her and not to anyone who might be seeking to steal them. They had served as a constant distraction and an unnecessary burden for most of her life. She was buoyant now, giddy with the irony of the whole silly mess: Human beings competing against their friends, their frenemies, and total strangers for rewards that don't exist, hoping to win a game that can't be won. At least the winner of the baby shower games has a chance to walk away with a decent party gift.

CHAPTER THIRTY- FOUR

Someone was speaking to her, telling a joke or gossiping, maybe, but she couldn't hear what they were saying. Her eyes were scanning the room, imagining how everyone would look without their clothespins, if they were all to mingle around the room wearing nothing but their truths.

Her life was certainly a lie, but so were the lives of almost everyone around her. They were frauds, all of them, not because they strived to live the good life, but because they were in denial about their humanity. Their secrecy and lies concealed the very details that made them human. They had problems, insecurities, infidelities and illnesses. They were poor decision makers, enablers, codependents, opportunists, pill poppers and porn addicts. They were just people, no one of them better than the next. They weren't honest with themselves, and they weren't honest with each other.

Her thoughts had become so loud, she couldn't hear anything except the sound of her own voice, tiny and clear.

"I was fired last Friday, and I might be facing criminal charges," she whispered to no one in particular.

In the small group, everyone's eyes widened.

"I'm sorry. What?" someone asked.

Julene, finding a stronger voice and not obligated to answer the previous question, dropped another one. "And Tristan left me. Again. He's gone."

Nearby, someone broke into a laugh and then stopped suddenly, realizing she wasn't joking.

"I've got an unbelievable amount of debt. I'm actually in bankruptcy, thanks to my parents," she continued. "I buy things I can't afford, I have a brother I've never met, I'm about to be evicted, my life is in shambles."

She had thought about this moment before. Not exactly like this, in this place, but something similar, and she'd imagined she would feel a sense of clarity and relief. She hadn't imagined, had no way of knowing, the moment would also come with such independence.

The wheels had come completely off her Cinderella carriage, and she believed she could move forward without it. She'd stunned them into silence and disrupted the celebration, although it hadn't been her intent. The time had come for her to leave. She walked to the play area to gather her children, pausing before her mother. Julene considered a few choice words for her, but decided against it. She'd choose a better time to unpack that baggage.

She called to her children. "Jada, Jacinta, and Jamison! Time to go, my loves."

They came running, drawn pictures and goody bags in hand, and she ushered them toward the front door while she checked her pocket for her valet ticket.

A familiar fear gripped her, just for a moment, while she waited for her car. *What if it had been repossessed already? What if…* She shook the fear loose, not allowing herself to consider potential embarrassment. If the car was gone, she'd call a cab. She'd be okay.

When the Audi arrived and the valet driver hopped out, she helped her children into the back seat, ensuring they were all belted and buckled, and then stepped around to the driver's side, where the valet driver stood, holding the door for her.

She drove away, her limbs humming with adrenaline. She'd behaved in a way she never had before, and though it had come with a sense of freedom, she hoped she hadn't ruined what was to be a festive occasion. Her regrets weren't strong enough to drive her back to the party to offer apologies, however. Instead, she found herself parked in front of the Jewel-Osco.

Her children, still clutching their coloring sheets and party favors, began peppering her with an endless stream of questions and requests.

"What are we getting from here?"

"Can we get cookies?"

"Can we ride in a shopping cart?"

Julene lifted the children one by one into a vacant shopping cart and wheeled them into the grocery store. She was too preoccupied to answer their never-ending questions, but she made a detour past the candy aisle and allowed them to each select a treat. When they were satisfied, she approached a young cashier and asked to purchase a reloadable gift card.

"How much would you like to put on it?" The young cashier's voice was monotone, and she didn't even bother looking at Julene. Her fingers hovered above the keypad, waiting.

"Umm… a thousand?" Julene faltered, unsure of the available credit on this particular charge card. This card, imprinted with the Legacy Builder's logo, had been lying on the antique console table in her parents' foyer. She'd taken it as something of an afterthought the night her mother had stood slurring about balloon flower and ginger tea rather than explaining why she'd chosen to destroy her own daughter's life.

"The limit is five hundred," the cashier stated and then waited, fingers hovering, for Julene to try again.

"I need more than that. Can't you just try for a thousand?" Julene fought to keep her voice calm, fought against the anxiety creeping up her spine.

The cashier looked up from the register, grabbed another card from the display rack, and placed it in front of Julene. "You just buy two cards. You can buy as many as you want, but I can only put five hundred on each one."

Julene smiled and relaxed her shoulders, permitting relief to replace the anxiety. "Of course. I understand. I'll take two cards." She remembered her children, enjoying their snacks in the cart. "And I need to pay for their stuff, too. I'm sorry they've already opened it."

The cashier shrugged her shoulders and began processing the gift cards. "Don't worry about it. I didn't see anything. There's a $2.95 service charge per card, though, so your total is $1,005.90."

Julene swiped the card and waited with bated breath. In seconds, the cash register produced a receipt and the cashier pushed the cards toward Julene. "Thank you. Have a nice day."

"I'm so sorry. I don't know what I was thinking. I need to purchase a few more of these," Julene said, selecting two more gift cards from the display rack. She thought for a moment and selected two more. "I'll take five hundred on each of these."

She emerged from the grocery store a full thirty minutes later, having learned how to successfully convert gift cards into money orders and then into cash. She had swiped the credit card until it wouldn't swipe anymore and deposited the now worthless card in the recycling bin.

In only fifteen minutes, she found herself standing at Ms. Marlene's front door again. When the older woman opened the door, Julene smiled timidly and extended her arms for a hug. Ms. Marlene hugged her warmly, releasing her embrace after a while and patting Julene on her hip as though she were a child.

"To what do I owe this surprise?" Ms. Marlene asked, peering over Julene's shoulder and noticing the children inside the car. "You brought the babies with you?"

Julene hadn't rehearsed what she planned to say. The words came out disjointedly. "Yes, Ma'am. I have them with me, but I need to ask a favor."

The older woman stepped out of her house and pulled the door closed behind her. "What is it, baby?"

Julene looked over her shoulder at her car and then turned back toward Ms. Marlene. "That's not my car. I need to give it back to the owner and I need to find a new car today. I was wondering if you wouldn't mind watching my children for just a few hours while I get things straightened out. They're really well-behaved and I won't be long. I just don't have anyone else to keep them right now."

Ms. Marlene was quiet for a long while and Julene instantly regretted the decision to ask for her help. She didn't really know this woman beyond a few conversations in the hallways. Julene took a step toward her car and Ms. Marlene reached out to stop her.

"Hang on, hang on. Here's the thing: I don't babysit. I'm sure your children are perfect angels, but I just don't keep kids."

Julene nodded. "I understand. I shouldn't have asked."

"Now, hold on," Ms. Marlene said again. "I didn't say I couldn't help you. I just said I don't babysit, but take a look at this."

She took Julene's hand and led her to a covered carport on the side of her home. "You see that minivan there? I was planning to donate it to the Good Mission. It runs perfectly, but I don't need it anymore. My old man keeps it serviced and I drive it once a month just to keep the battery from dying. If you need a vehicle, why don't *you* take it?"

Julene pulled the wad of cash from her purse and began counting. "Ms. Marlene, are you sure? I can pay you. I have—"

"I didn't offer to sell it to you. I said you can take it. I have the title upstairs. I can sign it over to you real quick. Keep your money for those babies. I don't know what you're planning, but I think you'll need the money."

The older woman disappeared inside the house and returned in just a few minutes, title and registration in an envelope, keys in her hand. She unlocked the van and allowed Julene to look inside. "It's not the fanciest car, but it's dependable and safe. I can leave the insurance on it for a few more days to give you time to get your own policy. How does that sound?"

New tears poured down Julene's cheeks while she transferred her children and their car seats to the minivan. *Don't cry, mommy. What's wrong? Did you get an ouchie?* They were concerned about her tears, and she explained the concept of happy tears while she buckled them in. "Everything is fine, you guys. I don't have an ouchie. It's just—you know how we cry when we feel very, very sad? Well, we can also cry when we feel very, very happy. Today, I'm feeling very, very happy."

"I wanna feel very, very happy! Can I cry happy tears, too, mommy?" Jacinda's voice piped up and her feet swung, kicking the seat in front of her.

Julene reached over to tickle her daughter. "You wanna cry? I know something that will make you very, very happy. It's a surprise for later. But, first, I have to take care of a few things. Be a good girl for mommy and you might just cry some happy tears soon, okay?"

She moved the Audi to a parking spot on the street and texted Tiller with the location. She placed the phone and the key inside the glove box. When she finished, she turned to Ms. Marlene. "How can I thank you? Please let me pay you."

"I can't take your money. I'm just being obedient to the Word of the Lord. Take the van and do what you must for yourself and your children. Just let me know when you get the insurance."

The two women hugged and repeated their goodbyes in the driveway until the children began to get restless. Finally, Julene backed her first car from Ms. Marlene's driveway.

At home, she kicked off her shoes and removed her jacket, letting it slip from her arms. The jacket hit the floor and a clothespin tumbled out. She was certain she'd lost them all during the game and she could fathom how this one had landed in her pocket. Her impulse was to throw it into the garbage, and then she thought better of it. She wasn't mad at the clothespin. It held no more power than she was willing to grant. She slipped it onto her key ring, saving it as a reminder that she could live a life that she loved. What was there to lose?

She helped the children shed their unforgiving party clothes and dressed them in their pajamas. Then, she allowed each one to grab their favorite toy before she ushered them back into the minivan and buckled them into their car seats.

Once they were racing down the highway, Jada's tiny voice rang from the back seat. "Mommy where are we going with our night clothes on?"

Julene replied, never taking her eyes off the road, "We're going to Savannah, baby. Let's go be with daddy."

EPILOGUE

Five years after her daughter and grandchildren disappeared into the night, Layla pulled into the valet lane at a restaurant situated sixty-five miles beyond the city's limits, bringing her car to a hard stop just inches from the bumper of the Bentley Mulsanne ahead of her in line. The valet, a spindly kid dressed in a crisp, white sports coat, black bowtie, and black tuxedo pants, waved to her, motioning instructions to wait while he attended to the cars ahead of her in line.

He ran from one car to the next, greeting guests, exchanging key fobs for valet tickets, ushering the guests toward the revolving door at the front of the restaurant. When he returned, she was not inside her own, but a different car, rifling through the glove box.

Confused for a moment, he leaned into the car and whispered to her, "Hey! What are you doing there? That's not your car."

She paused to glance at him and shrug one shoulder. "Oh, nothing. It's subliminal. I'm here to avenge Michael Jackson's death."

She lowered her voice a bit and whispered, "At least, that's what they *told* me."

The young man, unable to make sense of the disjointed explanation and too busy to question her further, ushered her out of the car and into the restaurant.

Inside, she asked the hostess for a table for one. She ordered a sixty-five dollar steak, medium-rare, and a perfect Makers Manhattan up. Not long after, she noticed a lively bunch sitting in the booth next to hers. A group of friends, both men and women, were laughing and drinking good-naturedly. She invited herself into the group, smiling, friendly, exuding happiness. "Can I join you guys?"

They transferred an expression of mild surprise from one to another around the table and decided they were just tipsy enough to add this interesting woman to their party. Layla chatted with them about the weather, astrological signs, and The Illuminati. While her conversation didn't compute, her eccentric behavior amused the strangers.

They asked her questions. "So, where are you from?"

She entertained them with her answers. "I don't know. Mars?"

She told them her mother was Earth, that the ocean was calling her. The strangers peppered her with more questions, encouraging her wild responses.

"I know I look like I'm from Venus, but I'm actually from Mars," she told them.

When they'd had their fill of fine foods and drinks, the party of seven strangers settled their checks and left. Alone at the table, she finished her own drink and made her way to the door, but the manager stopped her. "Ma'am. How do you plan on paying for your bill?"

She explained politely, "They paid for me."

To which he replied. "I don't think so. We can't allow you to leave without settling your bill."

She didn't try to run. She wasn't hostile. She simply could not help solve this dilemma. In an attempt to settle the ninety-six dollar check, and having observed her curious behavior all evening, the manager asked if there was anyone he could call.

She had no purse and no cellphone, only a carefree spirit and a vacant smile, but she gave him her daughter's phone number—the only number she'd committed to memory. The call went unanswered.

The staff, having already begun their closing duties and anxious to end the night, offered to chip in to pay the debt. The manager, concerned for Layla's well-being, decided it best to leave the situation to the authorities.

He called the police. "Hi, we have a guest here who is refusing to pay her bill. I think she may—she sounds a little crazy. We think she may be on drugs or something. We were wondering if someone could come by and pick her up."

When the deputies arrived, they asked, "Have you had much to drink tonight?" To which she replied, "Not really."

They escorted her outside, where they performed a sobriety test, and upon concluding that she was sober, asked again if there was any way she could cover her bill. Perhaps she had left her wallet in her vehicle. She asked the deputies to look for it. They searched her car and found her driver's license and cellphone. They noticed her car was a mess, but they did not find her wallet. Sorting through the clutter, the deputy uncovered scraps of marijuana in the console, and she was more than pleasant when she claimed ownership of it.

They arrested her after her confession, charging her with defrauding an innkeeper and the possession of less than an ounce of marijuana. They took her to the police station and towed her car to impound.

At the sheriff's department, Layla was released at three-fifteen a.m., upon determining that she had a clean record and showed no signs of mental incapacitation. They encouraged her to wait until someone could come and pick her up and informed her that she could stay there in a cell until she had a ride. She declined. She told the officers she was meeting up with some friends. She left the station in bare feet, having kicked off her heels in the back seat of the police car the night before, with only her driver's license and cellphone in hand.

When Julene finally answered the phone, the sun had only just begun to shrink behind the horizon. She'd been declining calls from strange phone numbers all day. Bill collectors, she'd assumed at first. But after five years of no contact, her mother's number had popped up while Julene was meeting with her book club at her friend Irene's house. She recognized the number, even after all these years, and she briefly wondered how her mother could have found her, but she pushed her curiosity aside. She'd need some time to gather herself before engaging in a conversation with her mother after so long. Now was not the time. She rejected the call during the meeting. She'd rejected it again while she celebrated with her friend Cynthia, who'd just found out she would finally become a mother. Only when she was alone in her car, driving away from Irene's house, did she finally take a deep breath and answer. "I swear to the Lord this better be important."

There was a pause on the other end of the line, and then a young man's voice, hesitant at first. "Um, my name is Bruce. Bruce Collins. My wife and I—there was a woman in our back yard earlier this afternoon. She seems pretty disoriented."

A young woman's voice echoed in the background. "Tell them she doesn't have any shoes on, but she's okay. She's not hurt."

He continued, "She's fine. I mean, she doesn't appear to be hurt; she's just lost. But she had her cell phone and she said it had died. The phone was dead. We offered to charge it for her, and we asked if we could call anyone, a family member or something. She only seemed to know your number. We've been calling all day."

Hysteria rose in Julene's throat, and she pulled her car off the road into the vacant lot of an old laundromat. She held the phone in silence, unable to form a thought or express a response.

"Hello. Are you there?" The young woman's voice replaced Bruce's.

"Um hm. Yesyesyes. I'm still here." Julene wrestled between her fears and her reality, wanting desperately to prevent the two from merging.

"Hey! I'm Bruce's wife, Annette. We couldn't get anyone on the phone when we called from our phone, but most people don't answer unknown numbers, so that was no big deal. When we finally got her phone charged, we figured we'd call someone from her contacts, from her phone, and let someone know where she is. But she didn't have any numbers saved in her phone. It's like it's been wiped clean. Your number was in her recent calls though. It looks like yours is the only number she ever calls. It's kind of heart-breaking."

Julene used the hem of her sweatshirt to wipe her face, pressing and holding it against the corner of each eye to absorb the tears. "She's my mother. It's—we have—it's complicated. Thank you for keeping her safe. Would you mind if—can I speak to her?"

There were rustling, muffled noises for a second, voices and barking dogs and a distant siren, and then… "Darling? Julene, honey? I don't know where I am. I don't know where you are. Can you…?"

Layla's question hung in the air, open ended, not needing to be completed. It was a question between a mother and a daughter. It was a question for a daughter who was born to protect her mother. It only required one response. "I'm on the way."

She spoke to Bruce and Annette Collins again, briefly. She steadied her nerves and called her new husband, Andrew, on the way home.

So much had changed since she'd arrived in Savannah five years ago. She'd found Tristan to be a thief and a drug-addict whom she couldn't trust to care for their children or even himself. She'd found a circle of friends whom she trusted, and she'd found a new man, made perfectly for her, who saw fit to make her his wife. They'd welcomed a new baby together and he protected Jada, Jacinta, and Jamison as though his blood coursed through their veins. She had fled from her old life and designed a new one. It was still imperfect, but it was hers, and on most days, when she focused on the present, she survived without reliving the pain of her past. Still, the past forced its way into her new life from time to time, as it had today, and she knew exactly what she had to do.

At home, she kissed her children while Andrew checked her tire pressure and oil. Then she headed toward the intersection where MLK Boulevard merges with I-16 West and began the 967-mile journey back to the place she'd vowed never to return.

About the Author

What do you do when you cannot live without books? You write them, of course!

Author Daines L. Reed, a wildly optimistic lover of words, resides in a small town just outside of Charlotte, NC with her husband, daughters, and pair of miniature Schnauzers. She is an avid reader, lifelong learner, and emerging storyteller.

By trade, Daines L. Reed is a registered dental hygienist. By birth, she is a writer, an observer of people, and a lover of words. She cannot live without books and cannot go a single day without asking, "What if?

Through her debut novel, *Trust*, Daines has exposed a cultural issue which deserves to be addressed. She hopes this novel will provide the spark for a dialogue that can push individuals to take a more active interest in the legacies they leave for their children.

The subsequent novels in the *Trust* series, *Good Morning Beautiful* and *It All Falls Down*, will entertain and enlighten readers as they explore the personal stories of the core characters, providing an intimate glimpse of the issues that impact their lives.

Did you enjoy *It All Falls Down*?
You won't want to miss these novels by Daines L. Reed:

Purchase these titles at www.BooksByDaines.com
or your favorite bookseller.

Made in the USA
Las Vegas, NV
30 April 2024

89340776R00152